Garfield
throws his
weight around

BY JIM DAVIS

Ballantine Books • New York

2017 Ballantine Books Trade Paperback Edition

Published in the United States by Ballantine Books, an imprint of Random House,
a division of Penguin Random House LLC, New York.

Originally published in slightly different form in the United States by Ballantine Books,
an imprint of Random House, a division of Penguin Random House LLC, in 1998.

ISBN 978-0-425-28559-6
Ebook ISBN 978-0-425-28560-2

Printed in China on acid-free paper

randomhousebooks.com

9 8 7 6 5 4 3 2 1

First Colorized Edition

ODIE'S PAST LIVES

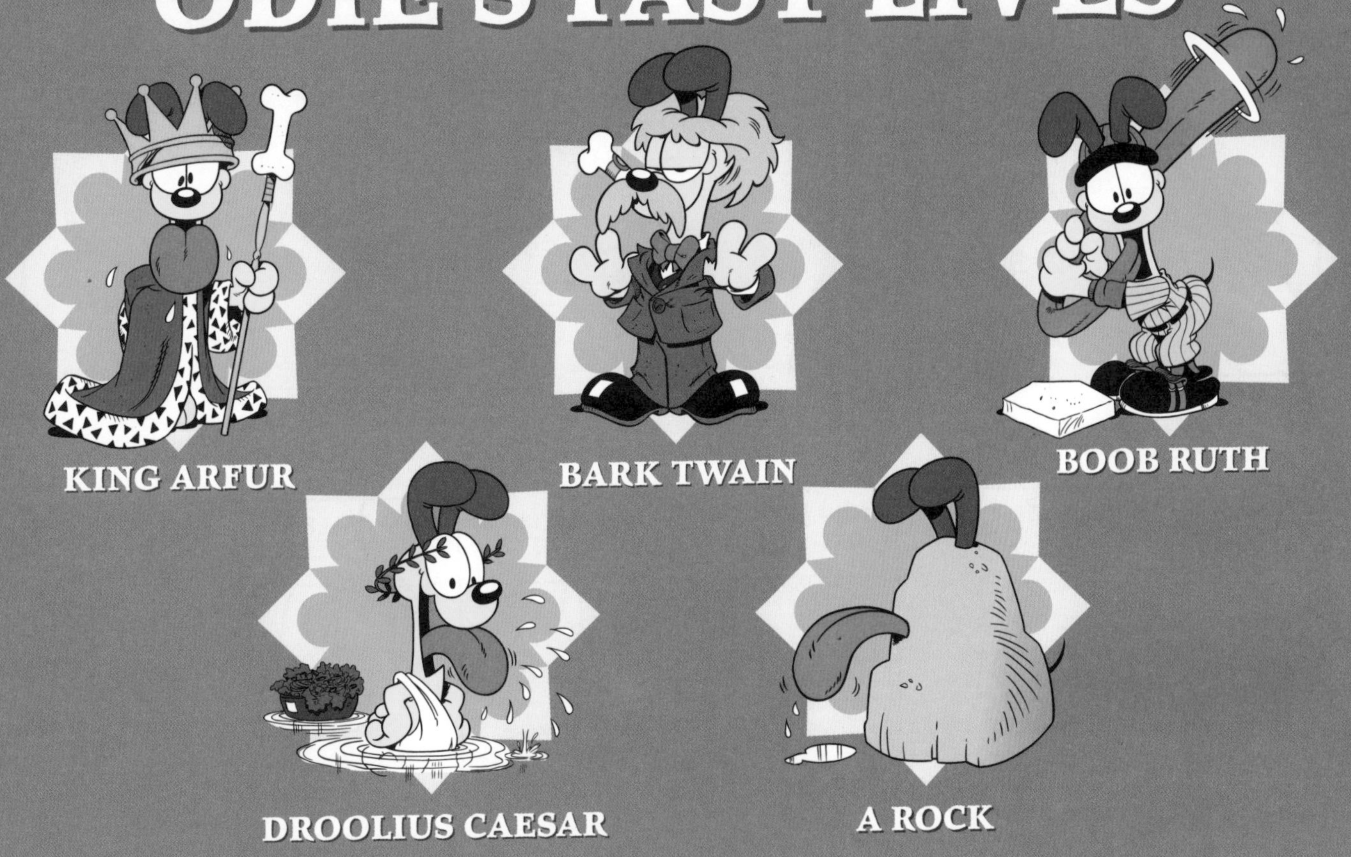
KING ARFUR
BARK TWAIN
BOOB RUTH
DROOLIUS CAESAR
A ROCK

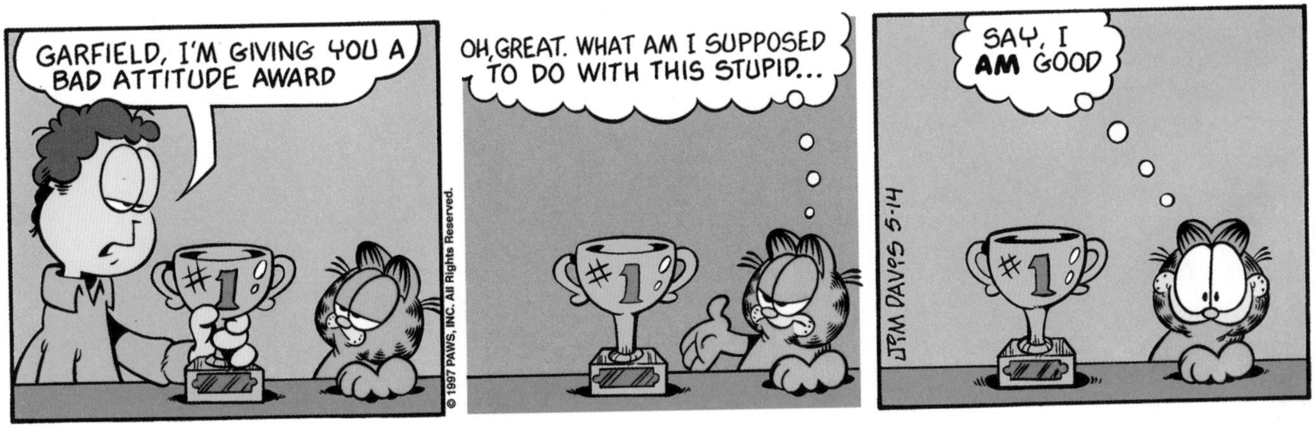
GARFIELD, I'M GIVING YOU A BAD ATTITUDE AWARD
#1
© 1997 PAWS, INC. All Rights Reserved.
OH, GREAT. WHAT AM I SUPPOSED TO DO WITH THIS STUPID...
#1
JPM DAVIS 5-14
SAY, I **AM** GOOD
#1

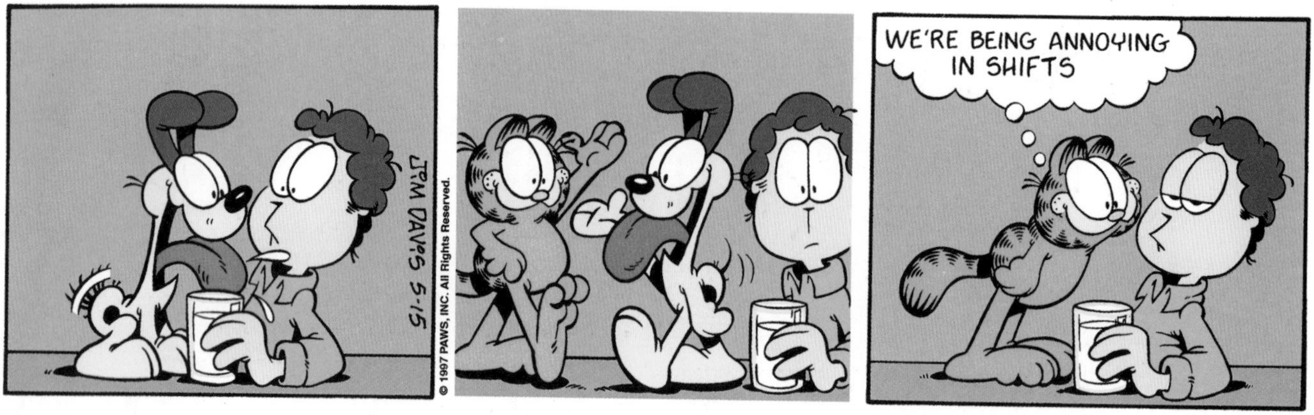
JIM DAVIS 5-15
© 1997 PAWS, INC. All Rights Reserved.
WE'RE BEING ANNOYING IN SHIFTS

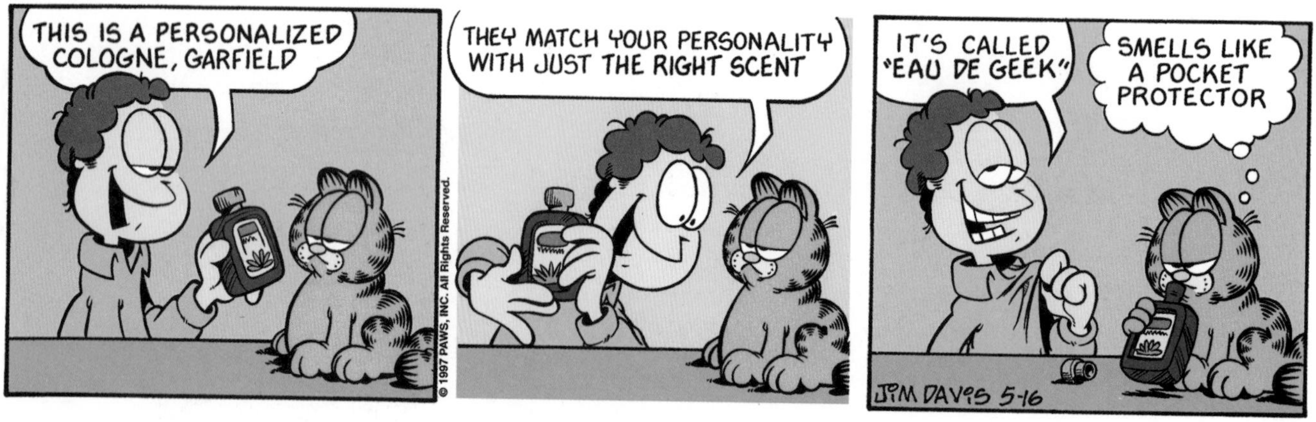
THIS IS A PERSONALIZED COLOGNE, GARFIELD
© 1997 PAWS, INC. All Rights Reserved.
THEY MATCH YOUR PERSONALITY WITH JUST THE RIGHT SCENT
IT'S CALLED "EAU DE GEEK"
SMELLS LIKE A POCKET PROTECTOR
JIM DAVIS 5-16

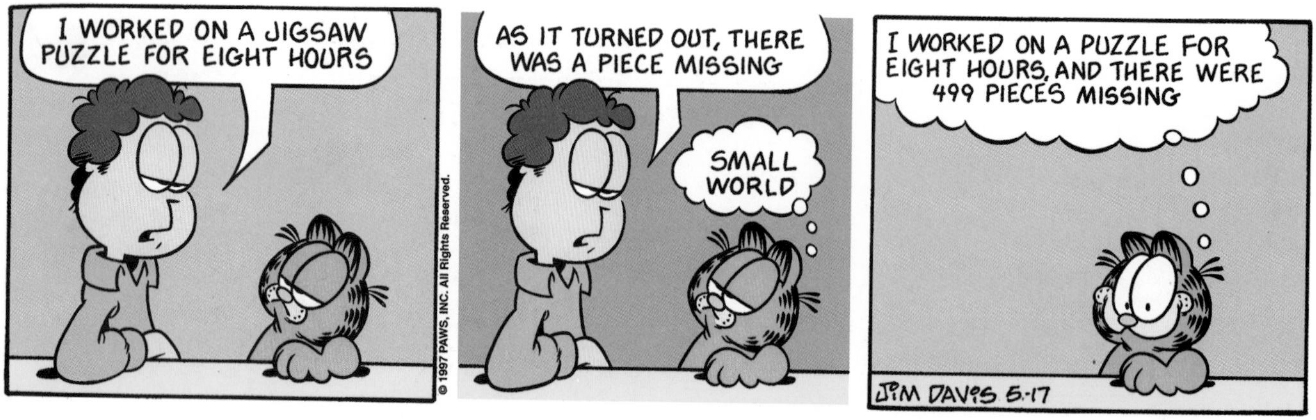
I WORKED ON A JIGSAW PUZZLE FOR EIGHT HOURS
© 1997 PAWS, INC. All Rights Reserved.
AS IT TURNED OUT, THERE WAS A PIECE MISSING
SMALL WORLD
I WORKED ON A PUZZLE FOR EIGHT HOURS, AND THERE WERE 499 PIECES MISSING
JIM DAVIS 5-17

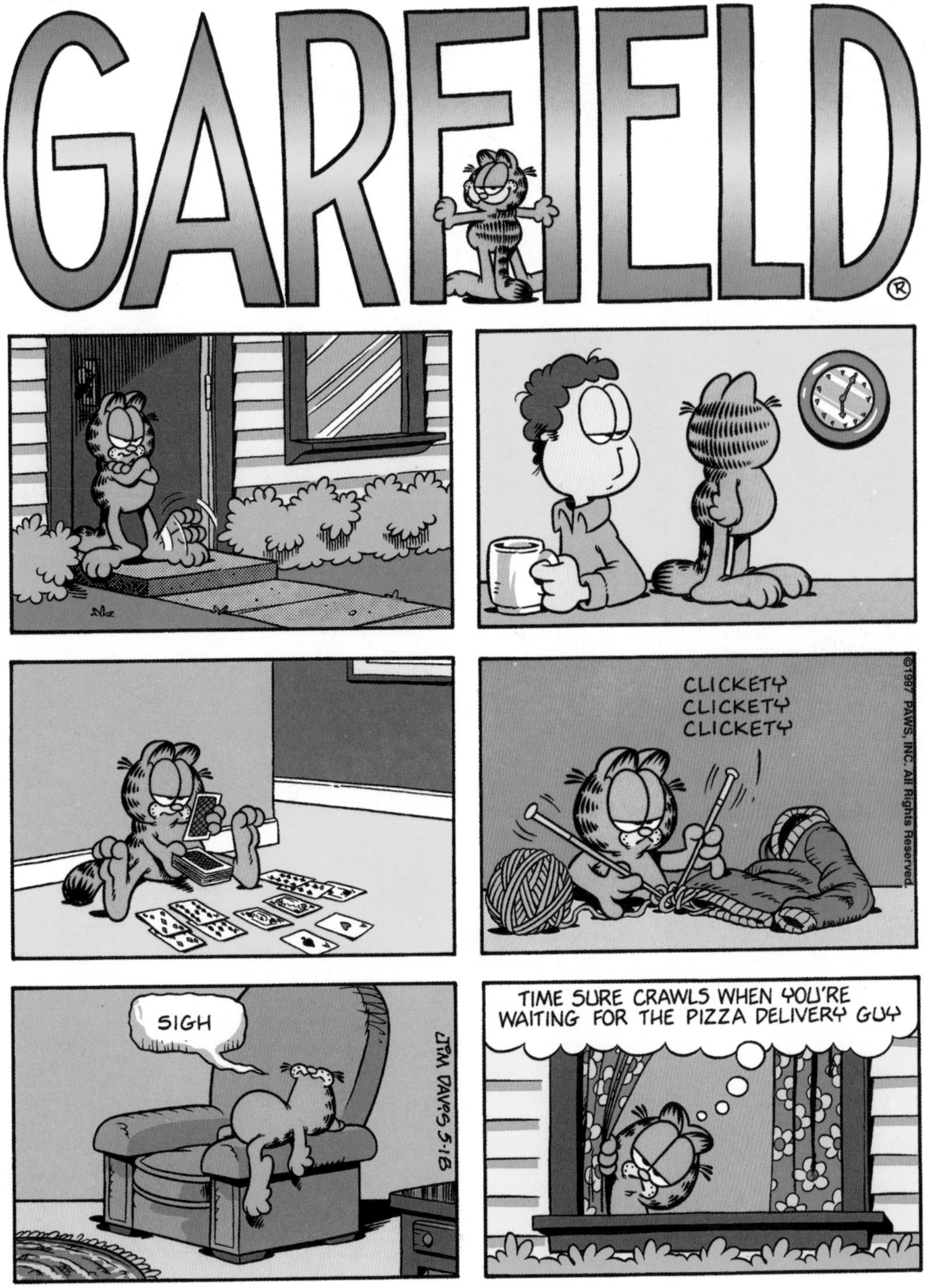
GARFIELD®
CLICKETY
CLICKETY
CLICKETY
©1997 PAWS, INC. All Rights Reserved.
SIGH
JIM DAVIS 5-18
TIME SURE CRAWLS WHEN YOU'RE WAITING FOR THE PIZZA DELIVERY GUY

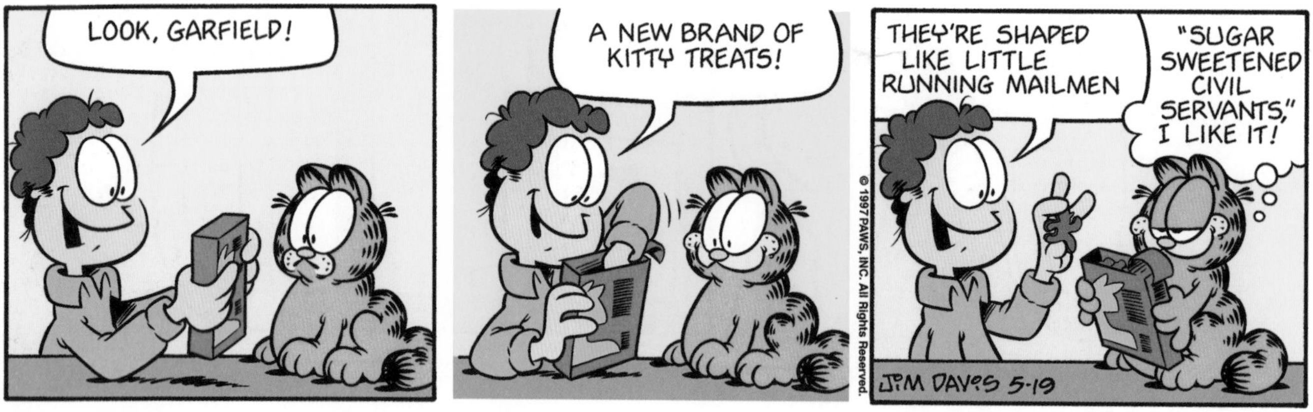
LOOK, GARFIELD!
A NEW BRAND OF KITTY TREATS!
THEY'RE SHAPED LIKE LITTLE RUNNING MAILMEN
"SUGAR SWEETENED CIVIL SERVANTS," I LIKE IT!
© 1997 PAWS, INC. All Rights Reserved.
JIM DAVIS 5-19

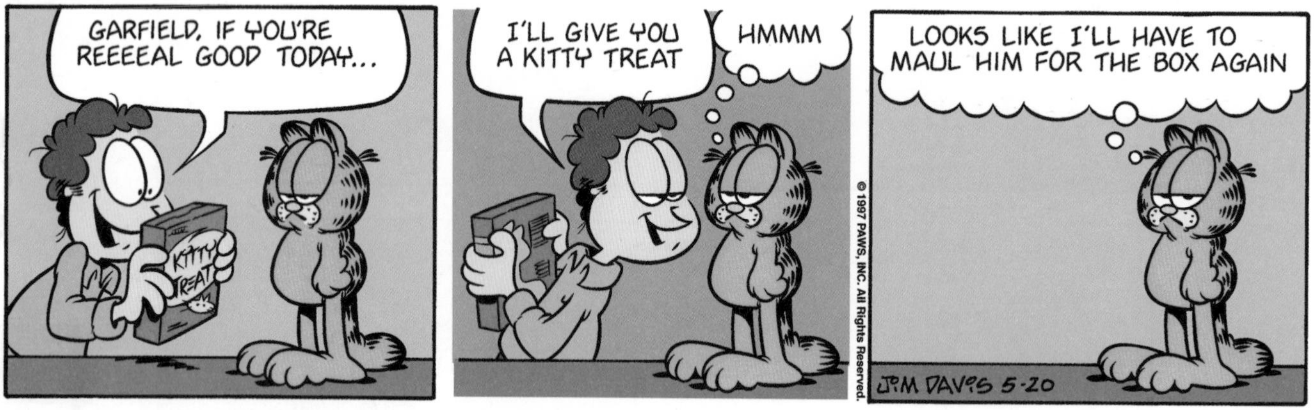
GARFIELD, IF YOU'RE REEEEAL GOOD TODAY...
KITTY TREAT
I'LL GIVE YOU A KITTY TREAT
HMMM
LOOKS LIKE I'LL HAVE TO MAUL HIM FOR THE BOX AGAIN
© 1997 PAWS, INC. All Rights Reserved.
JIM DAVIS 5-20

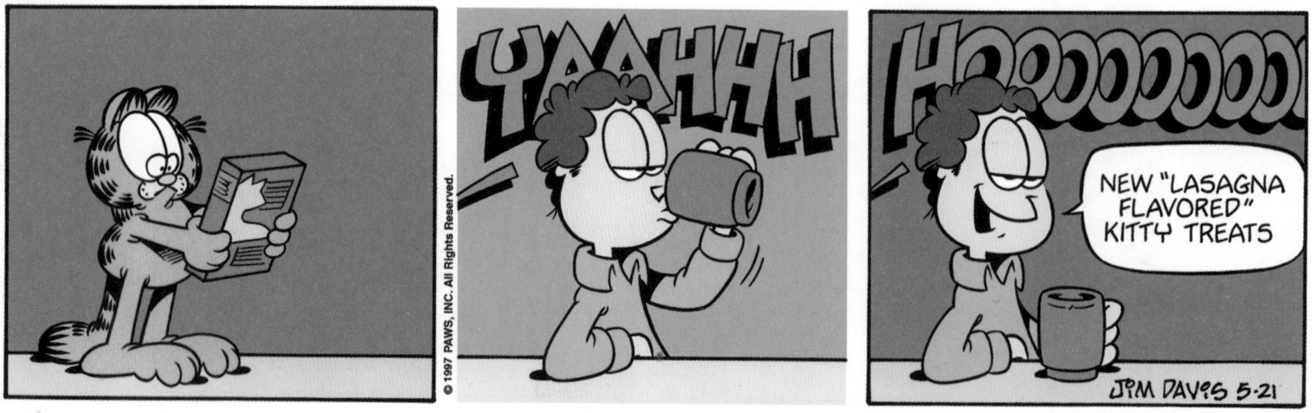
© 1997 PAWS, INC. All Rights Reserved.
YAAHHH
HOOOOOOOOO
NEW "LASAGNA FLAVORED" KITTY TREATS
JIM DAVIS 5-21

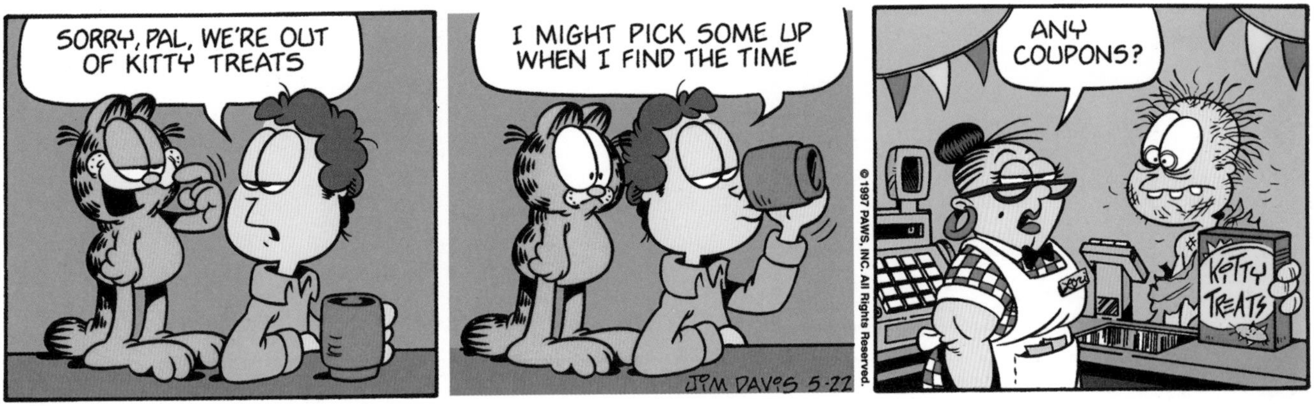
SORRY, PAL, WE'RE OUT OF KITTY TREATS
I MIGHT PICK SOME UP WHEN I FIND THE TIME
ANY COUPONS?
KITTY TREATS
JIM DAVIS 5-22
© 1997 PAWS, INC. All Rights Reserved.

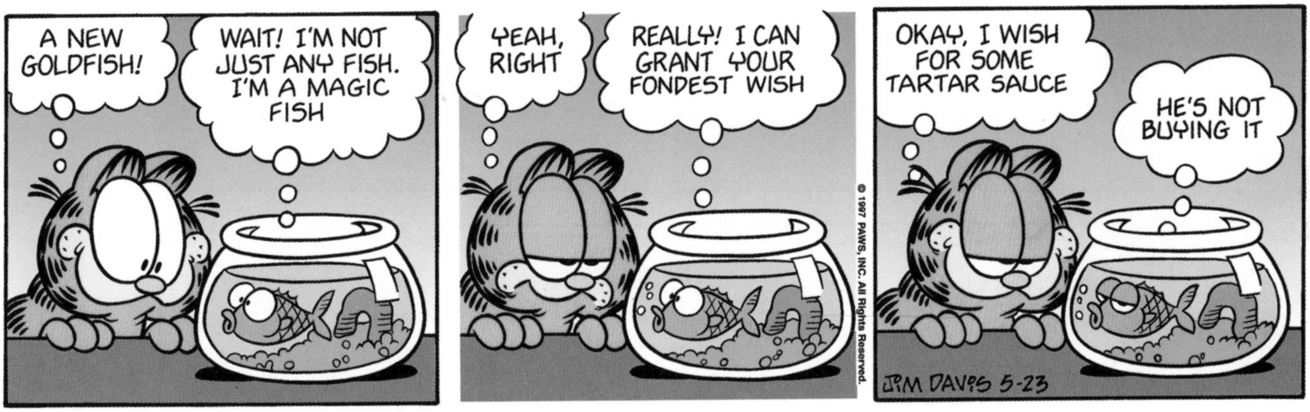
A NEW GOLDFISH!
WAIT! I'M NOT JUST ANY FISH. I'M A MAGIC FISH
YEAH, RIGHT
REALLY! I CAN GRANT YOUR FONDEST WISH
OKAY, I WISH FOR SOME TARTAR SAUCE
HE'S NOT BUYING IT
JIM DAVIS 5-23
© 1997 PAWS, INC. All Rights Reserved.

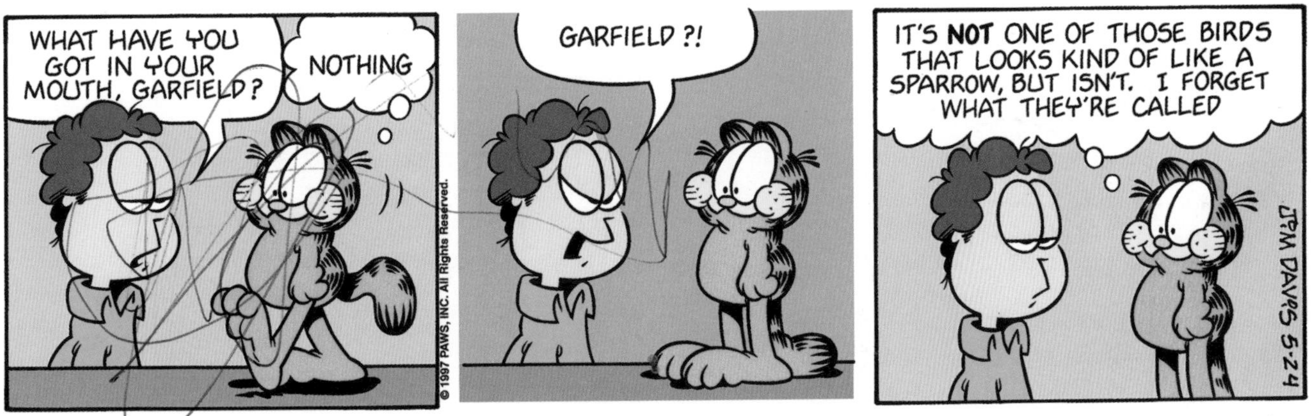
WHAT HAVE YOU GOT IN YOUR MOUTH, GARFIELD?
NOTHING
GARFIELD ?!
IT'S **NOT** ONE OF THOSE BIRDS THAT LOOKS KIND OF LIKE A SPARROW, BUT ISN'T. I FORGET WHAT THEY'RE CALLED
JIM DAVIS 5-24
© 1997 PAWS, INC. All Rights Reserved.

GARFIELD®

LOOK AT YOU, YOU LAZY LUMP!
GET UP! MOVE AROUND! EXERCISE!
GO OUTSIDE! BREATHE SOME FRESH AIR!
GO TO THE LIBRARY! READ A BOOK!
YOU'RE STILL SITTING THERE, AREN'T YOU?
YUP
GOOOOOD. I HAVE TRAINED YOU WELL
JIM DAVIS 5-25
©1997 PAWS, INC. All Rights Reserved.

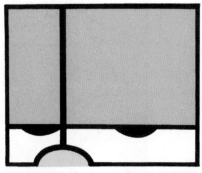

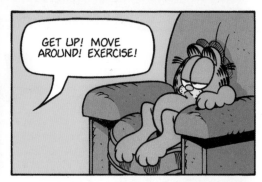

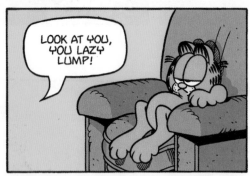

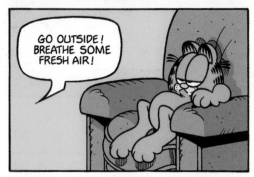

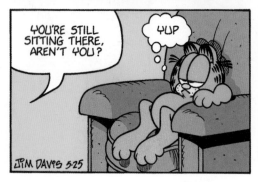

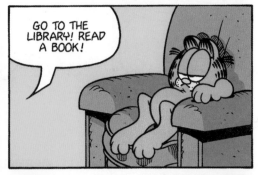

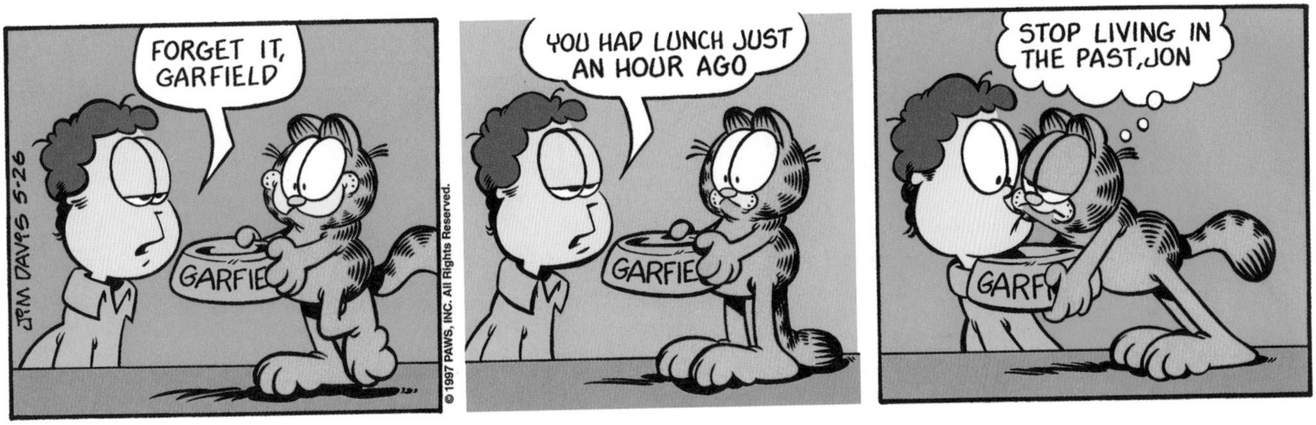
JIM DAVIS 5-26
FORGET IT, GARFIELD
GARFIE
© 1997 PAWS, INC. All Rights Reserved.
YOU HAD LUNCH JUST AN HOUR AGO
GARFIE
STOP LIVING IN THE PAST, JON
GARF

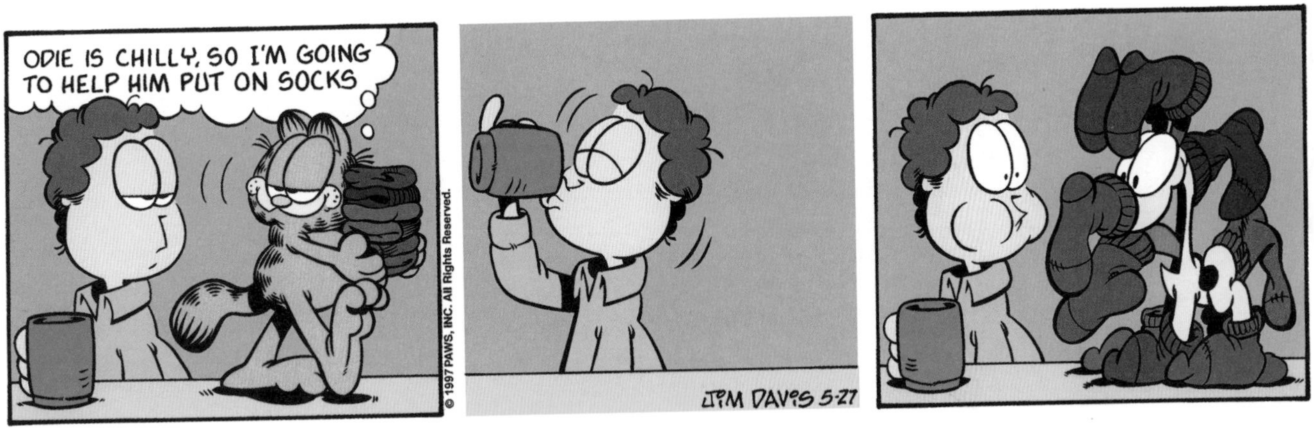
ODIE IS CHILLY, SO I'M GOING TO HELP HIM PUT ON SOCKS
© 1997 PAWS, INC. All Rights Reserved.
JIM DAVIS 5-27

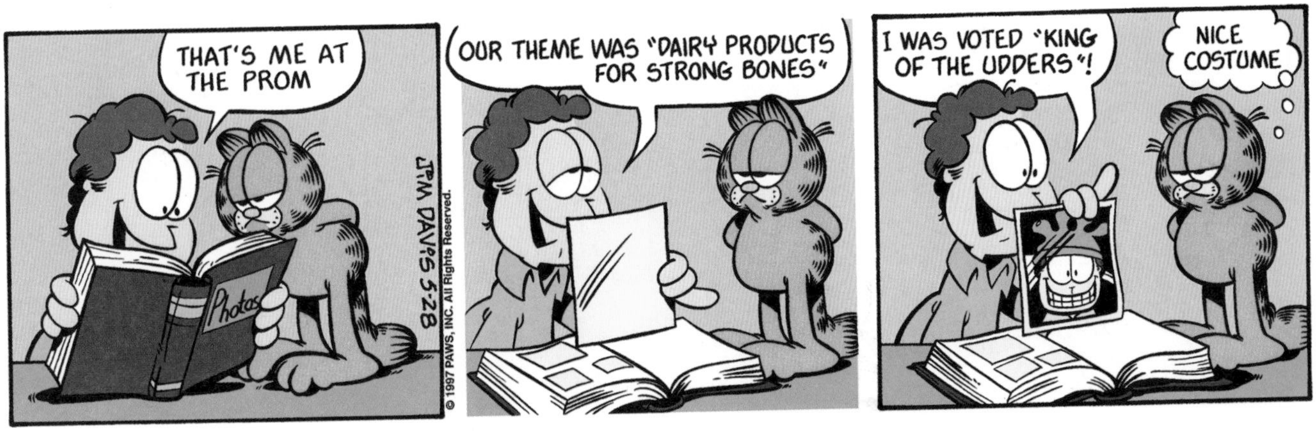
THAT'S ME AT THE PROM
Photos
JIM DAVIS 5-28
© 1997 PAWS, INC. All Rights Reserved.
OUR THEME WAS "DAIRY PRODUCTS FOR STRONG BONES"
I WAS VOTED "KING OF THE UDDERS"!
NICE COSTUME

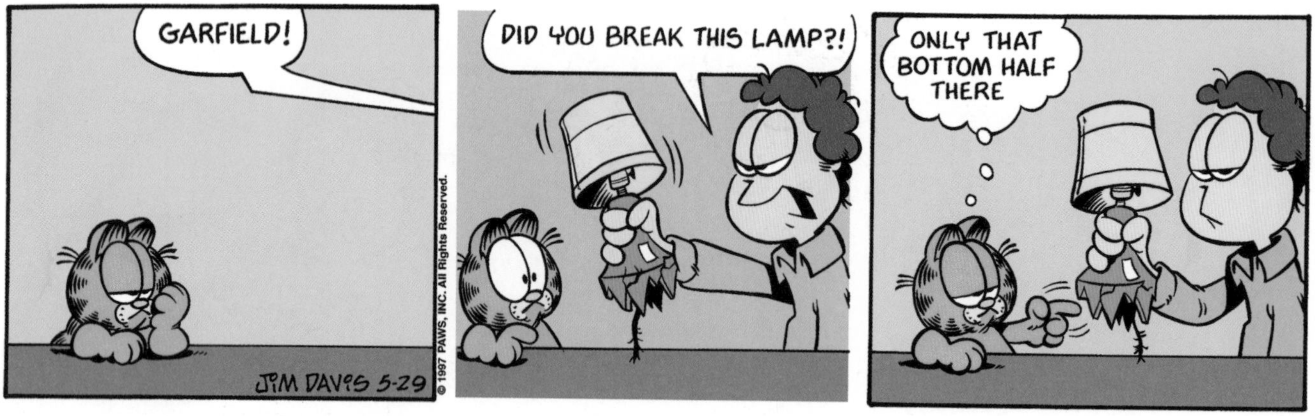
GARFIELD!
JIM DAVIS 5-29
DID YOU BREAK THIS LAMP?!
ONLY THAT BOTTOM HALF THERE

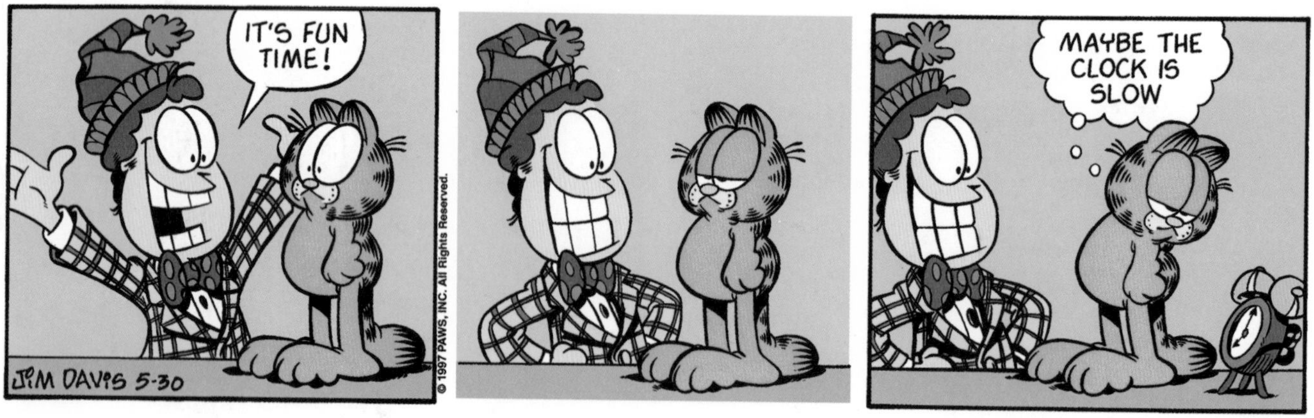
IT'S FUN TIME!
JIM DAVIS 5-30
MAYBE THE CLOCK IS SLOW

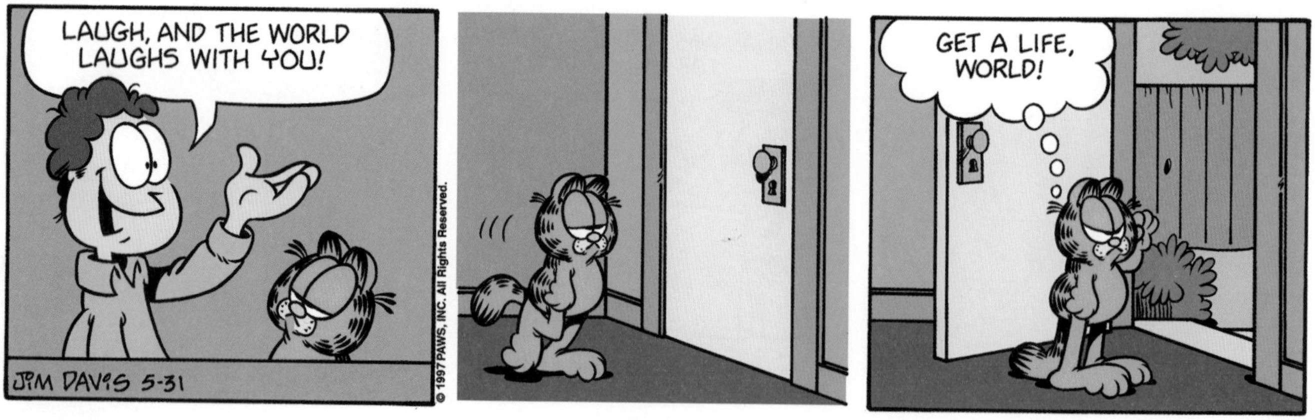
LAUGH, AND THE WORLD LAUGHS WITH YOU!
JIM DAVIS 5-31
GET A LIFE, WORLD!

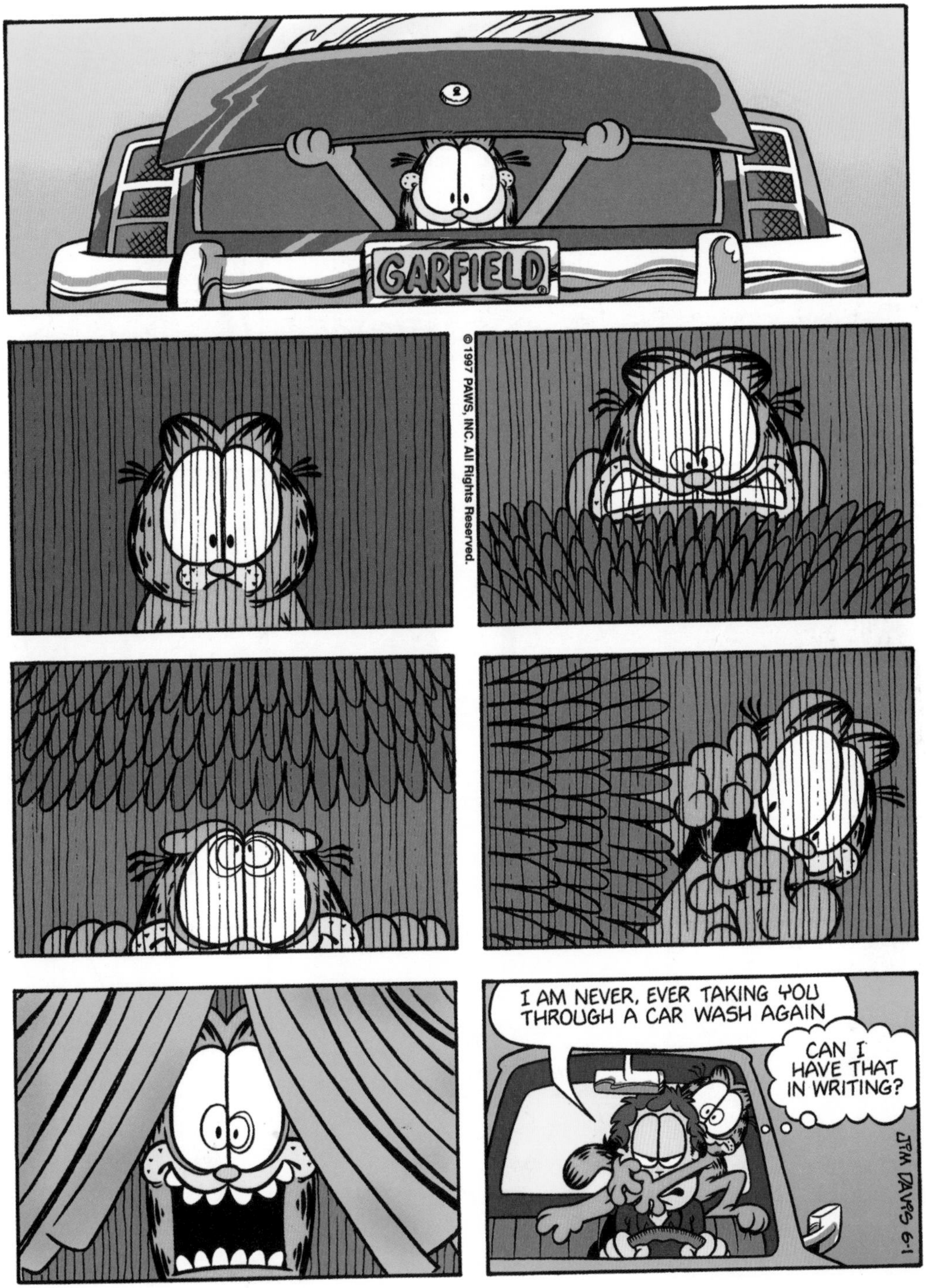
GARFIELD®
I AM NEVER, EVER TAKING YOU THROUGH A CAR WASH AGAIN
CAN I HAVE THAT IN WRITING?
JIM DAVIS 6-1

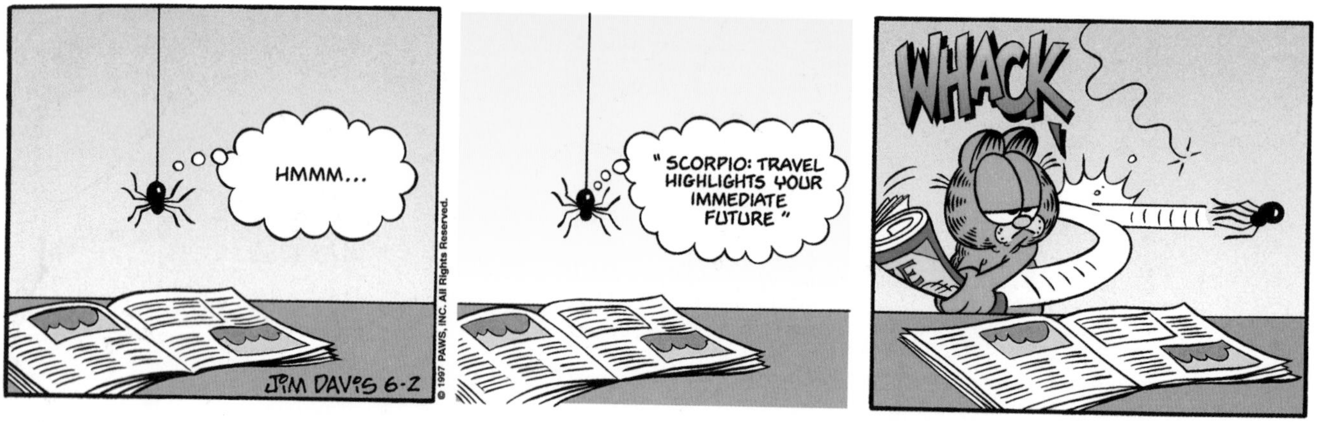
HMMM...
JIM DAVIS 6-2
© 1997 PAWS, INC. All Rights Reserved.
"SCORPIO: TRAVEL HIGHLIGHTS YOUR IMMEDIATE FUTURE"
WHACK

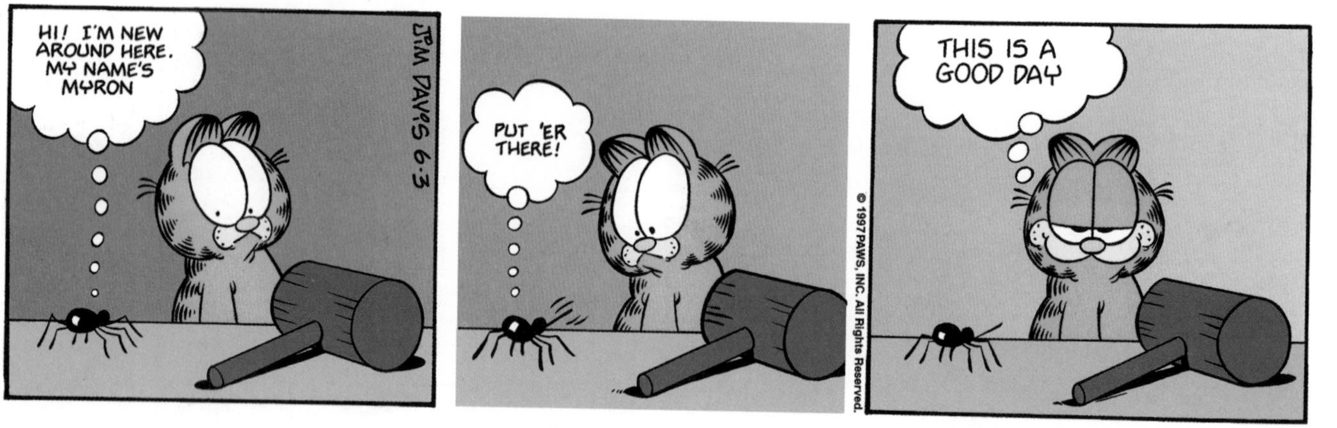
HI! I'M NEW AROUND HERE. MY NAME'S MYRON
JIM DAVIS 6-3
PUT 'ER THERE!
© 1997 PAWS, INC. All Rights Reserved.
THIS IS A GOOD DAY

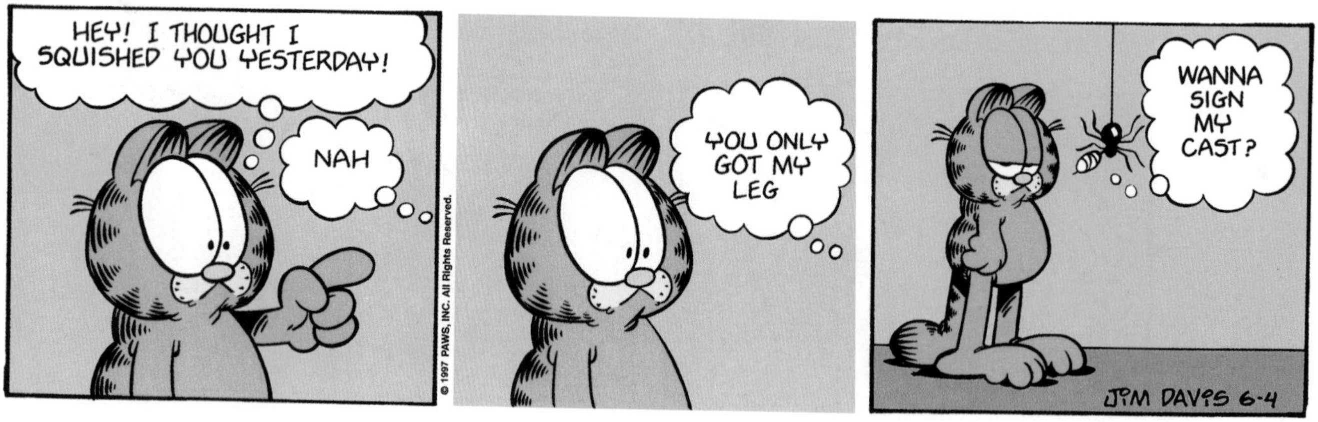
HEY! I THOUGHT I SQUISHED YOU YESTERDAY!
NAH
© 1997 PAWS, INC. All Rights Reserved.
YOU ONLY GOT MY LEG
WANNA SIGN MY CAST?
JIM DAVIS 6-4

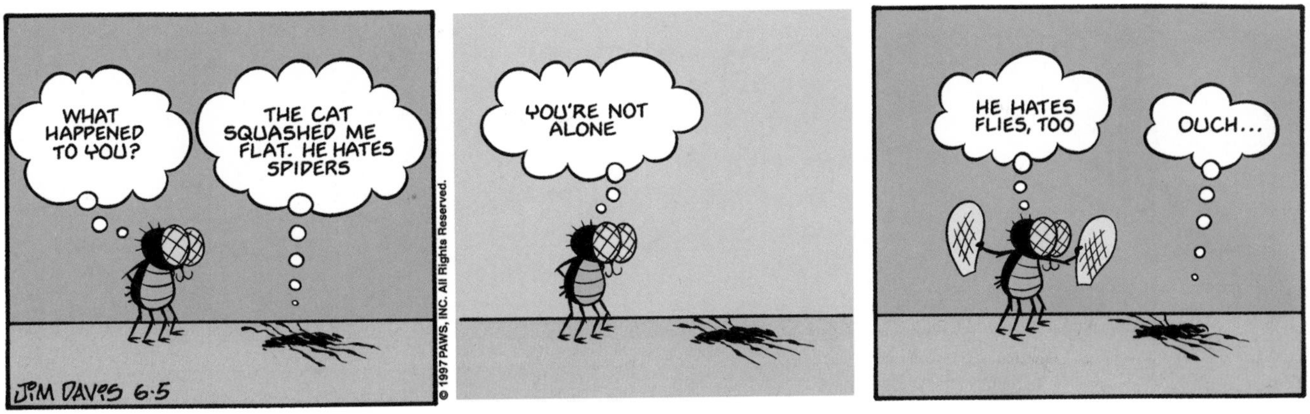
WHAT HAPPENED TO YOU?
THE CAT SQUASHED ME FLAT. HE HATES SPIDERS
JIM DAVIS 6-5
© 1997 PAWS, INC. All Rights Reserved.
YOU'RE NOT ALONE
HE HATES FLIES, TOO
OUCH...

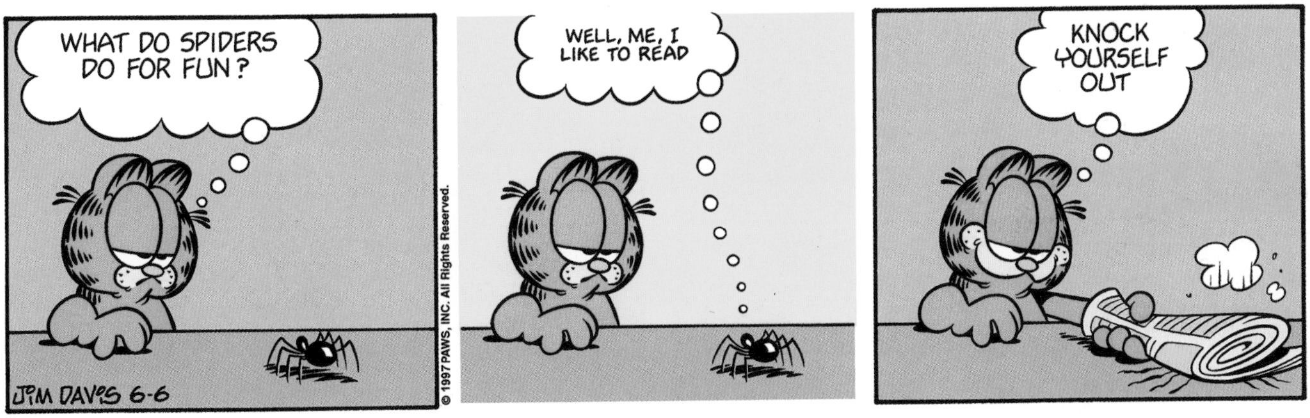
WHAT DO SPIDERS DO FOR FUN?
JIM DAVIS 6-6
© 1997 PAWS, INC. All Rights Reserved.
WELL, ME, I LIKE TO READ
KNOCK YOURSELF OUT

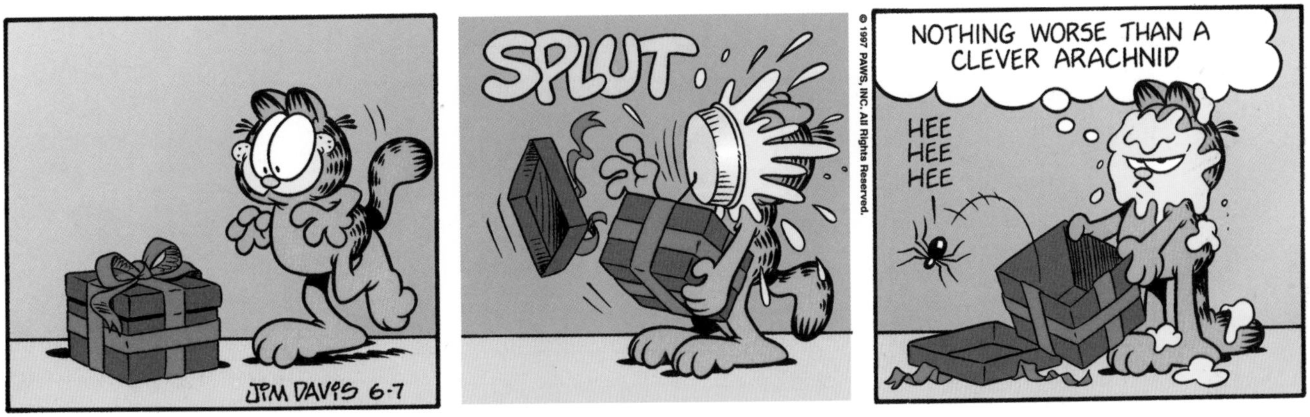
JIM DAVIS 6-7
SPLUT
© 1997 PAWS, INC. All Rights Reserved.
NOTHING WORSE THAN A CLEVER ARACHNID
HEE HEE HEE !

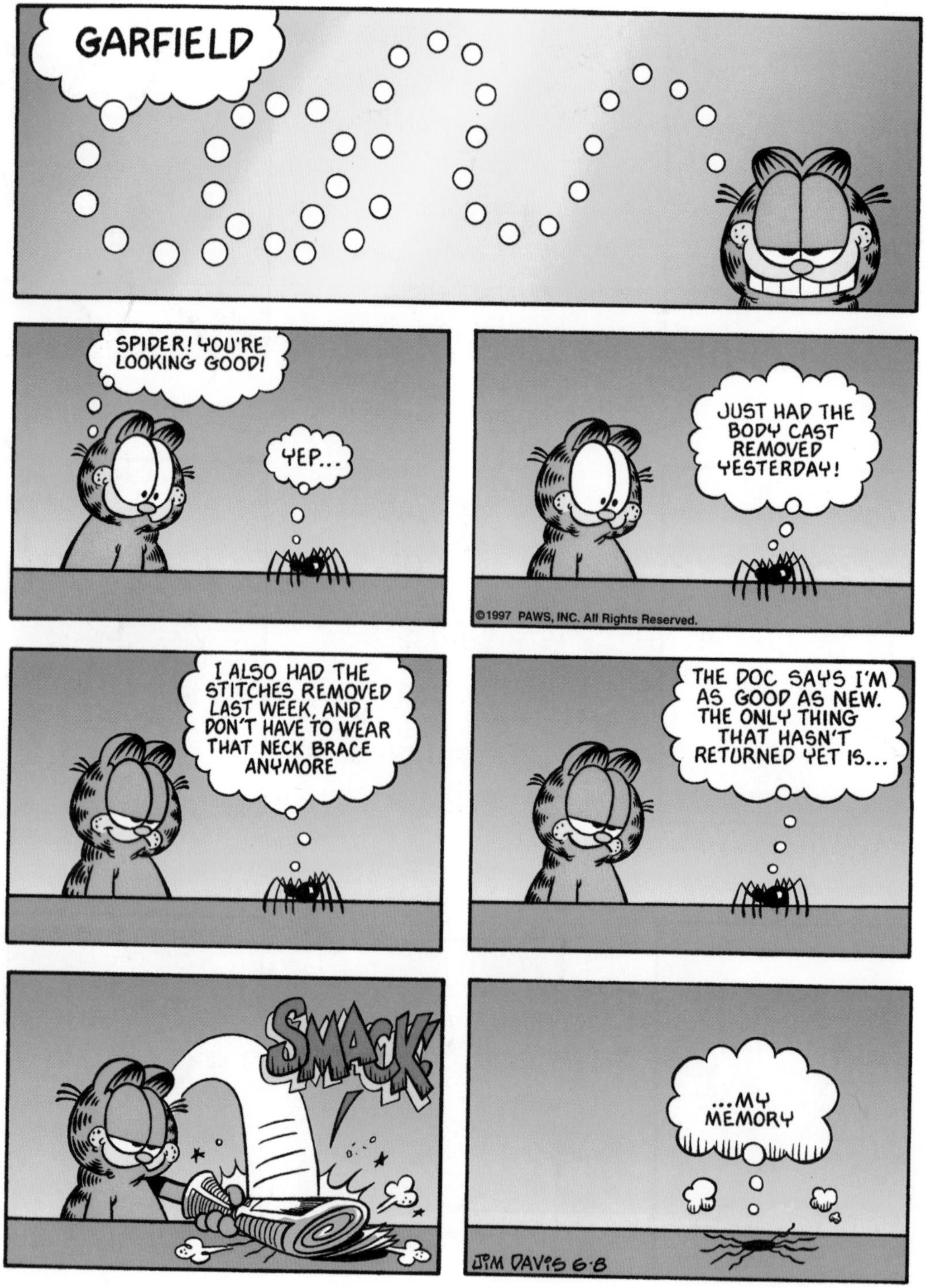
GARFIELD
SPIDER! YOU'RE LOOKING GOOD!
YEP...
JUST HAD THE BODY CAST REMOVED YESTERDAY!
©1997 PAWS, INC. All Rights Reserved.
I ALSO HAD THE STITCHES REMOVED LAST WEEK, AND I DON'T HAVE TO WEAR THAT NECK BRACE ANYMORE
THE DOC SAYS I'M AS GOOD AS NEW. THE ONLY THING THAT HASN'T RETURNED YET IS...
SMACK!
...MY MEMORY
JIM DAVIS 6-8

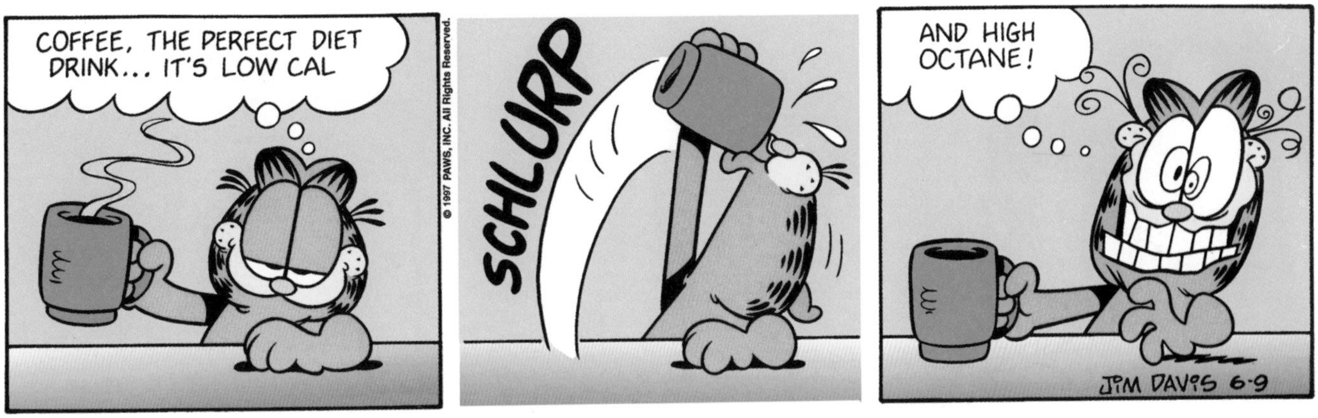
COFFEE, THE PERFECT DIET DRINK... IT'S LOW CAL
© 1997 PAWS, INC. All Rights Reserved.
SCHLURP
AND HIGH OCTANE!
JIM DAVIS 6-9

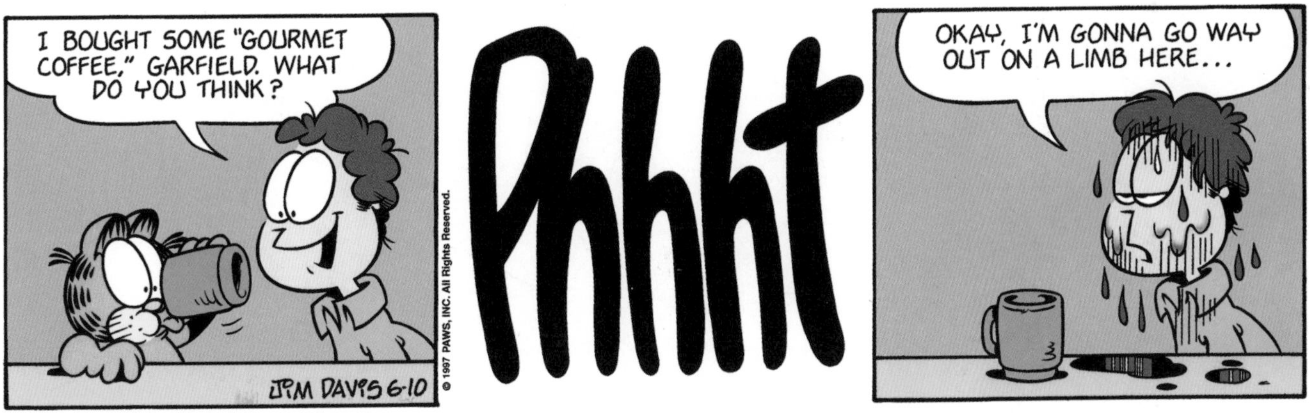
I BOUGHT SOME "GOURMET COFFEE," GARFIELD. WHAT DO YOU THINK?
JIM DAVIS 6-10
© 1997 PAWS, INC. All Rights Reserved.
Phhht
OKAY, I'M GONNA GO WAY OUT ON A LIMB HERE...

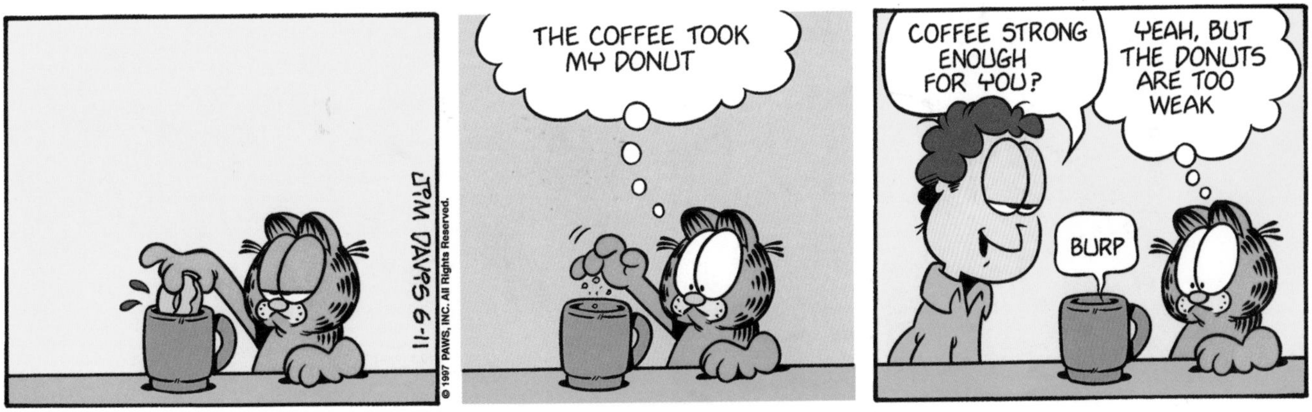
JIM DAVIS 6-11
© 1997 PAWS, INC. All Rights Reserved.
THE COFFEE TOOK MY DONUT
COFFEE STRONG ENOUGH FOR YOU?
YEAH, BUT THE DONUTS ARE TOO WEAK
BURP

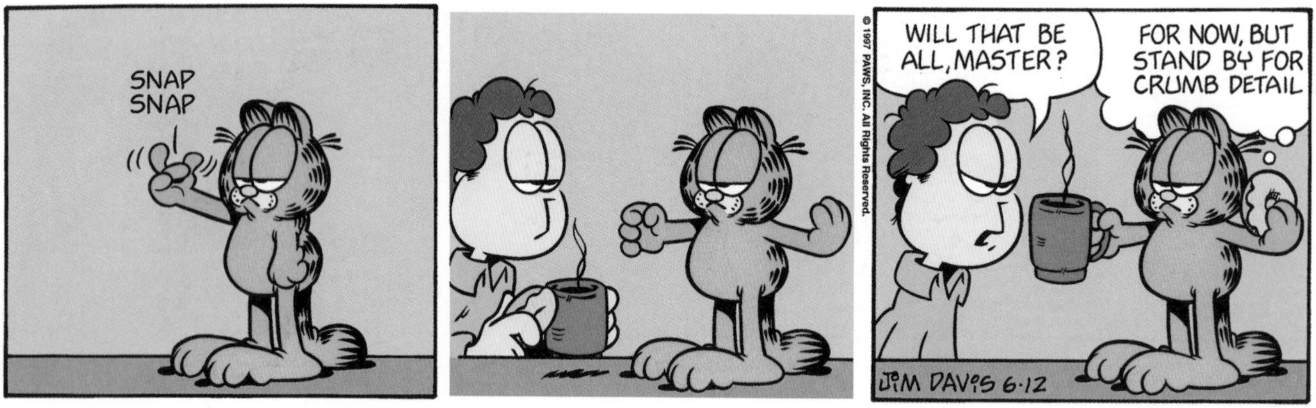
SNAP
SNAP
WILL THAT BE ALL, MASTER?
FOR NOW, BUT STAND BY FOR CRUMB DETAIL
© 1997 PAWS, INC. All Rights Reserved.
JIM DAVIS 6-12

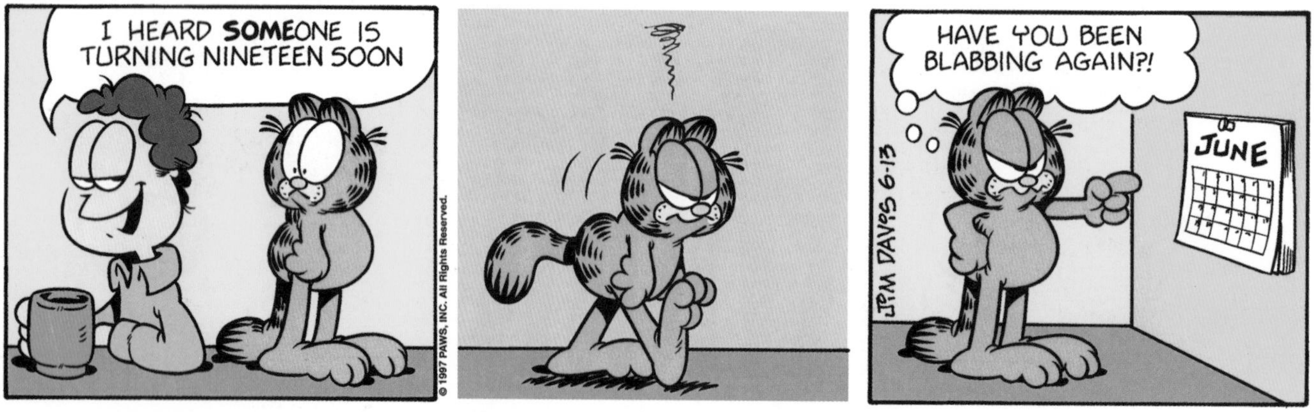
I HEARD **SOME**ONE IS TURNING NINETEEN SOON
HAVE YOU BEEN BLABBING AGAIN?!
JUNE
© 1997 PAWS, INC. All Rights Reserved.
JIM DAVIS 6-13

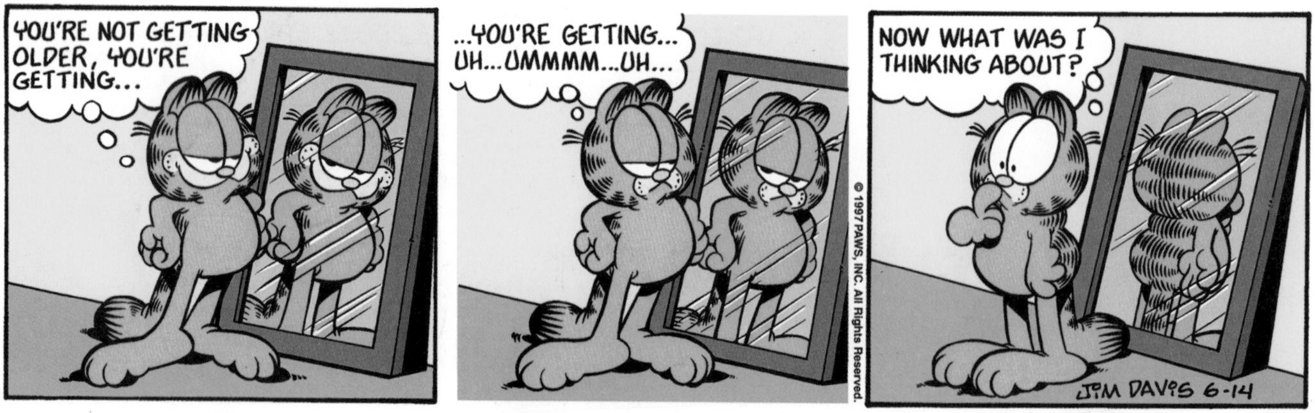
YOU'RE NOT GETTING OLDER, YOU'RE GETTING...
...YOU'RE GETTING... UH...UMMMM...UH...
NOW WHAT WAS I THINKING ABOUT?
© 1997 PAWS, INC. All Rights Reserved.
JIM DAVIS 6-14

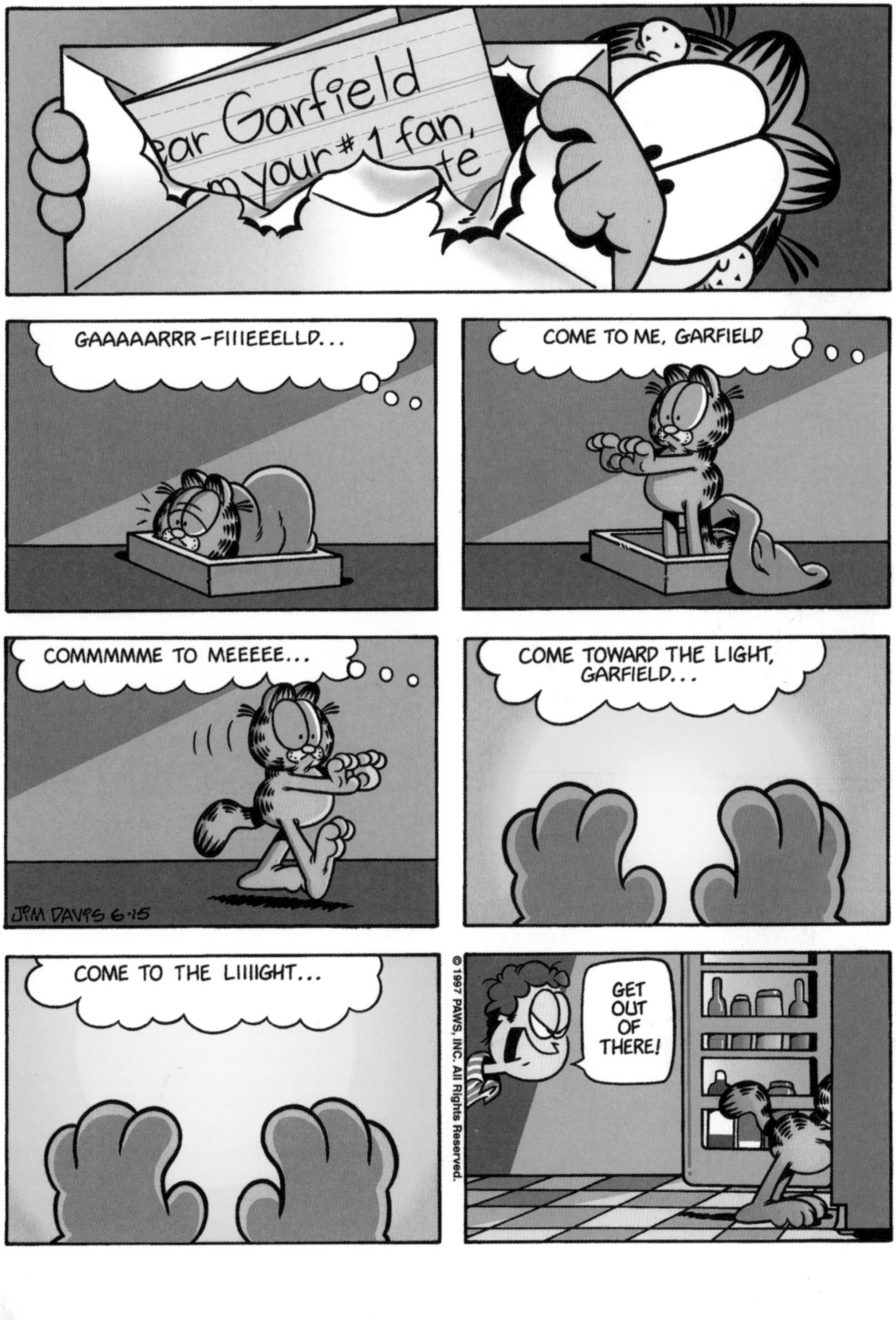
ear Garfield
m your # 1 fan,
te
GAAAAARRR-FIIIEEELLD...
COME TO ME, GARFIELD
COMMMME TO MEEEEE...
COME TOWARD THE LIGHT, GARFIELD...
COME TO THE LIIIGHT...
GET OUT OF THERE!
JIM DAVIS 6-15

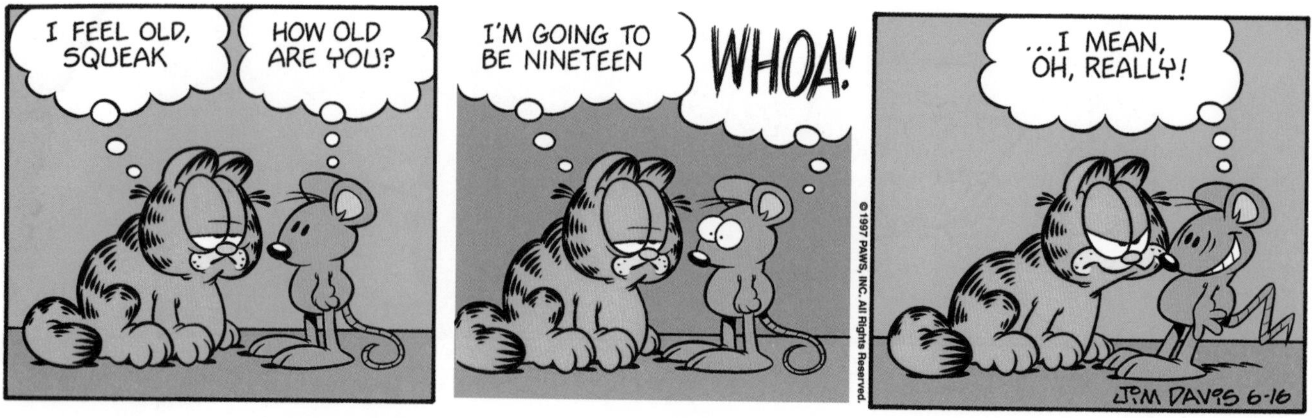
I FEEL OLD, SQUEAK
HOW OLD ARE YOU?
I'M GOING TO BE NINETEEN
WHOA!
...I MEAN, OH, REALLY!
© 1997 PAWS, INC. All Rights Reserved.
JIM DAVIS 6-16

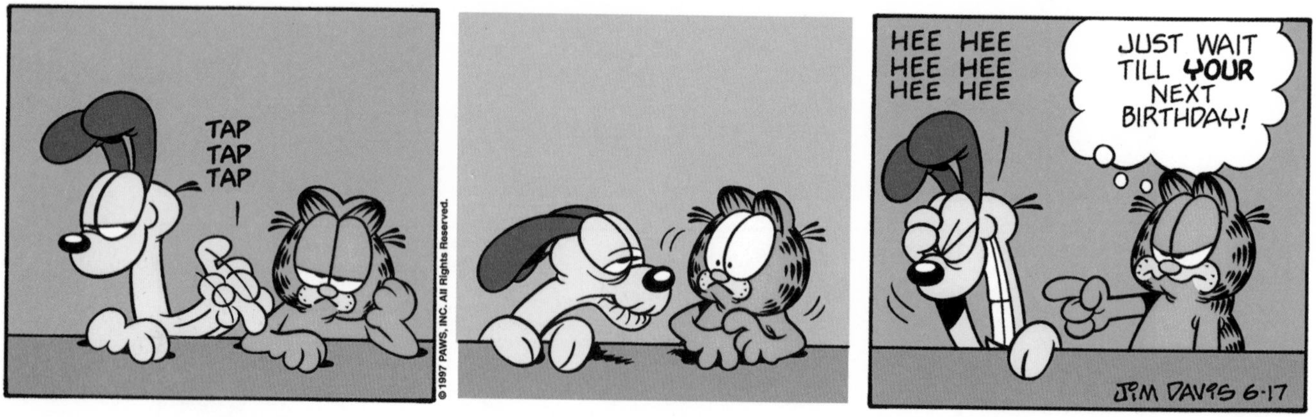
TAP TAP TAP
© 1997 PAWS, INC. All Rights Reserved.
HEE HEE HEE HEE HEE HEE
JUST WAIT TILL **YOUR** NEXT BIRTHDAY!
JIM DAVIS 6-17

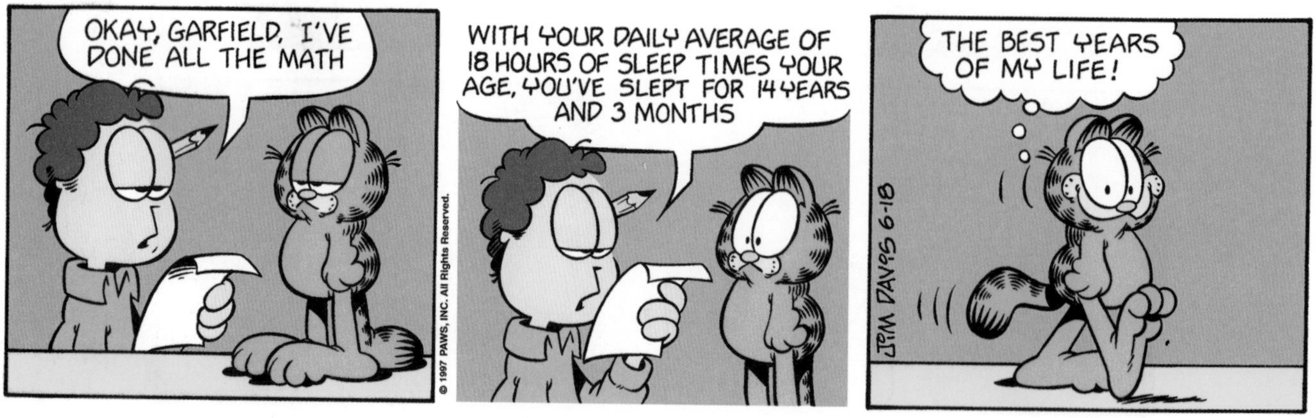
OKAY, GARFIELD, I'VE DONE ALL THE MATH
© 1997 PAWS, INC. All Rights Reserved.
WITH YOUR DAILY AVERAGE OF 18 HOURS OF SLEEP TIMES YOUR AGE, YOU'VE SLEPT FOR 14 YEARS AND 3 MONTHS
THE BEST YEARS OF MY LIFE!
JIM DAVIS 6-18

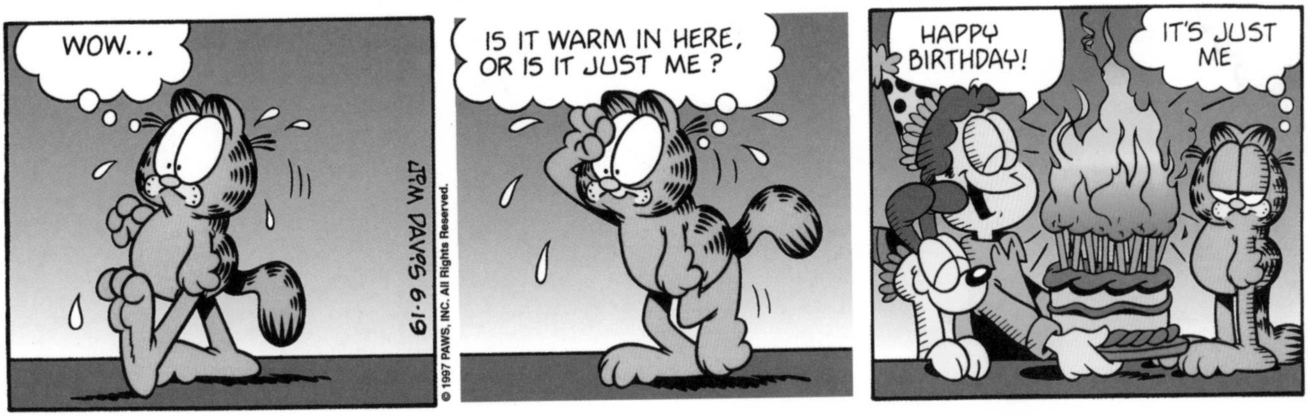
WOW...
JIM DAVIS 6-19
© 1997 PAWS, INC. All Rights Reserved.
IS IT WARM IN HERE, OR IS IT JUST ME ?
HAPPY BIRTHDAY!
IT'S JUST ME

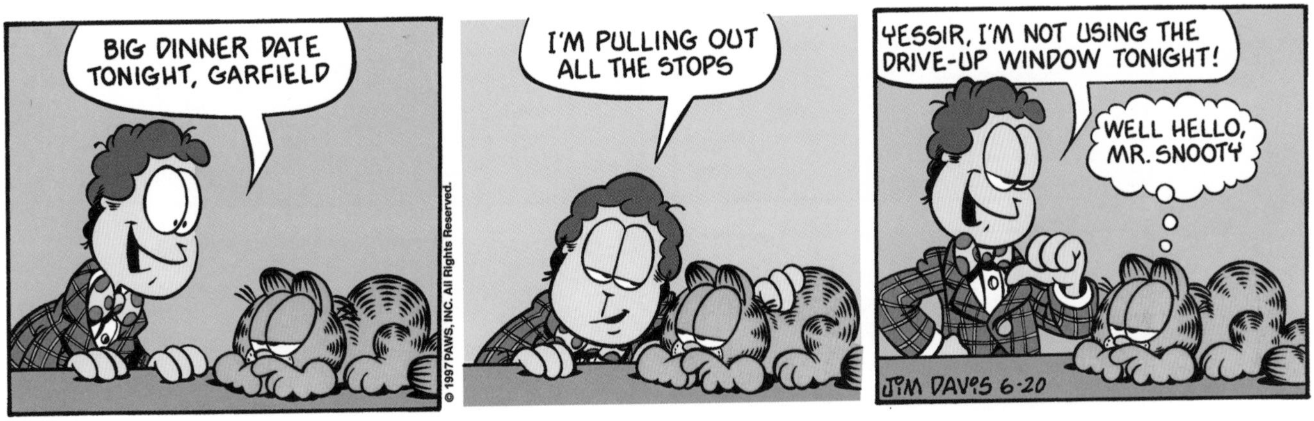
BIG DINNER DATE TONIGHT, GARFIELD
© 1997 PAWS, INC. All Rights Reserved.
I'M PULLING OUT ALL THE STOPS
YESSIR, I'M NOT USING THE DRIVE-UP WINDOW TONIGHT!
WELL HELLO, MR. SNOOTY
JIM DAVIS 6-20

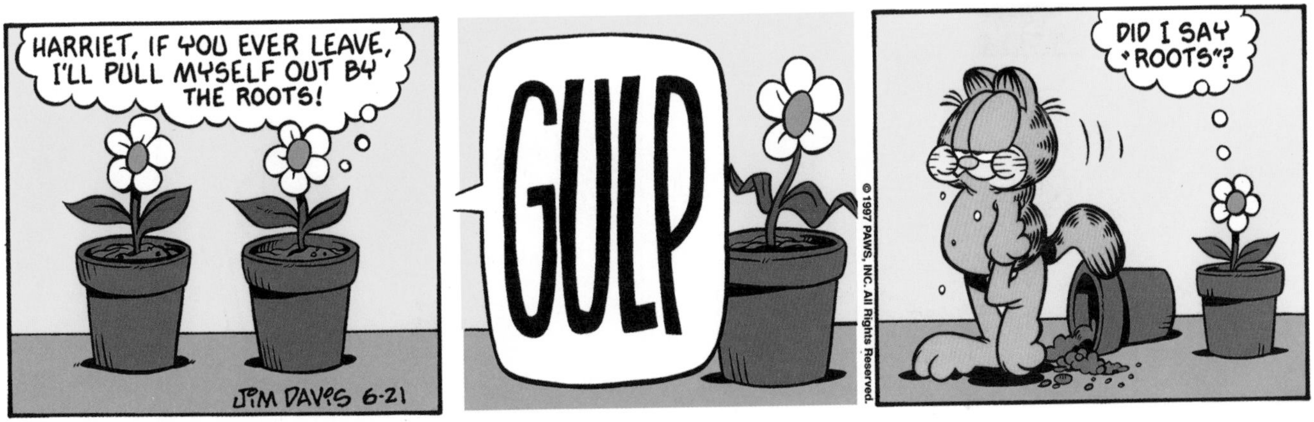
HARRIET, IF YOU EVER LEAVE, I'LL PULL MYSELF OUT BY THE ROOTS!
JIM DAVIS 6-21
GULP
© 1997 PAWS, INC. All Rights Reserved.
DID I SAY "ROOTS"?

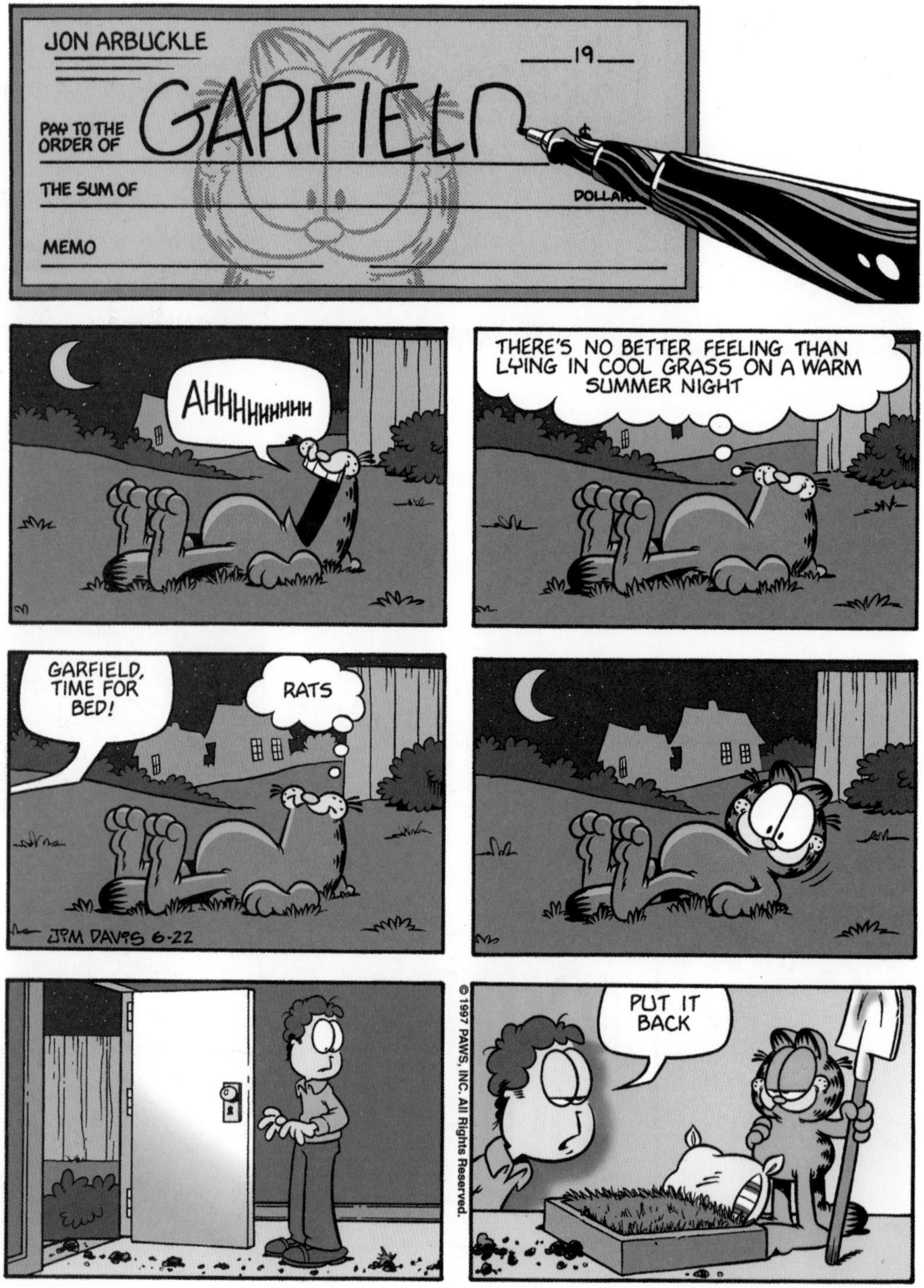
JON ARBUCKLE
19
PAY TO THE ORDER OF
GARFIELD
$
THE SUM OF
DOLLARS
MEMO
AHHHHHHHHH
THERE'S NO BETTER FEELING THAN LYING IN COOL GRASS ON A WARM SUMMER NIGHT
GARFIELD, TIME FOR BED!
RATS
JIM DAVIS 6-22
© 1997 PAWS, INC. All Rights Reserved.
PUT IT BACK

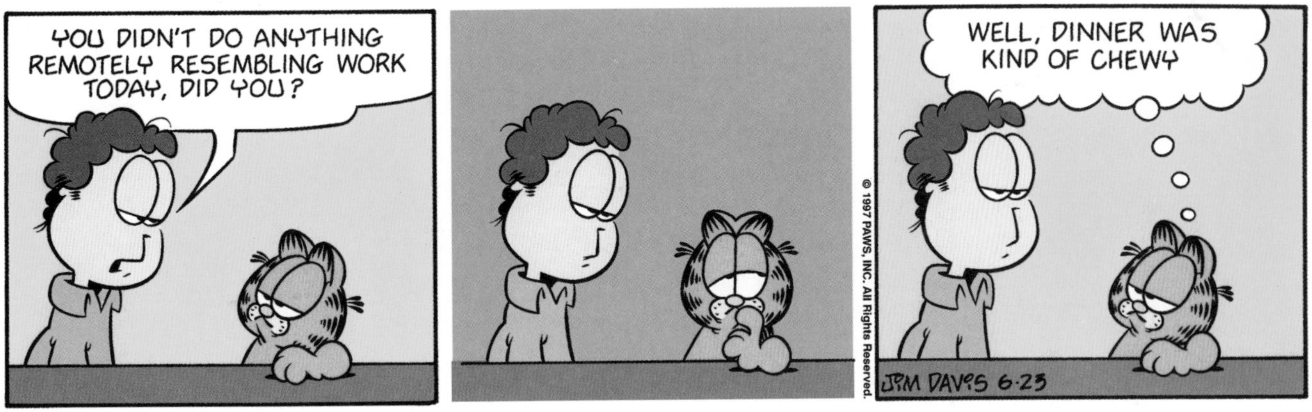
YOU DIDN'T DO ANYTHING REMOTELY RESEMBLING WORK TODAY, DID YOU?
© 1997 PAWS, INC. All Rights Reserved.
WELL, DINNER WAS KIND OF CHEWY
JIM DAVIS 6-23

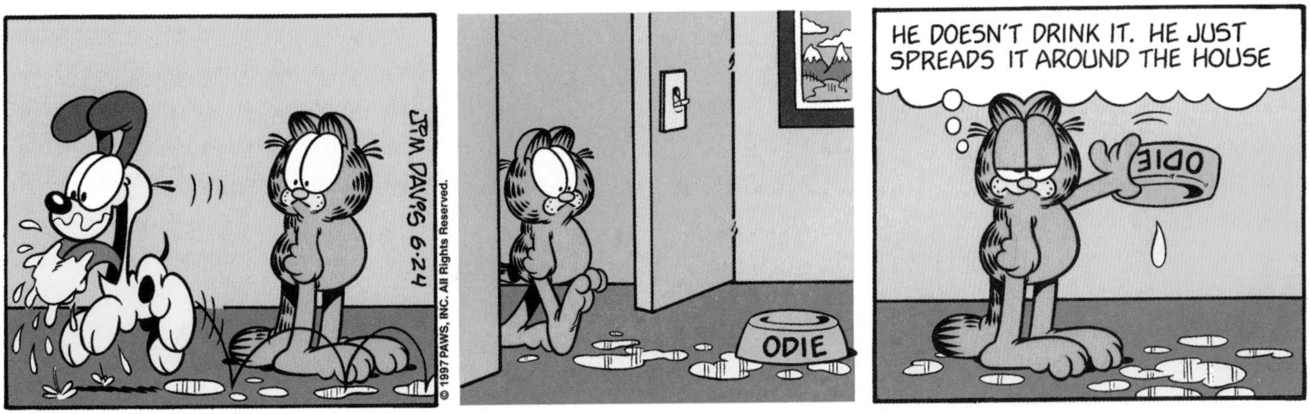
JIM DAVIS 6-24
© 1997 PAWS, INC. All Rights Reserved.
ODIE
HE DOESN'T DRINK IT. HE JUST SPREADS IT AROUND THE HOUSE
ODIE

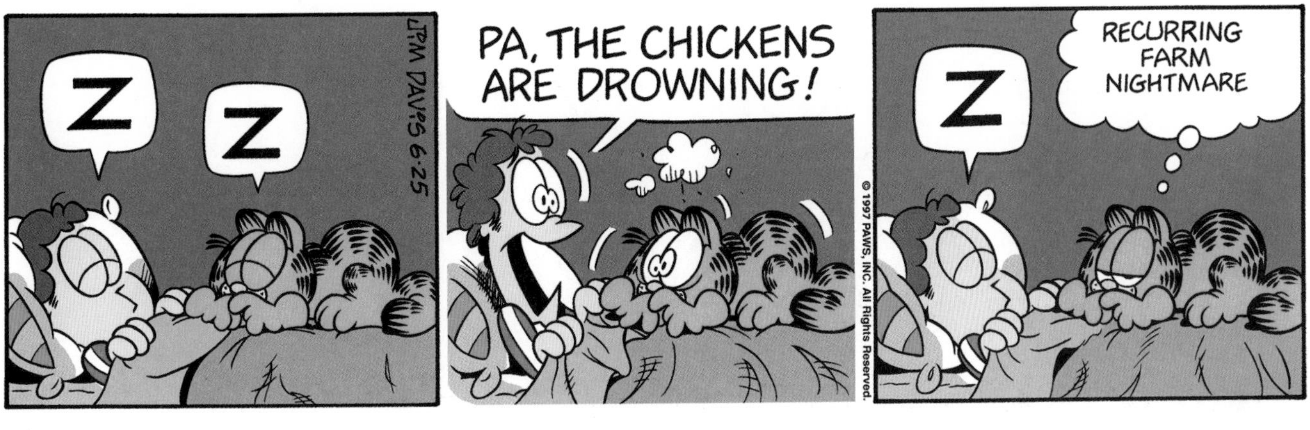
JIM DAVIS 6-25
Z
Z
PA, THE CHICKENS ARE DROWNING!
© 1997 PAWS, INC. All Rights Reserved.
Z
RECURRING FARM NIGHTMARE

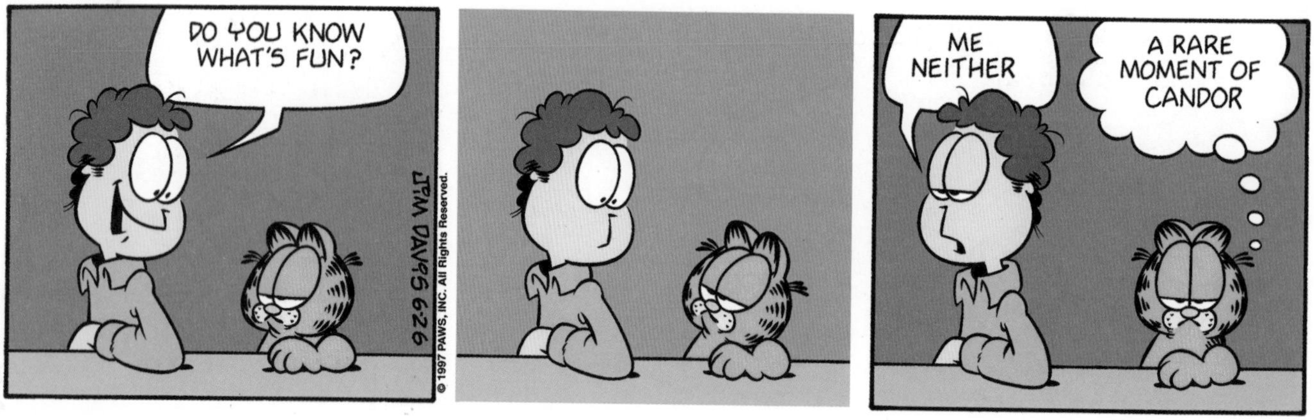
DO YOU KNOW WHAT'S FUN?
JIM DAVIS 6-26
© 1997 PAWS, INC. All Rights Reserved.
ME NEITHER
A RARE MOMENT OF CANDOR

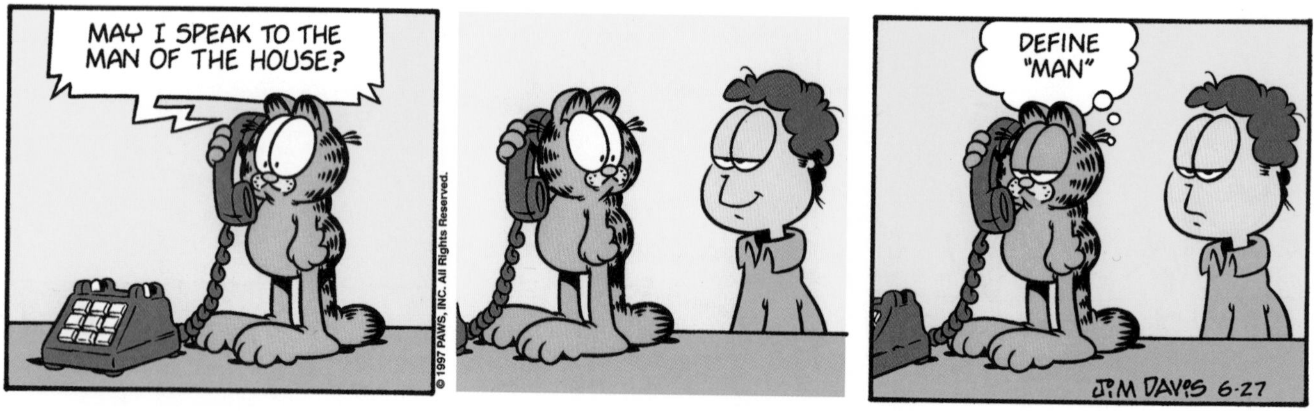
MAY I SPEAK TO THE MAN OF THE HOUSE?
© 1997 PAWS, INC. All Rights Reserved.
DEFINE "MAN"
JIM DAVIS 6-27

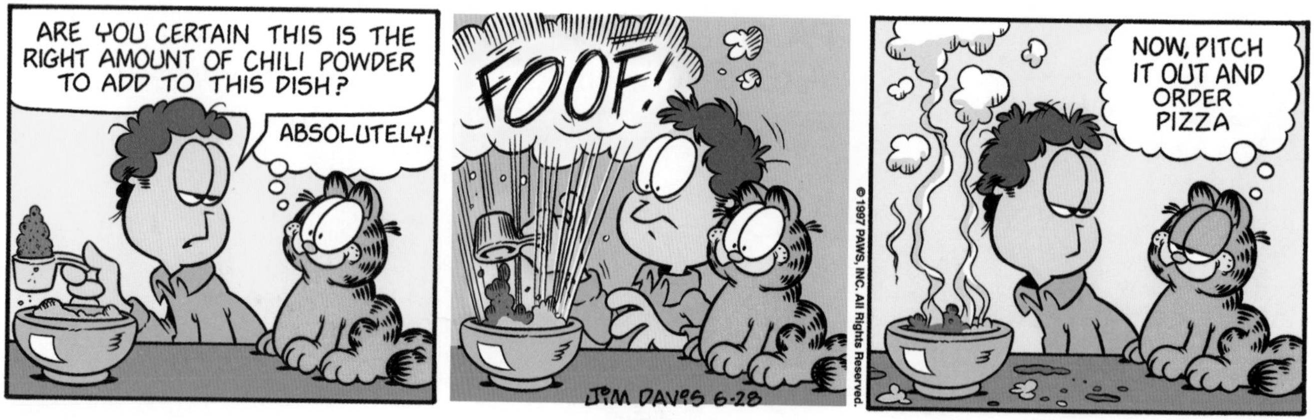
ARE YOU CERTAIN THIS IS THE RIGHT AMOUNT OF CHILI POWDER TO ADD TO THIS DISH?
ABSOLUTELY!
FOOF!
JIM DAVIS 6-28
© 1997 PAWS, INC. All Rights Reserved.
NOW, PITCH IT OUT AND ORDER PIZZA

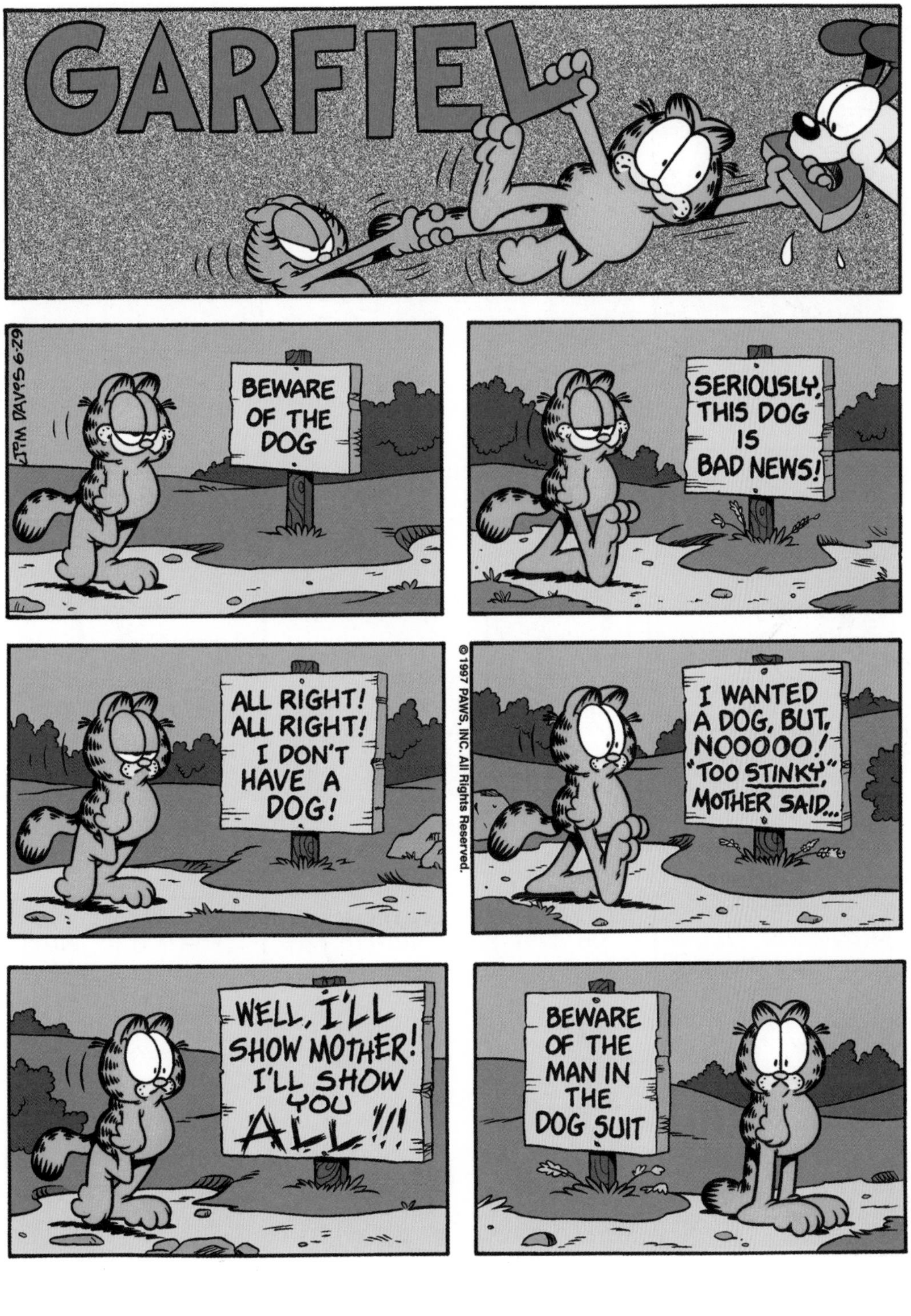
GARFIEL
JPM DAVIS 6-29
BEWARE OF THE DOG
SERIOUSLY, THIS DOG IS BAD NEWS!
ALL RIGHT! ALL RIGHT! I DON'T HAVE A DOG!
I WANTED A DOG, BUT, NOOOOO! "TOO STINKY," MOTHER SAID...
WELL, I'LL SHOW MOTHER! I'LL SHOW YOU ALL!!!
BEWARE OF THE MAN IN THE DOG SUIT

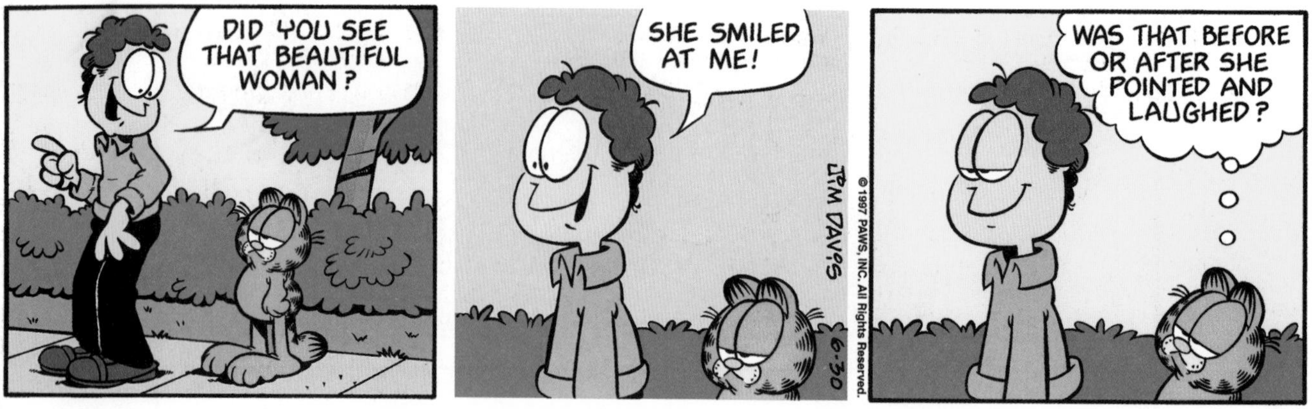
DID YOU SEE THAT BEAUTIFUL WOMAN?
SHE SMILED AT ME!
JIM DAVIS 6-30
© 1997 PAWS, INC. All Rights Reserved.
WAS THAT BEFORE OR AFTER SHE POINTED AND LAUGHED?

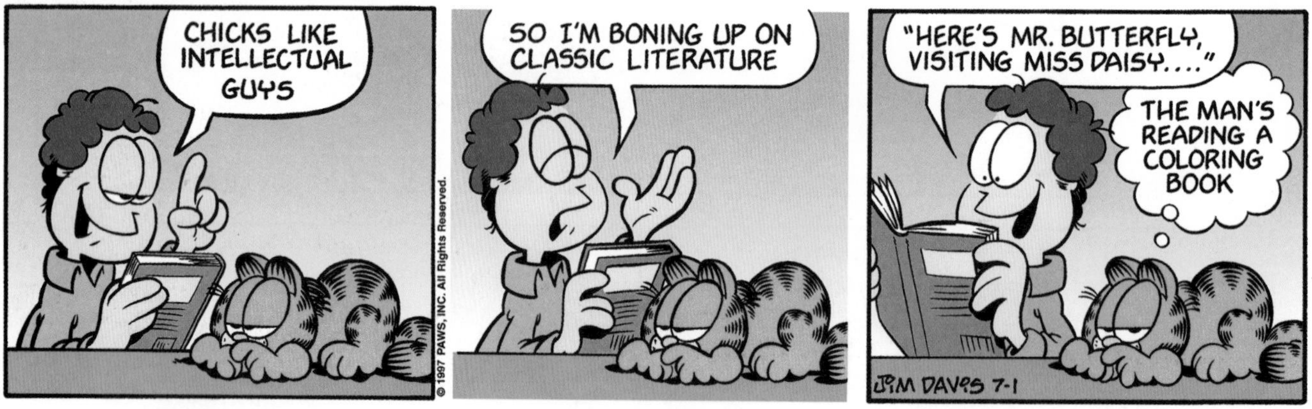
CHICKS LIKE INTELLECTUAL GUYS
© 1997 PAWS, INC. All Rights Reserved.
SO I'M BONING UP ON CLASSIC LITERATURE
"HERE'S MR. BUTTERFLY, VISITING MISS DAISY...."
THE MAN'S READING A COLORING BOOK
JIM DAVIS 7-1

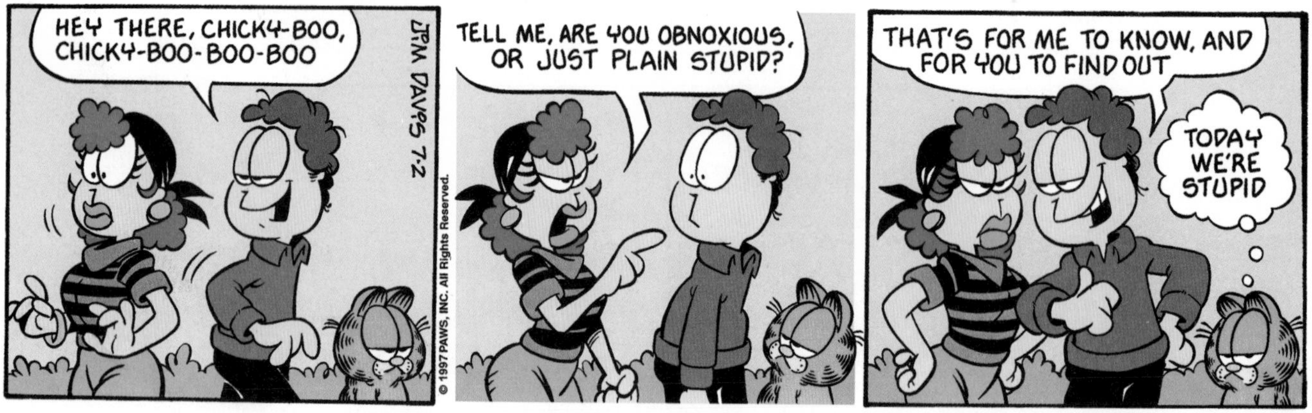
HEY THERE, CHICKY-BOO, CHICKY-BOO-BOO-BOO
JIM DAVIS 7-2
© 1997 PAWS, INC. All Rights Reserved.
TELL ME, ARE YOU OBNOXIOUS, OR JUST PLAIN STUPID?
THAT'S FOR ME TO KNOW, AND FOR YOU TO FIND OUT
TODAY WE'RE STUPID

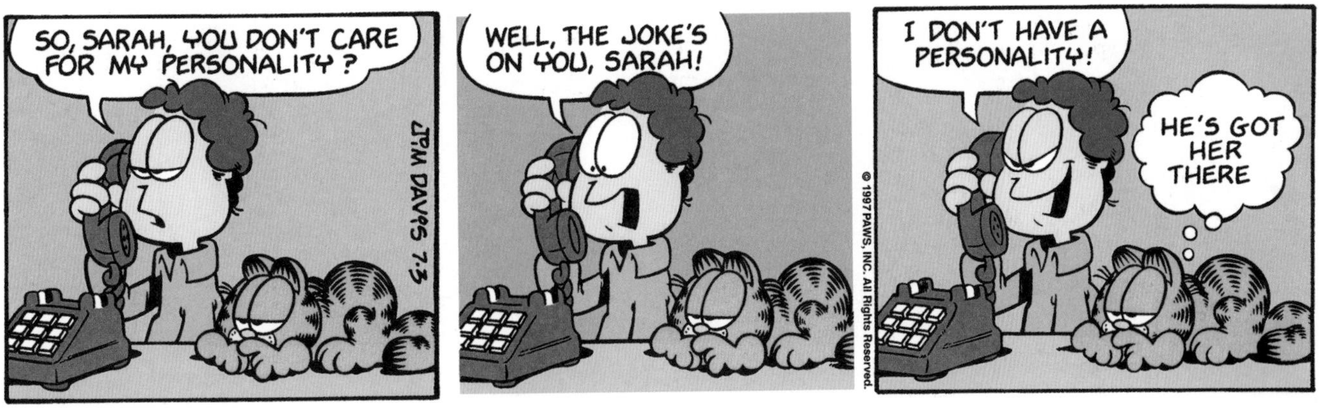
SO, SARAH, YOU DON'T CARE FOR MY PERSONALITY ?
JIM DAVIS 7-3
WELL, THE JOKE'S ON YOU, SARAH!
© 1997 PAWS, INC. All Rights Reserved.
I DON'T HAVE A PERSONALITY!
HE'S GOT HER THERE

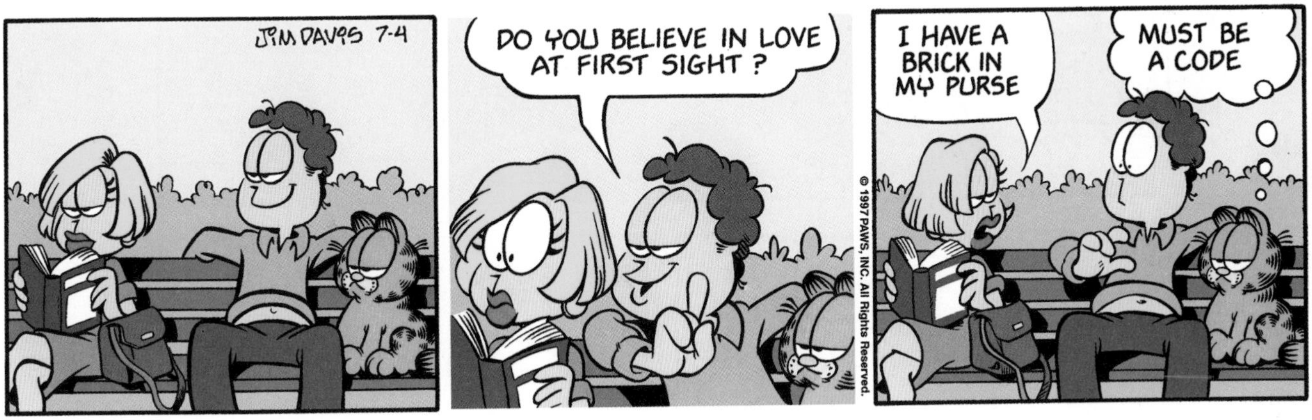
JIM DAVIS 7-4
DO YOU BELIEVE IN LOVE AT FIRST SIGHT ?
© 1997 PAWS, INC. All Rights Reserved.
I HAVE A BRICK IN MY PURSE
MUST BE A CODE

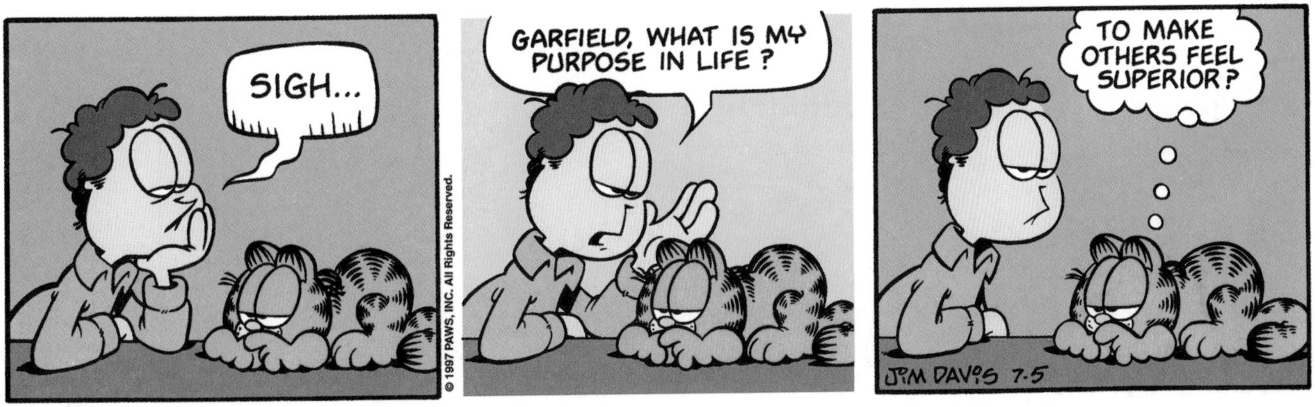
SIGH...
© 1997 PAWS, INC. All Rights Reserved.
GARFIELD, WHAT IS MY PURPOSE IN LIFE ?
TO MAKE OTHERS FEEL SUPERIOR ?
JIM DAVIS 7-5

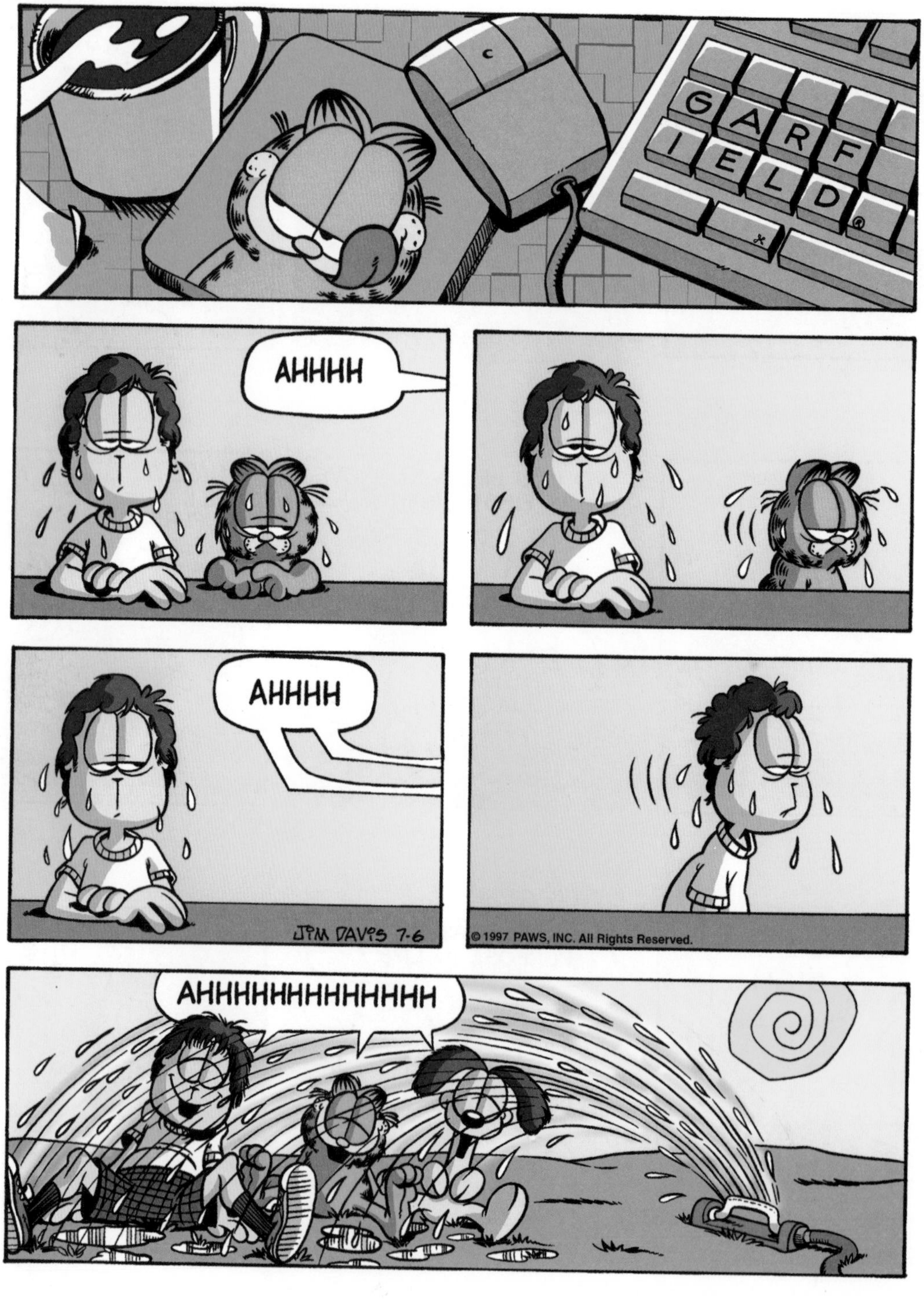
GARFIELD
AHHHH
AHHHH
JIM DAVIS 7-6
© 1997 PAWS, INC. All Rights Reserved.
AHHHHHHHHHHHHH

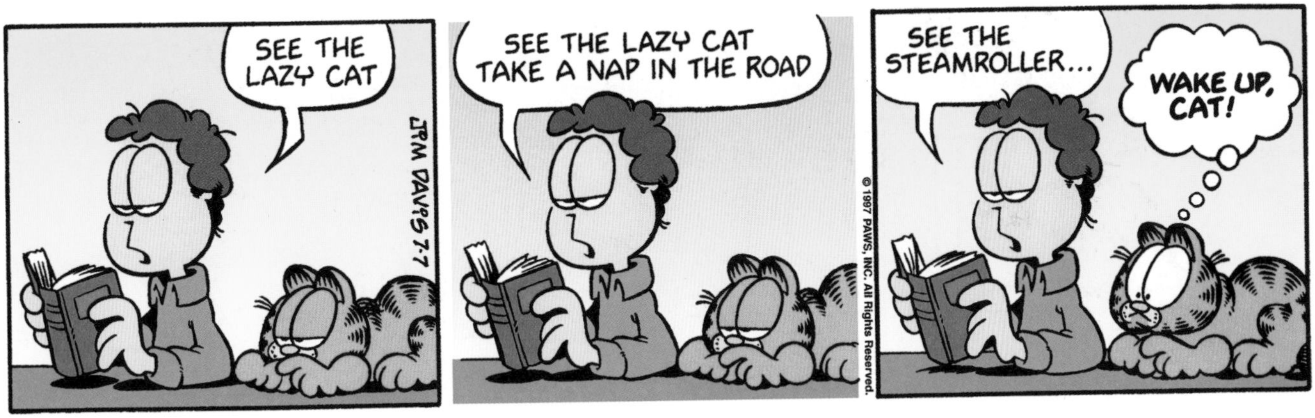
SEE THE LAZY CAT
JIM DAVIS 7-7
SEE THE LAZY CAT TAKE A NAP IN THE ROAD
© 1997 PAWS, INC. All Rights Reserved.
SEE THE STEAMROLLER...
WAKE UP, CAT!

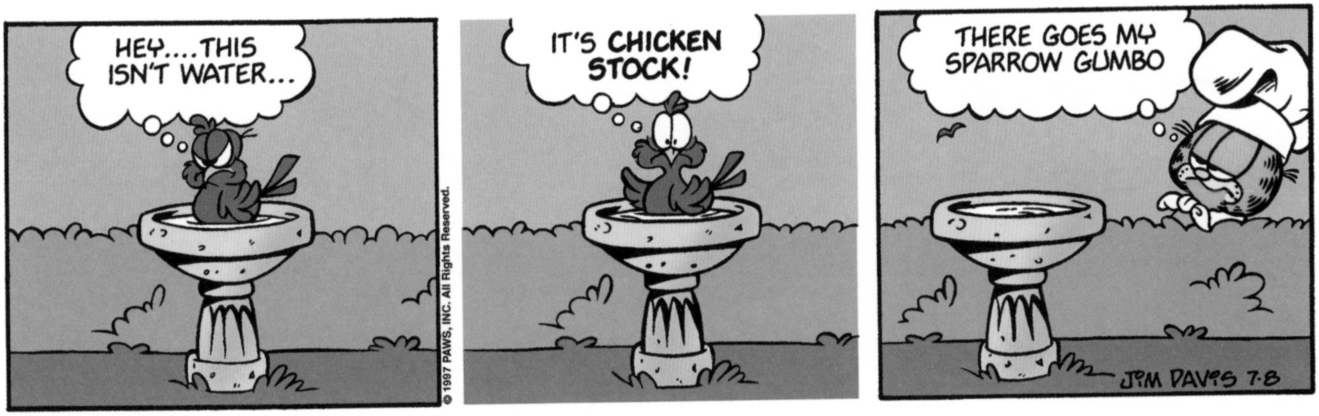
HEY....THIS ISN'T WATER...
© 1997 PAWS, INC. All Rights Reserved.
IT'S CHICKEN STOCK!
THERE GOES MY SPARROW GUMBO
JIM DAVIS 7-8

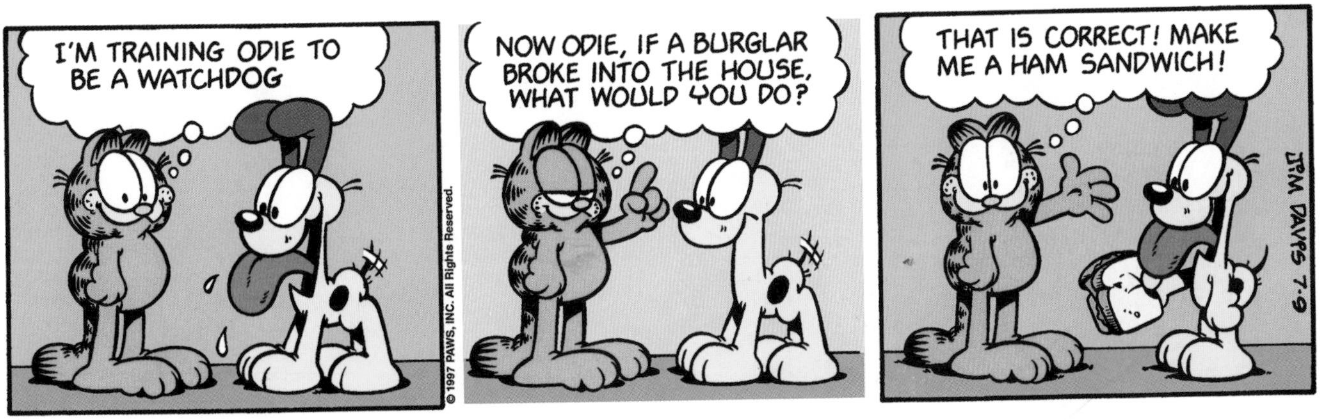
I'M TRAINING ODIE TO BE A WATCHDOG
© 1997 PAWS, INC. All Rights Reserved.
NOW ODIE, IF A BURGLAR BROKE INTO THE HOUSE, WHAT WOULD YOU DO?
THAT IS CORRECT! MAKE ME A HAM SANDWICH!
JIM DAVIS 7-9

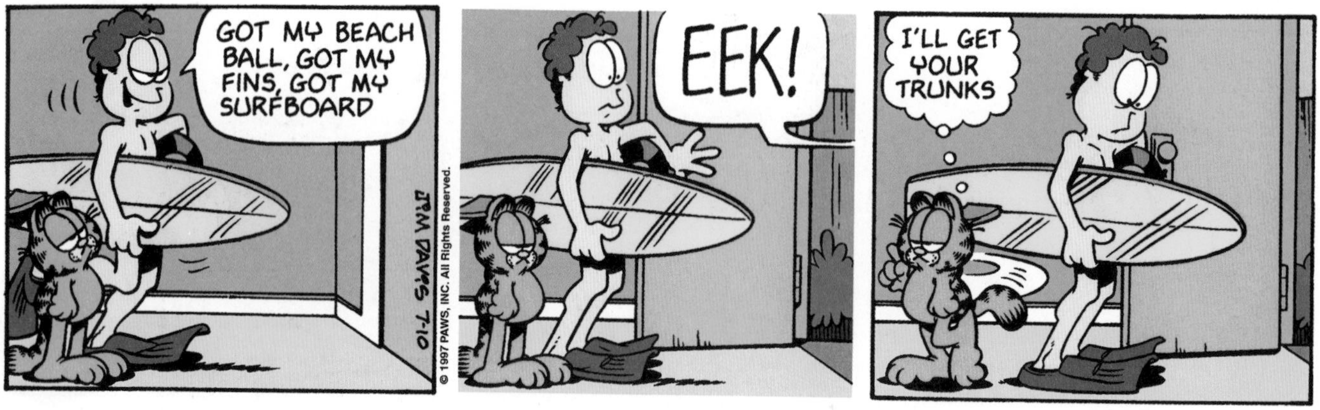
GOT MY BEACH BALL, GOT MY FINS, GOT MY SURFBOARD
JIM DAVIS 7-10
© 1997 PAWS, INC. All Rights Reserved.
EEK!
I'LL GET YOUR TRUNKS

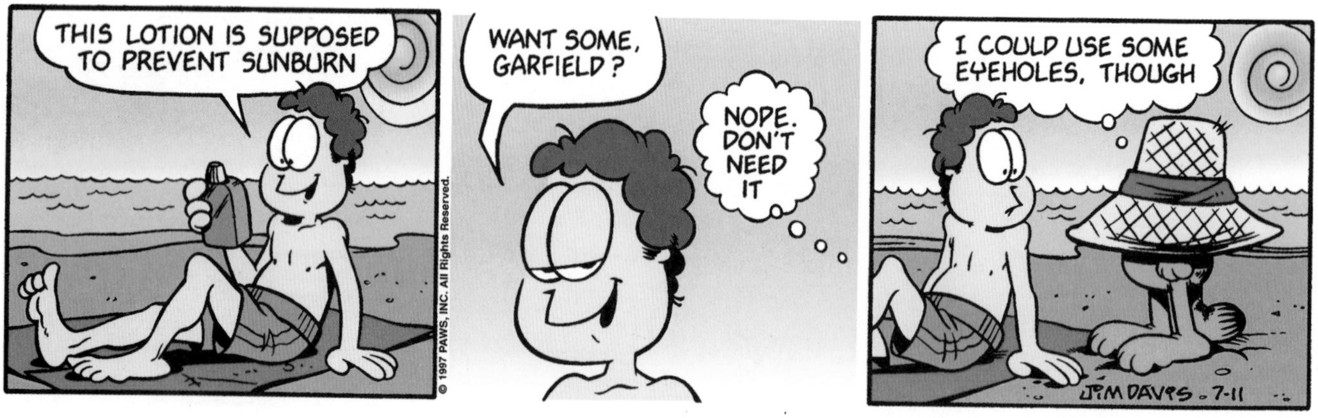
THIS LOTION IS SUPPOSED TO PREVENT SUNBURN
© 1997 PAWS, INC. All Rights Reserved.
WANT SOME, GARFIELD?
NOPE. DON'T NEED IT
I COULD USE SOME EYEHOLES, THOUGH
JIM DAVIS 7-11

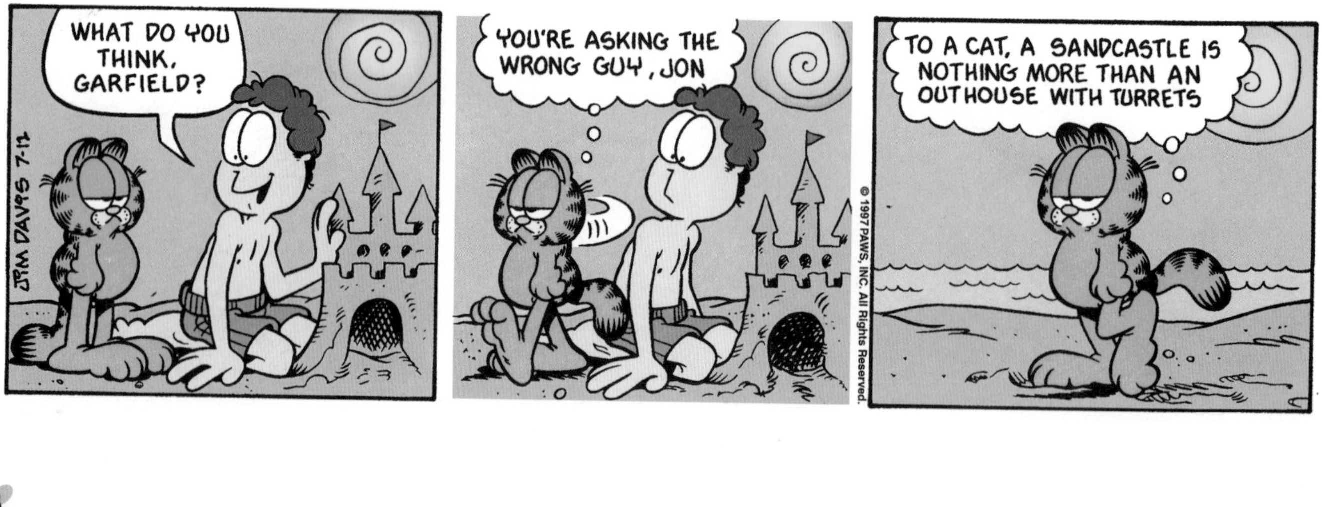
WHAT DO YOU THINK, GARFIELD?
JIM DAVIS 7-12
YOU'RE ASKING THE WRONG GUY, JON
© 1997 PAWS, INC. All Rights Reserved.
TO A CAT, A SANDCASTLE IS NOTHING MORE THAN AN OUTHOUSE WITH TURRETS

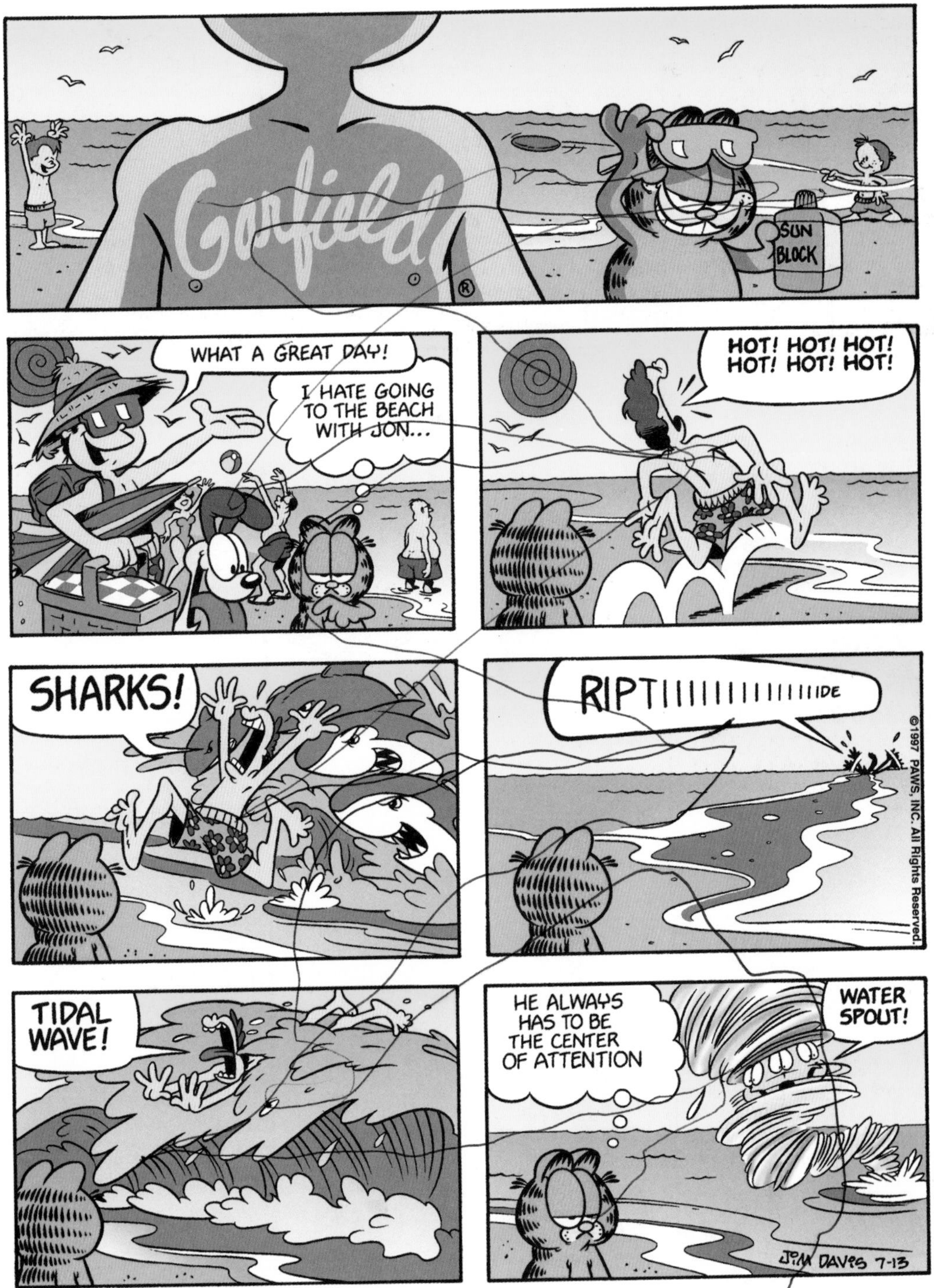
Garfield®
SUN BLOCK
WHAT A GREAT DAY!
I HATE GOING TO THE BEACH WITH JON...
HOT! HOT! HOT! HOT! HOT! HOT!
SHARKS!
RIPTIIIIIIIIIIIIIIIIIDE
TIDAL WAVE!
HE ALWAYS HAS TO BE THE CENTER OF ATTENTION
WATER SPOUT!
JIM DAVIS 7-13

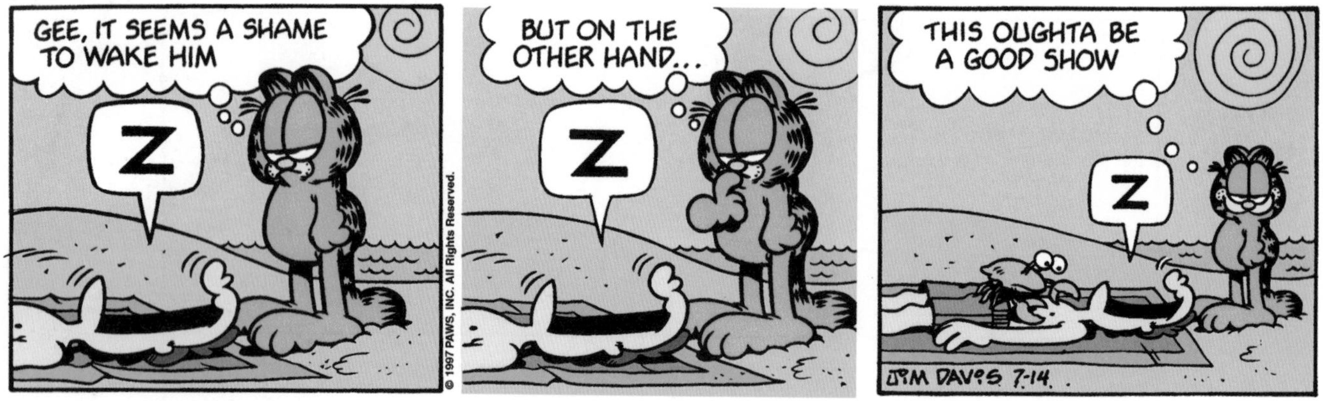
GEE, IT SEEMS A SHAME TO WAKE HIM
Z
BUT ON THE OTHER HAND...
Z
© 1997 PAWS, INC. All Rights Reserved.
THIS OUGHTA BE A GOOD SHOW
Z
JIM DAVIS 7-14

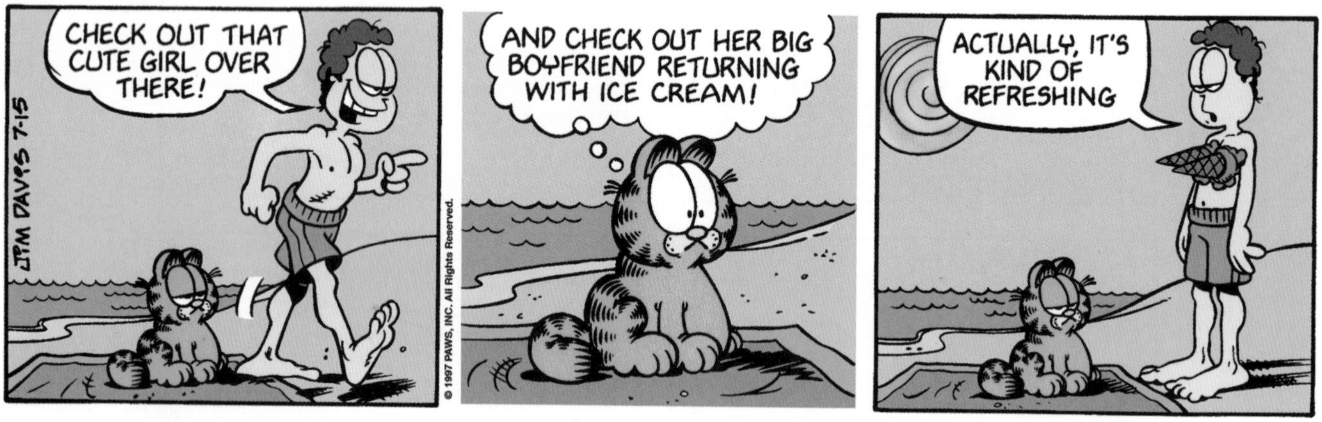
JIM DAVIS 7-15
CHECK OUT THAT CUTE GIRL OVER THERE!
© 1997 PAWS, INC. All Rights Reserved.
AND CHECK OUT HER BIG BOYFRIEND RETURNING WITH ICE CREAM!
ACTUALLY, IT'S KIND OF REFRESHING

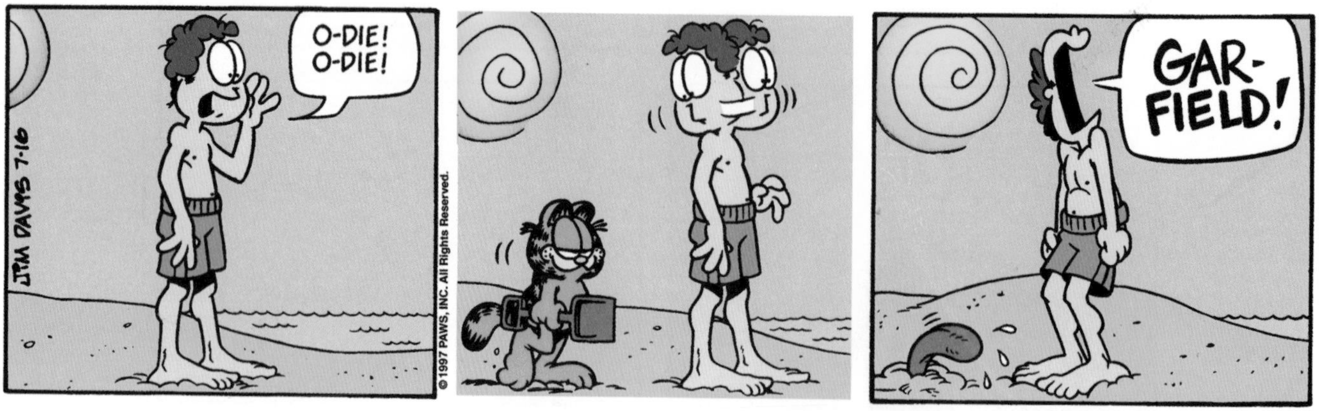
JIM DAVIS 7-16
O-DIE! O-DIE!
© 1997 PAWS, INC. All Rights Reserved.
GAR-FIELD!

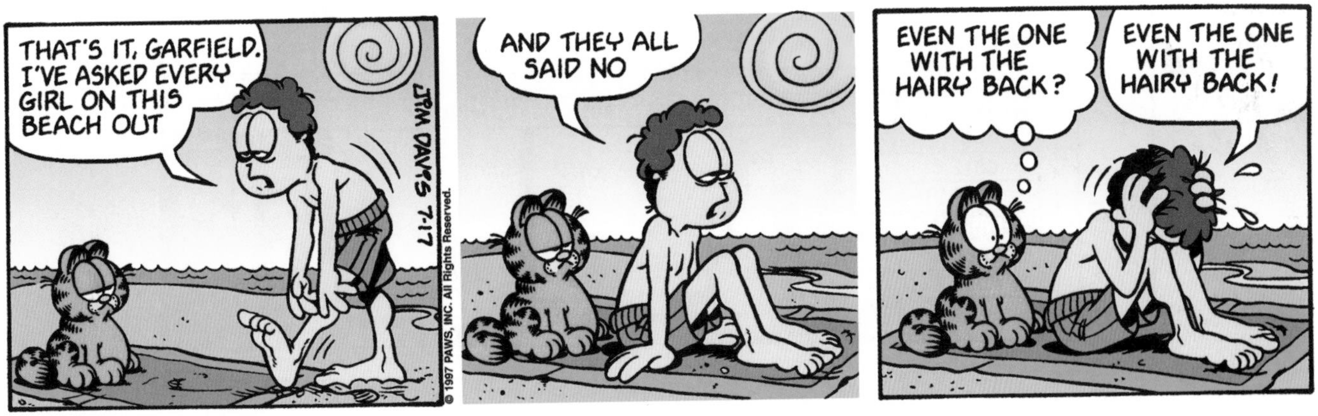
THAT'S IT, GARFIELD. I'VE ASKED EVERY GIRL ON THIS BEACH OUT
JIM DAVIS 7-17
© 1997 PAWS, INC. All Rights Reserved.
AND THEY ALL SAID NO
EVEN THE ONE WITH THE HAIRY BACK?
EVEN THE ONE WITH THE HAIRY BACK!

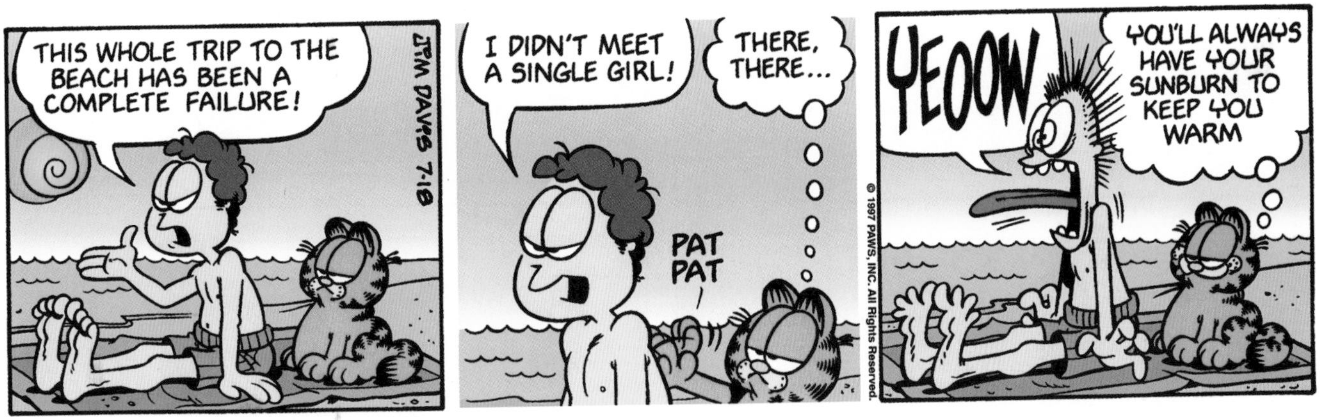
THIS WHOLE TRIP TO THE BEACH HAS BEEN A COMPLETE FAILURE!
JIM DAVIS 7-18
I DIDN'T MEET A SINGLE GIRL!
THERE, THERE...
PAT PAT
© 1997 PAWS, INC. All Rights Reserved.
YEOOW
YOU'LL ALWAYS HAVE YOUR SUNBURN TO KEEP YOU WARM

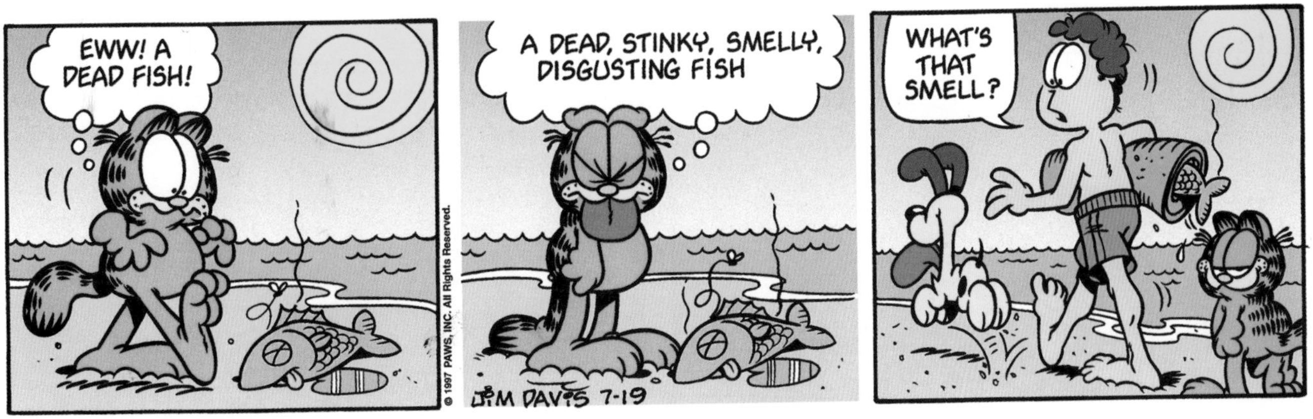
EWW! A DEAD FISH!
© 1997 PAWS, INC. All Rights Reserved.
A DEAD, STINKY, SMELLY, DISGUSTING FISH
JIM DAVIS 7-19
WHAT'S THAT SMELL?

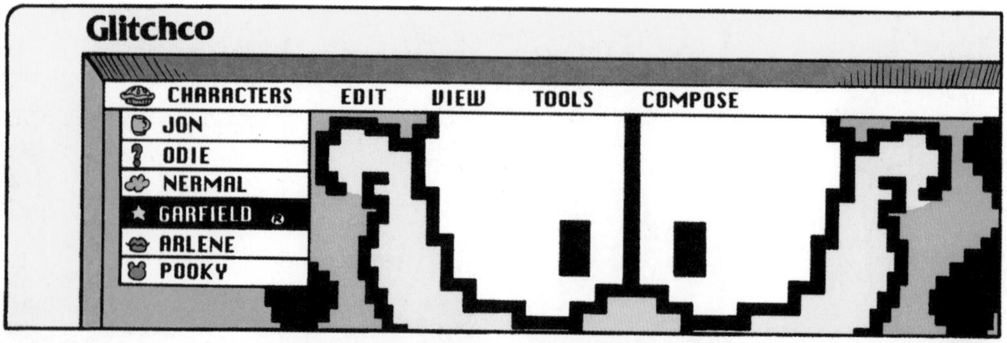

Glitchco
CHARACTERS
EDIT
VIEW
TOOLS
COMPOSE
JON
ODIE
NERMAL
GARFIELD
ARLENE
POOKY

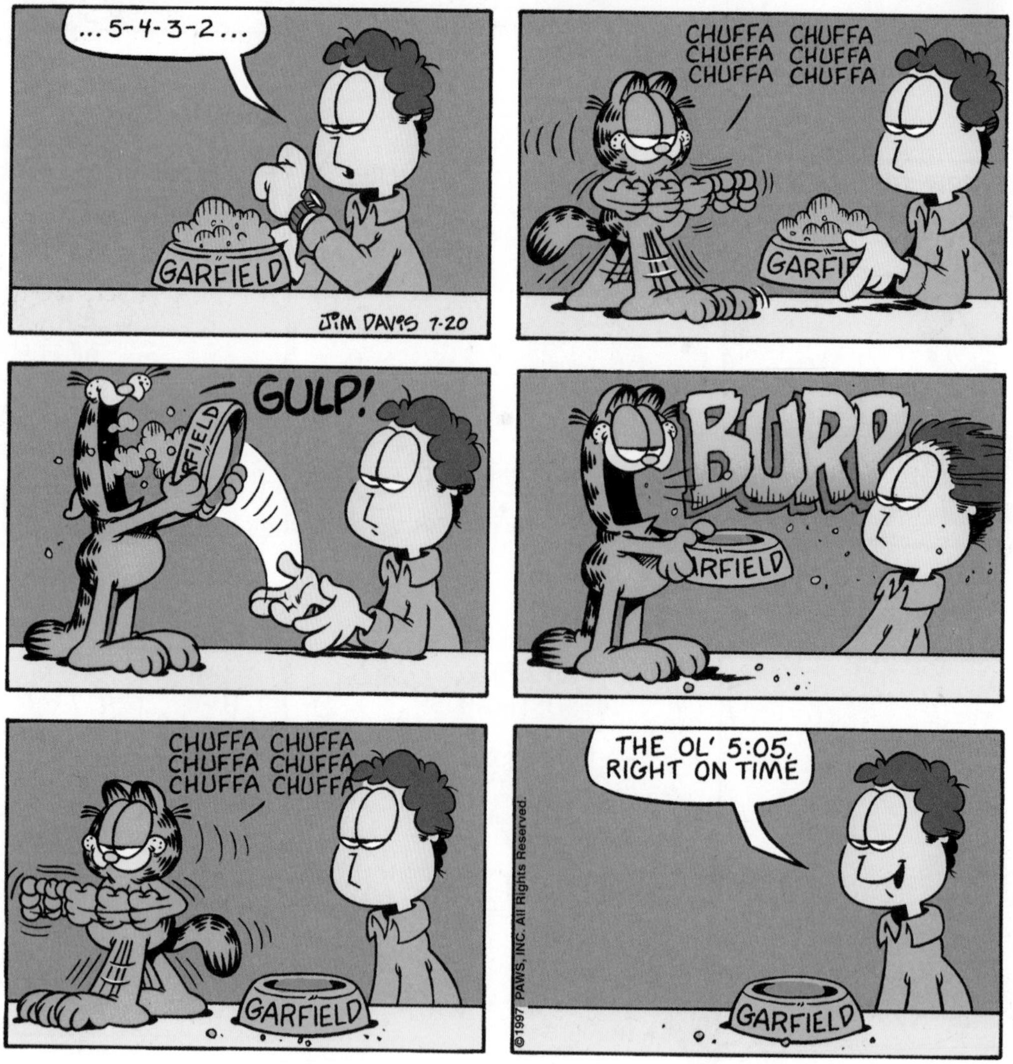

...5-4-3-2...
GARFIELD
JIM DAVIS 7-20
CHUFFA CHUFFA
CHUFFA CHUFFA
CHUFFA CHUFFA
GULP!
BURP
RFIELD
CHUFFA CHUFFA
CHUFFA CHUFFA
CHUFFA CHUFFA
GARFIELD
© 1997 PAWS, INC. All Rights Reserved.
THE OL' 5:05, RIGHT ON TIME
GARFIELD

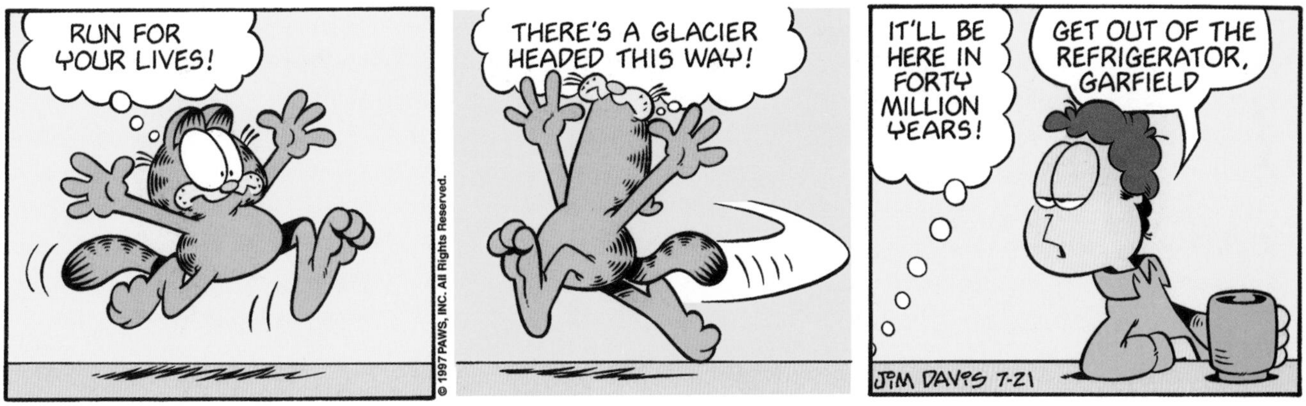
RUN FOR YOUR LIVES!
© 1997 PAWS, INC. All Rights Reserved.
THERE'S A GLACIER HEADED THIS WAY!
IT'LL BE HERE IN FORTY MILLION YEARS!
GET OUT OF THE REFRIGERATOR, GARFIELD
JIM DAVIS 7-21

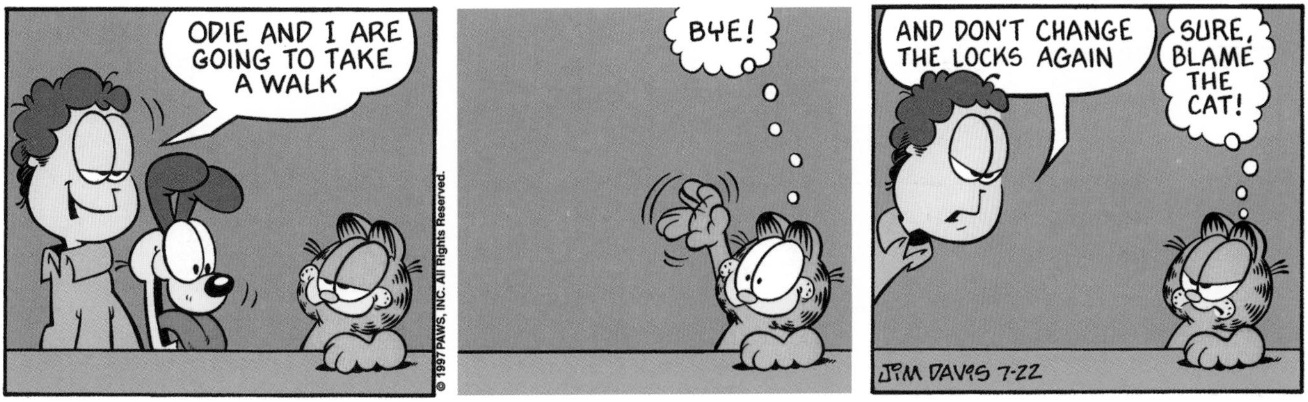
ODIE AND I ARE GOING TO TAKE A WALK
© 1997 PAWS, INC. All Rights Reserved.
BYE!
AND DON'T CHANGE THE LOCKS AGAIN
SURE, BLAME THE CAT!
JIM DAVIS 7-22

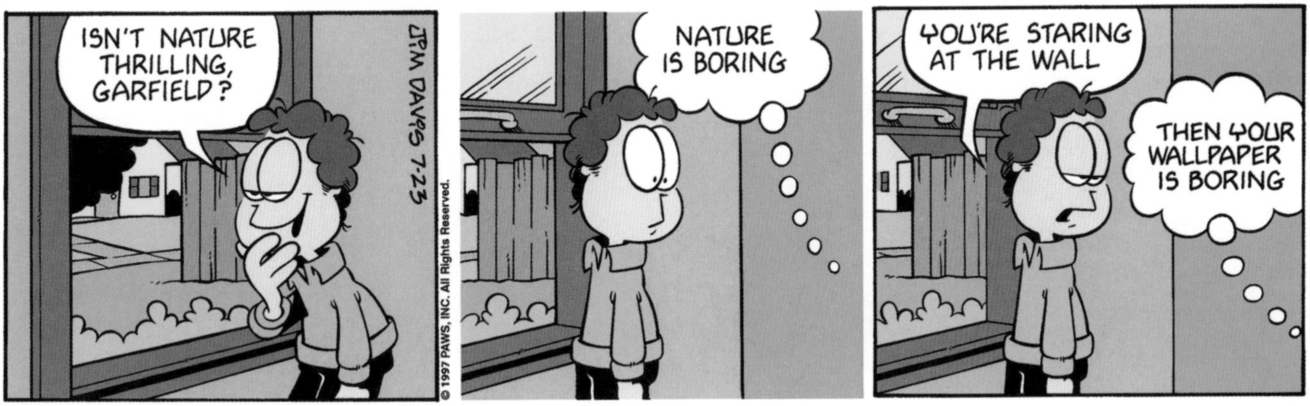
ISN'T NATURE THRILLING, GARFIELD?
JIM DAVIS 7-23
© 1997 PAWS, INC. All Rights Reserved.
NATURE IS BORING
YOU'RE STARING AT THE WALL
THEN YOUR WALLPAPER IS BORING

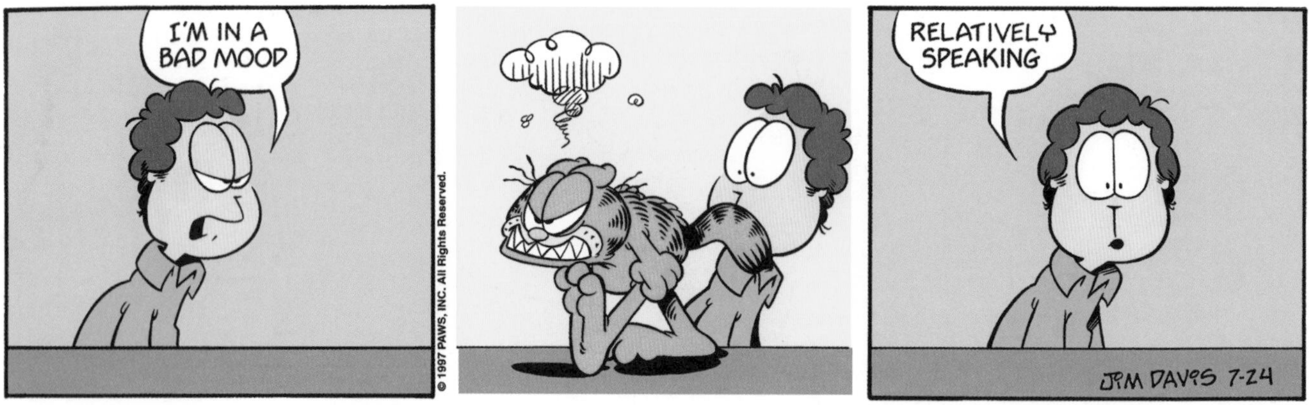
I'M IN A BAD MOOD
RELATIVELY SPEAKING
JIM DAVIS 7-24
© 1997 PAWS, INC. All Rights Reserved.

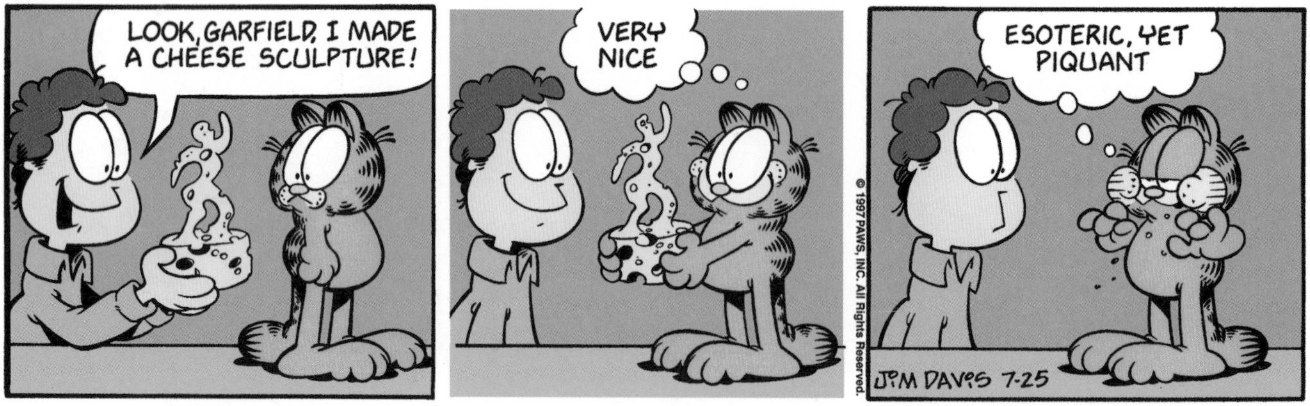
LOOK, GARFIELD, I MADE A CHEESE SCULPTURE!
VERY NICE
ESOTERIC, YET PIQUANT
JIM DAVIS 7-25
© 1997 PAWS, INC. All Rights Reserved.

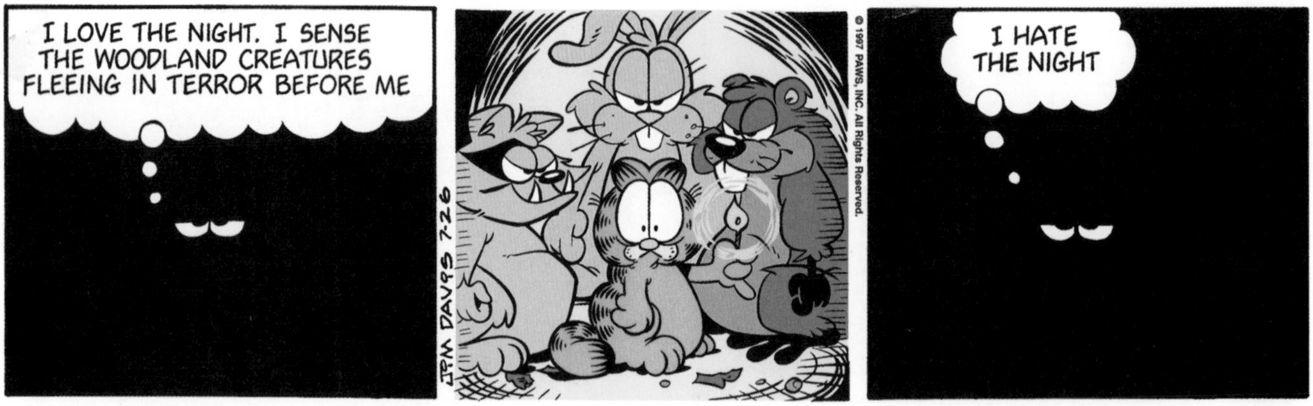
I LOVE THE NIGHT. I SENSE THE WOODLAND CREATURES FLEEING IN TERROR BEFORE ME
JIM DAVIS 7-26
I HATE THE NIGHT
© 1997 PAWS, INC. All Rights Reserved.

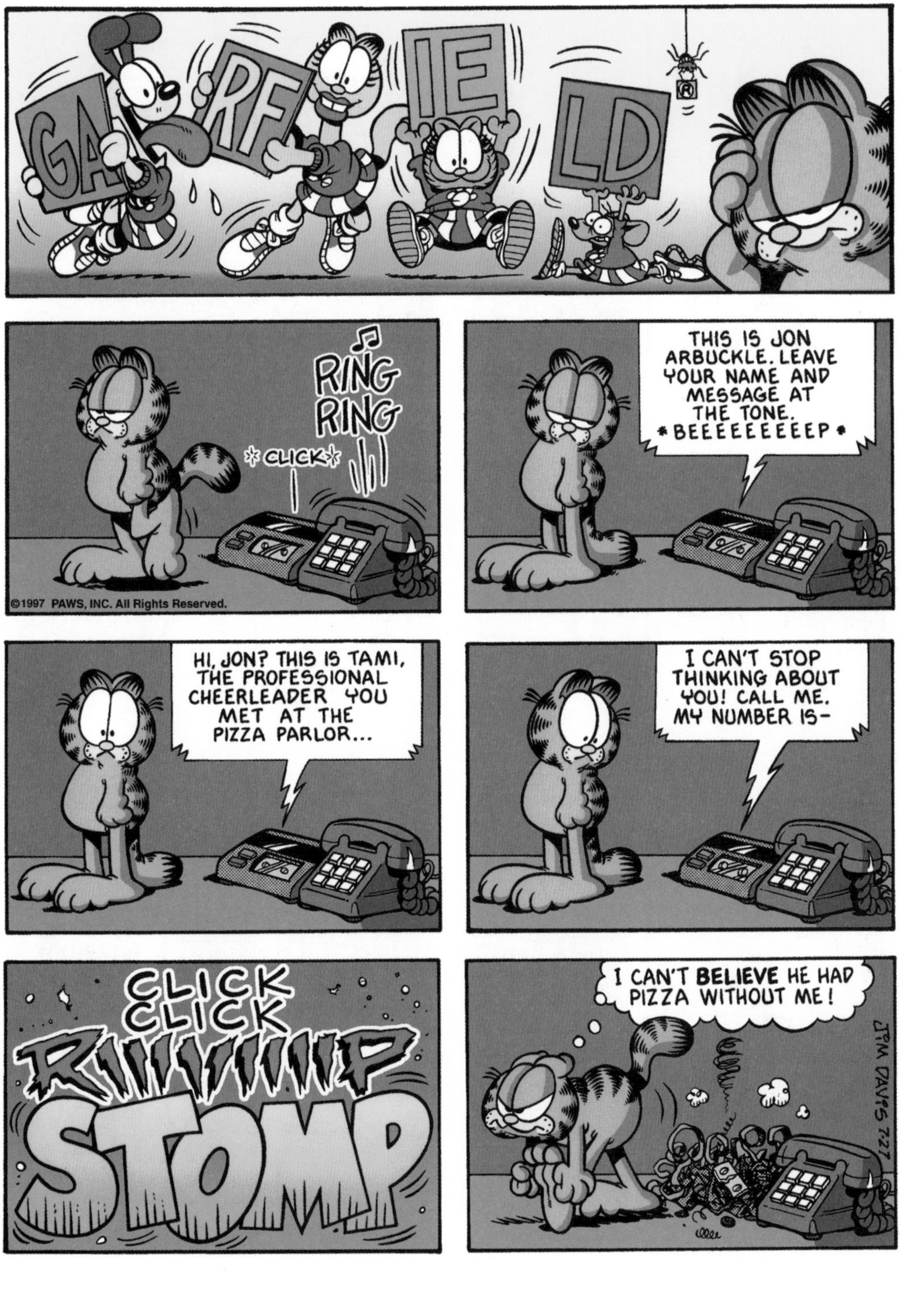
GA RF IE LD ®
RING RING
CLICK
©1997 PAWS, INC. All Rights Reserved.
THIS IS JON ARBUCKLE. LEAVE YOUR NAME AND MESSAGE AT THE TONE. *BEEEEEEEEEP*
HI, JON? THIS IS TAMI, THE PROFESSIONAL CHEERLEADER YOU MET AT THE PIZZA PARLOR...
I CAN'T STOP THINKING ABOUT YOU! CALL ME. MY NUMBER IS–
CLICK CLICK
RIIIIIIIP
STOMP
I CAN'T **BELIEVE** HE HAD PIZZA WITHOUT ME!
JIM DAVIS 7-27

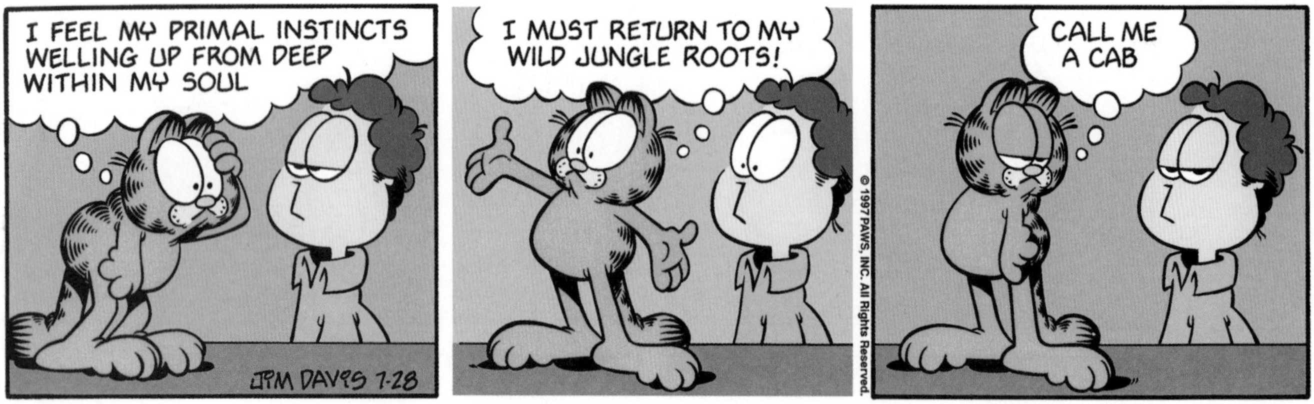
I FEEL MY PRIMAL INSTINCTS WELLING UP FROM DEEP WITHIN MY SOUL
I MUST RETURN TO MY WILD JUNGLE ROOTS!
CALL ME A CAB
JIM DAVIS 7-28
© 1997 PAWS, INC. All Rights Reserved.

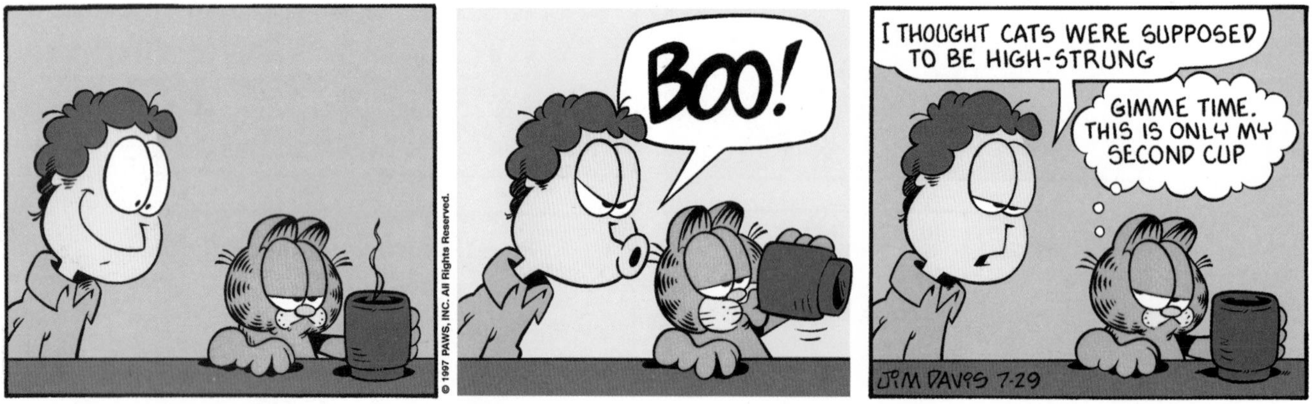
BOO!
I THOUGHT CATS WERE SUPPOSED TO BE HIGH-STRUNG
GIMME TIME. THIS IS ONLY MY SECOND CUP
JIM DAVIS 7-29
© 1997 PAWS, INC. All Rights Reserved.

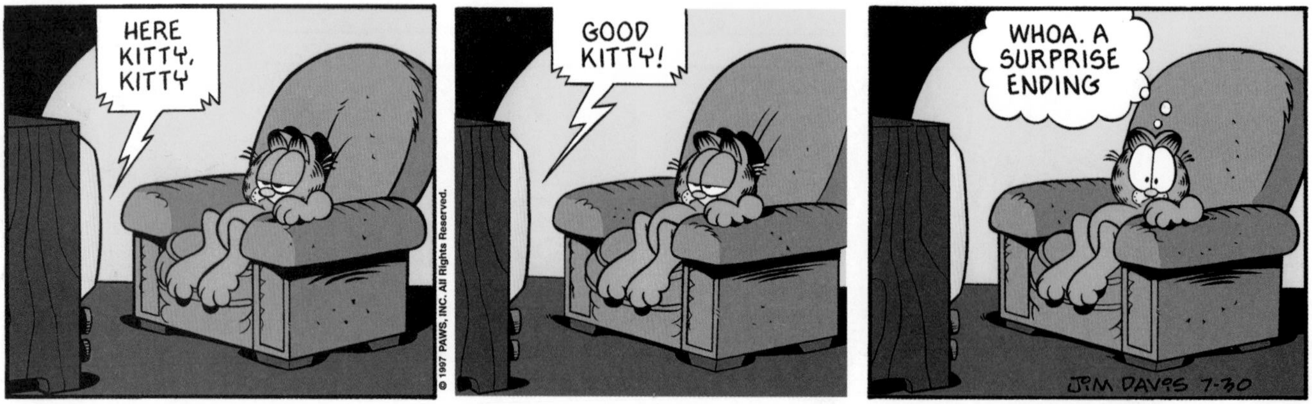
HERE KITTY, KITTY
GOOD KITTY!
WHOA. A SURPRISE ENDING
JIM DAVIS 7-30
© 1997 PAWS, INC. All Rights Reserved.

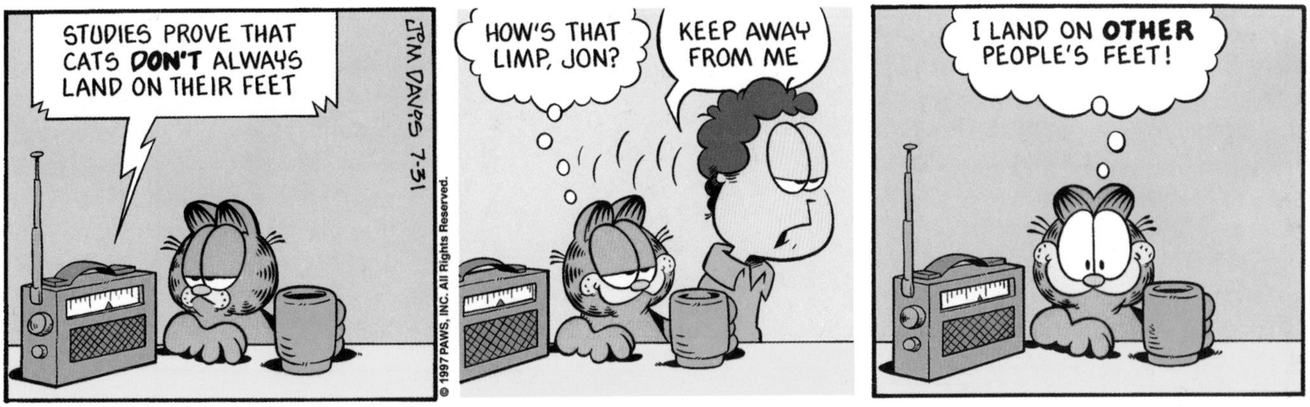
STUDIES PROVE THAT CATS **DON'T** ALWAYS LAND ON THEIR FEET
JIM DAVIS 7-31
© 1997 PAWS, INC. All Rights Reserved.
HOW'S THAT LIMP, JON?
KEEP AWAY FROM ME
I LAND ON **OTHER** PEOPLE'S FEET!

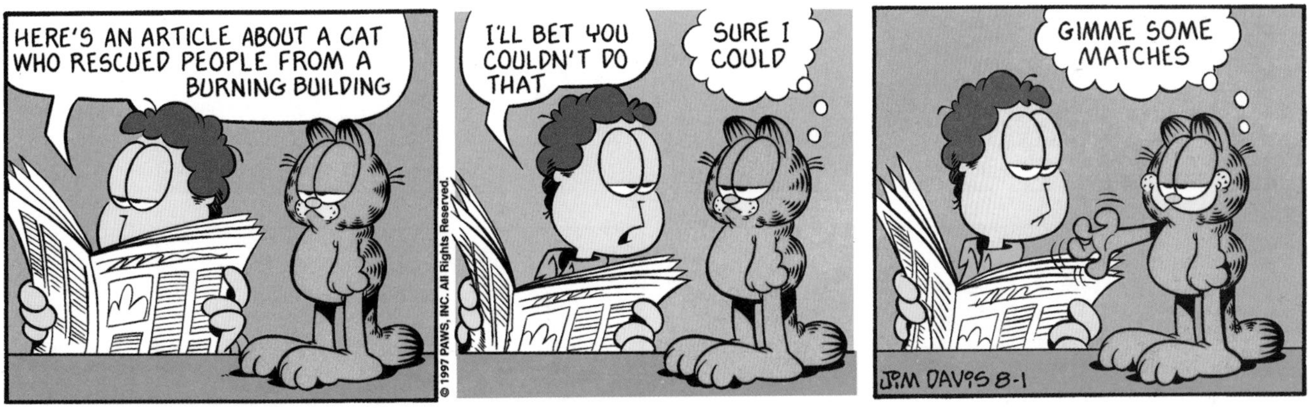
HERE'S AN ARTICLE ABOUT A CAT WHO RESCUED PEOPLE FROM A BURNING BUILDING
© 1997 PAWS, INC. All Rights Reserved.
I'LL BET YOU COULDN'T DO THAT
SURE I COULD
GIMME SOME MATCHES
JIM DAVIS 8-1

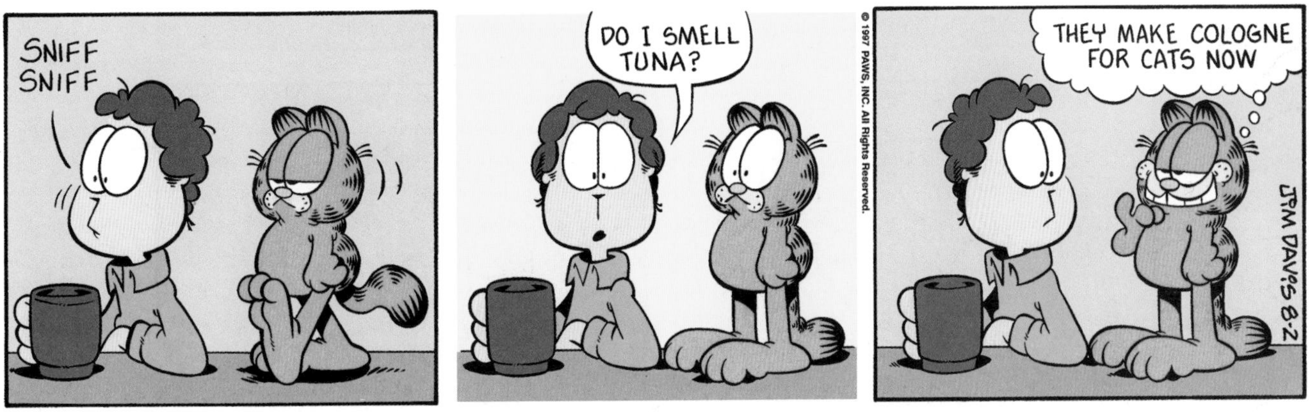
SNIFF SNIFF
DO I SMELL TUNA?
© 1997 PAWS, INC. All Rights Reserved.
THEY MAKE COLOGNE FOR CATS NOW
JIM DAVIS 8-2

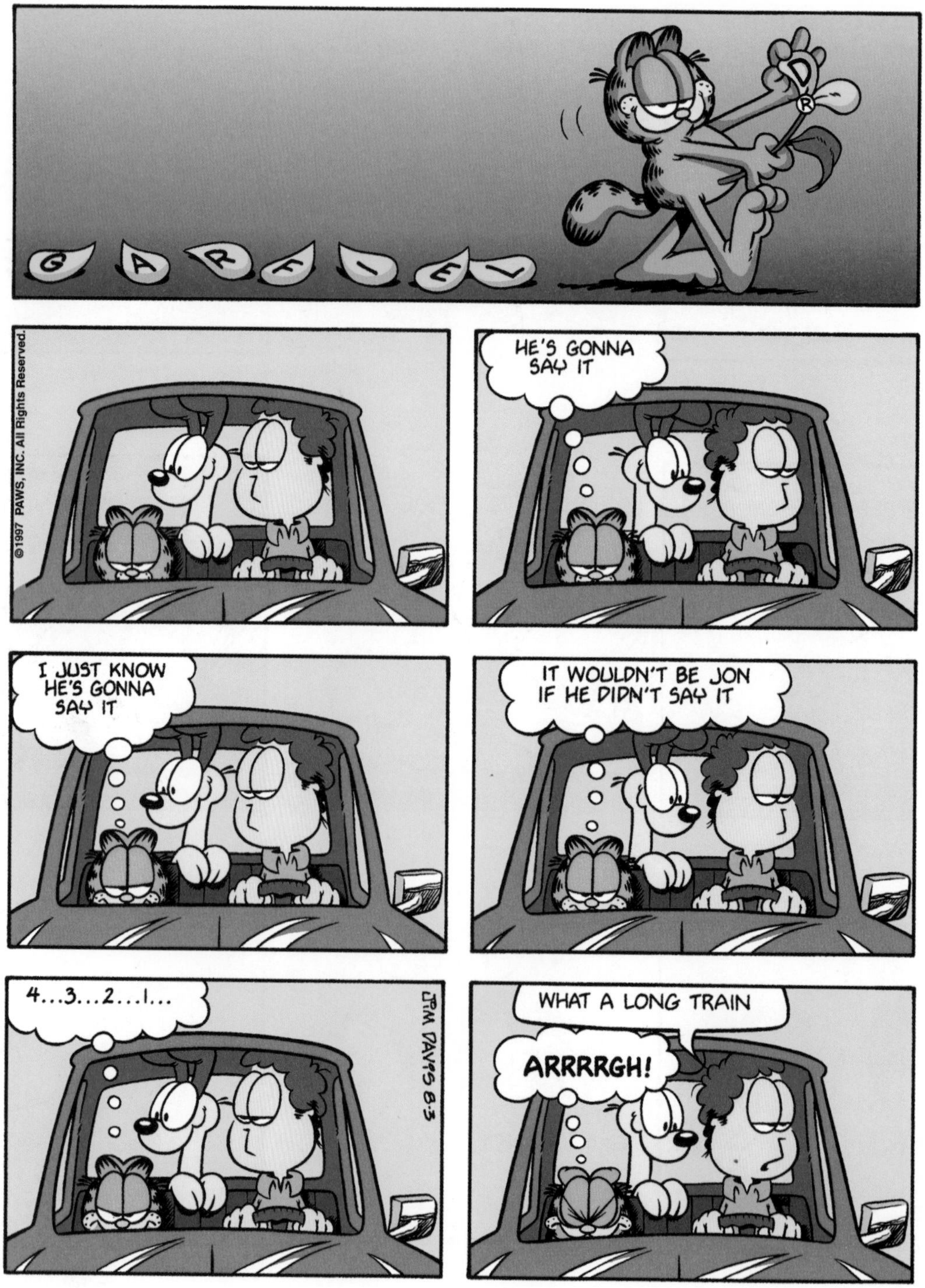
G A R F I E L D
©1997 PAWS, INC. All Rights Reserved.
HE'S GONNA SAY IT
I JUST KNOW HE'S GONNA SAY IT
IT WOULDN'T BE JON IF HE DIDN'T SAY IT
4...3...2...1...
JIM DAVIS 8-3
WHAT A LONG TRAIN
ARRRRGH!

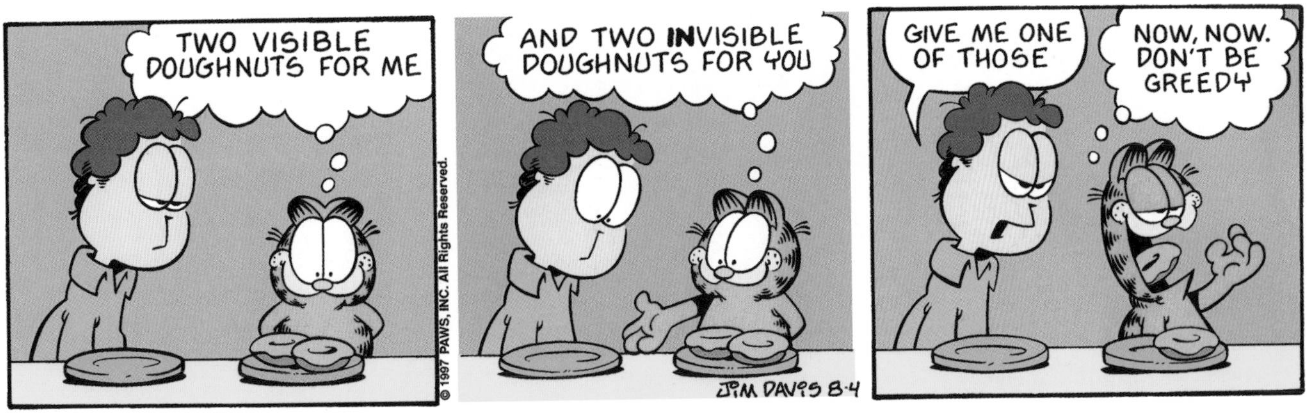
TWO VISIBLE DOUGHNUTS FOR ME
© 1997 PAWS, INC. All Rights Reserved.
AND TWO INVISIBLE DOUGHNUTS FOR YOU
JIM DAVIS 8-4
GIVE ME ONE OF THOSE
NOW, NOW. DON'T BE GREEDY

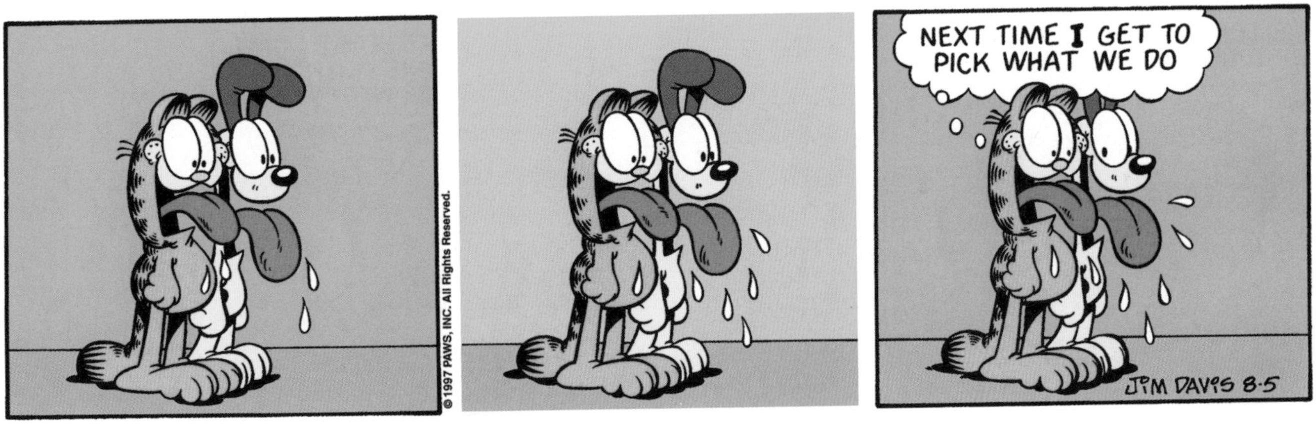
© 1997 PAWS, INC. All Rights Reserved.
NEXT TIME I GET TO PICK WHAT WE DO
JIM DAVIS 8-5

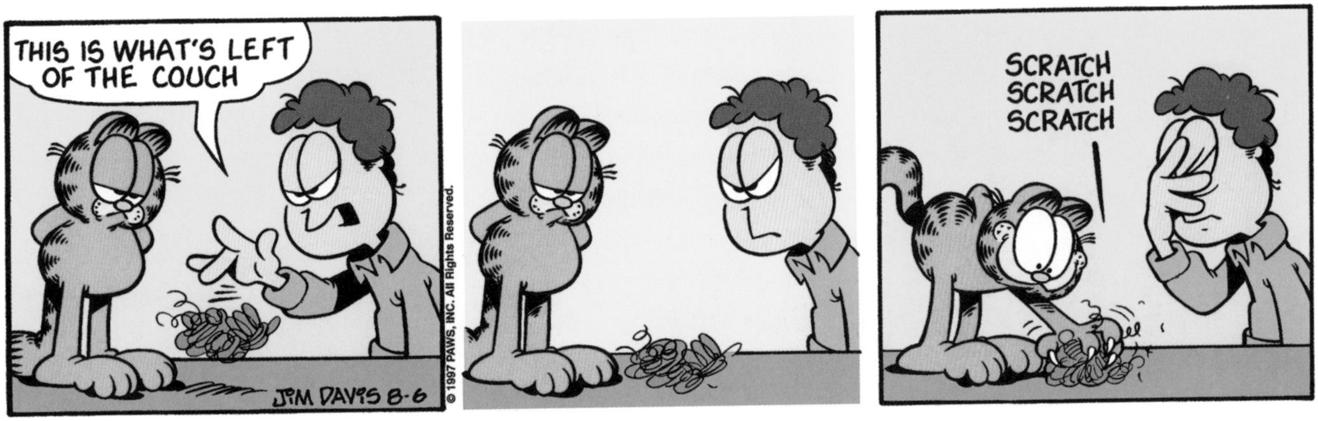
THIS IS WHAT'S LEFT OF THE COUCH
JIM DAVIS 8-6
© 1997 PAWS, INC. All Rights Reserved.
SCRATCH SCRATCH SCRATCH

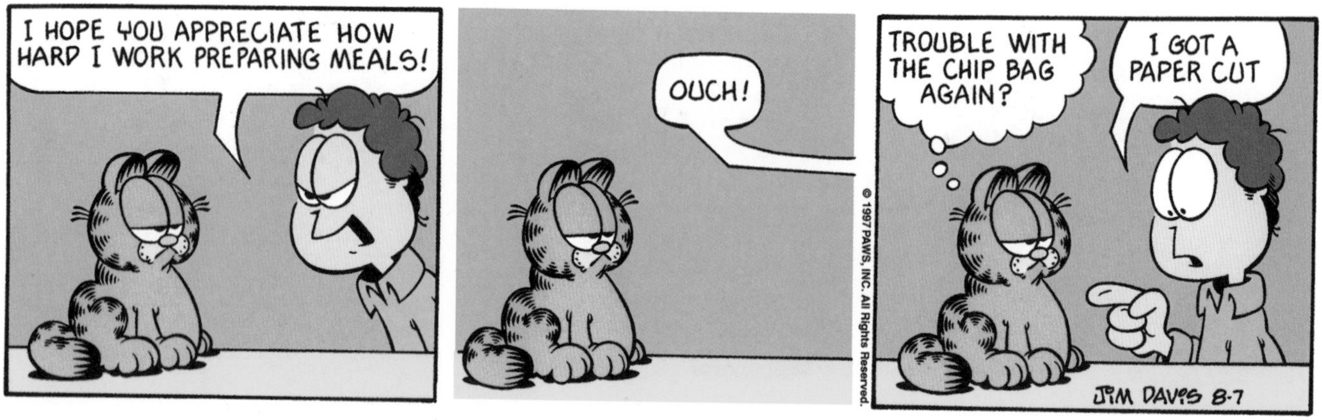
I HOPE YOU APPRECIATE HOW HARD I WORK PREPARING MEALS!
OUCH!
© 1997 PAWS, INC. All Rights Reserved.
TROUBLE WITH THE CHIP BAG AGAIN?
I GOT A PAPER CUT
JIM DAVIS 8-7

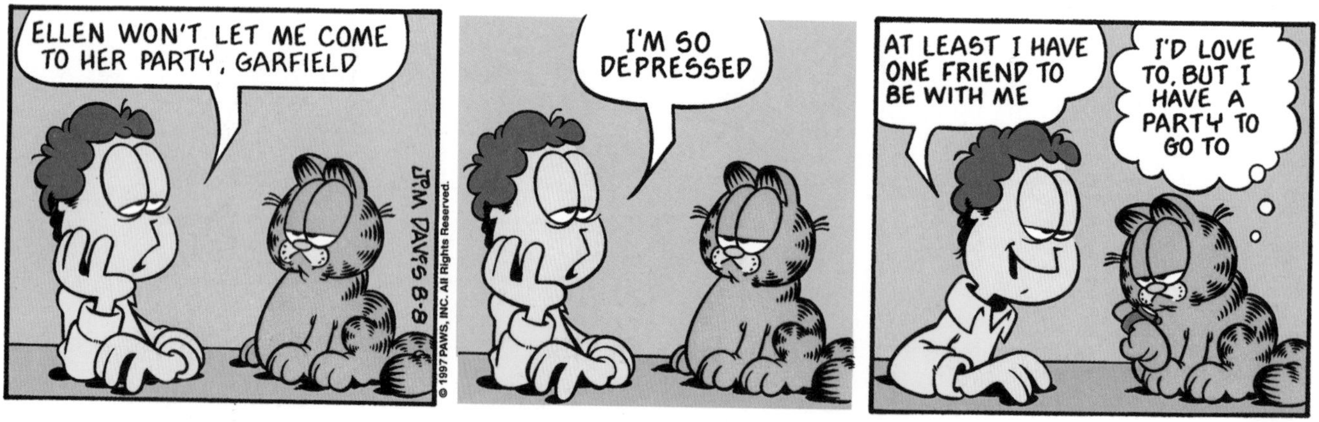
ELLEN WON'T LET ME COME TO HER PARTY, GARFIELD
JIM DAVIS 8-8
© 1997 PAWS, INC. All Rights Reserved.
I'M SO DEPRESSED
AT LEAST I HAVE ONE FRIEND TO BE WITH ME
I'D LOVE TO, BUT I HAVE A PARTY TO GO TO

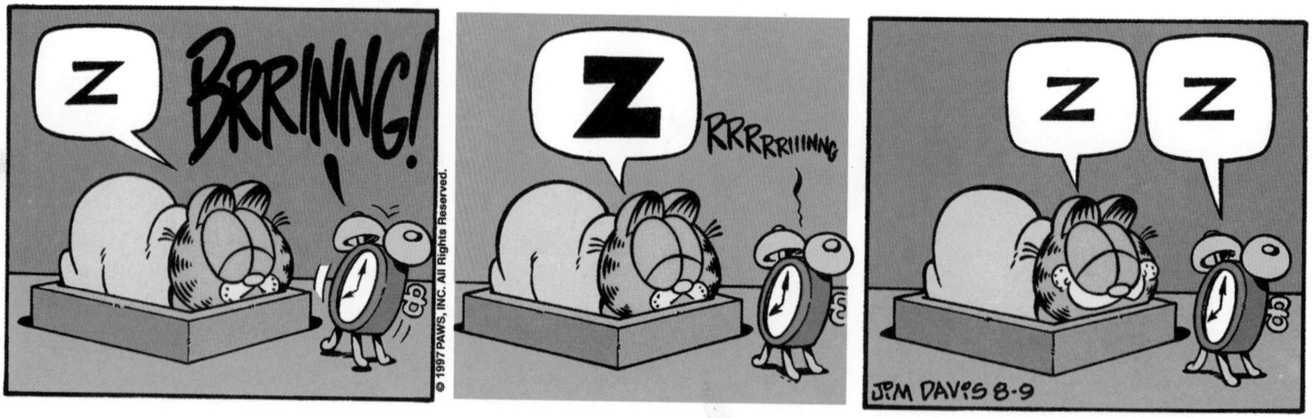
Z
BRRINNG!
© 1997 PAWS, INC. All Rights Reserved.
Z
RRRRRIIINNG
Z
Z
JIM DAVIS 8-9

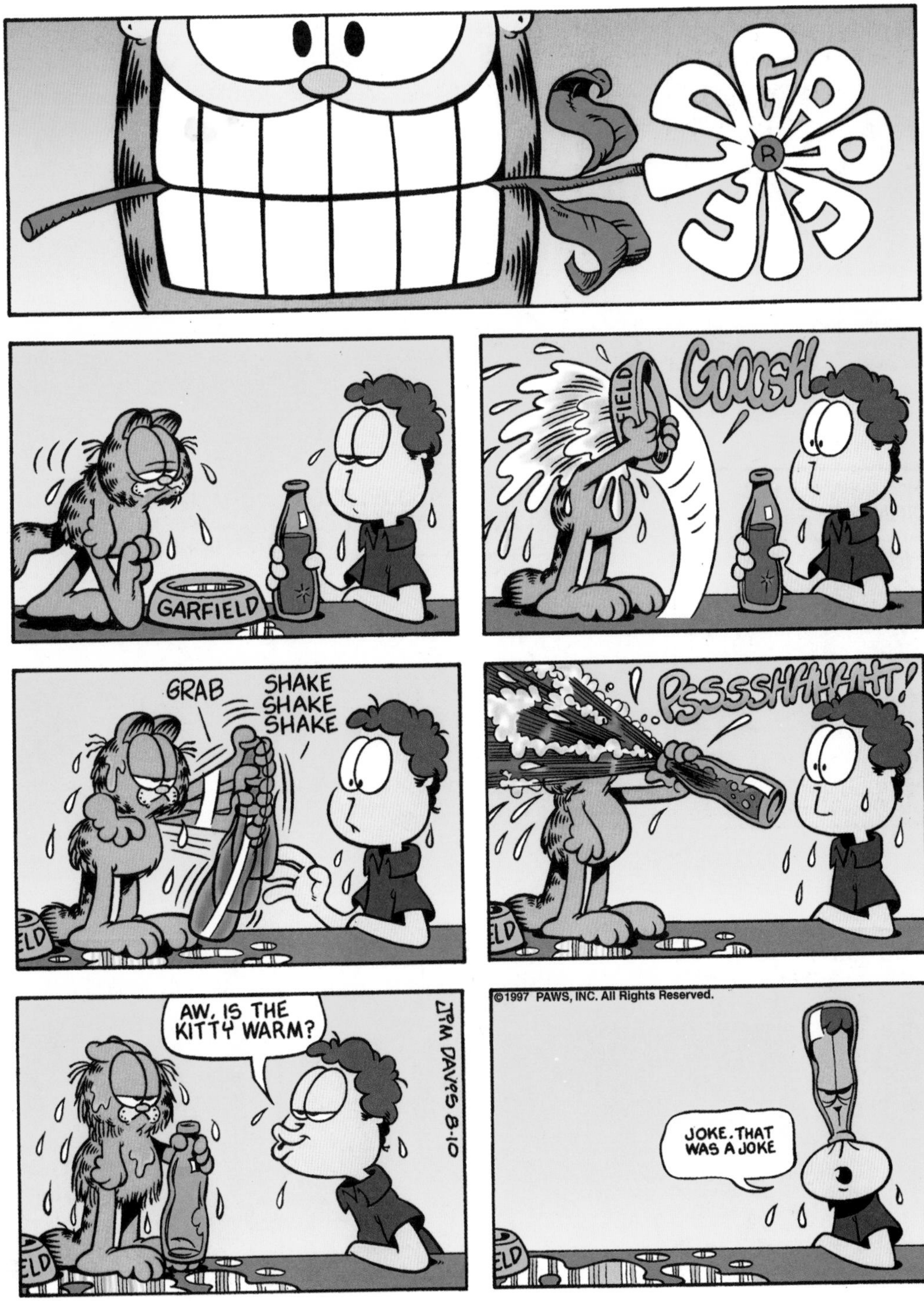
GARFIELD
GARFIELD
GOOOSH
FIELD
GRAB
SHAKE
SHAKE
SHAKE
PSSSSHHHHHT!
AW, IS THE KITTY WARM?
JIM DAVIS 8-10
©1997 PAWS, INC. All Rights Reserved.
JOKE. THAT WAS A JOKE

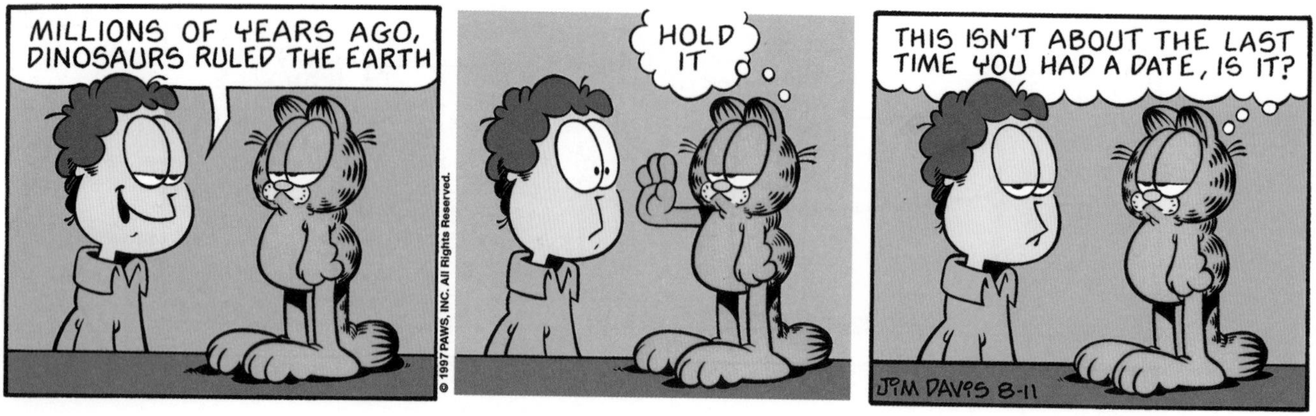
MILLIONS OF YEARS AGO, DINOSAURS RULED THE EARTH
HOLD IT
THIS ISN'T ABOUT THE LAST TIME YOU HAD A DATE, IS IT?
© 1997 PAWS, INC. All Rights Reserved.
JIM DAVIS 8-11

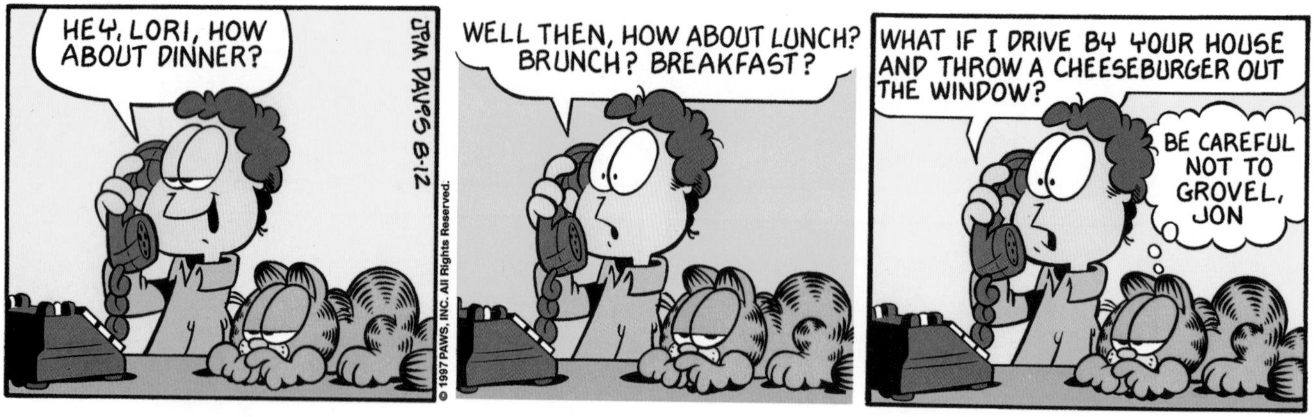
HEY, LORI, HOW ABOUT DINNER?
JIM DAVIS 8-12
© 1997 PAWS, INC. All Rights Reserved.
WELL THEN, HOW ABOUT LUNCH? BRUNCH? BREAKFAST?
WHAT IF I DRIVE BY YOUR HOUSE AND THROW A CHEESEBURGER OUT THE WINDOW?
BE CAREFUL NOT TO GROVEL, JON

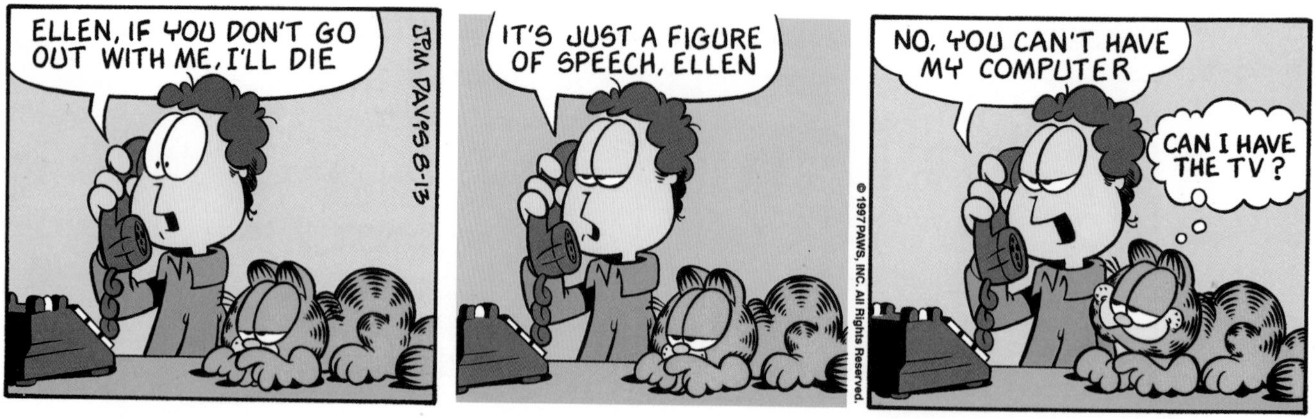
ELLEN, IF YOU DON'T GO OUT WITH ME, I'LL DIE
JIM DAVIS 8-13
IT'S JUST A FIGURE OF SPEECH, ELLEN
© 1997 PAWS, INC. All Rights Reserved.
NO, YOU CAN'T HAVE MY COMPUTER
CAN I HAVE THE TV?

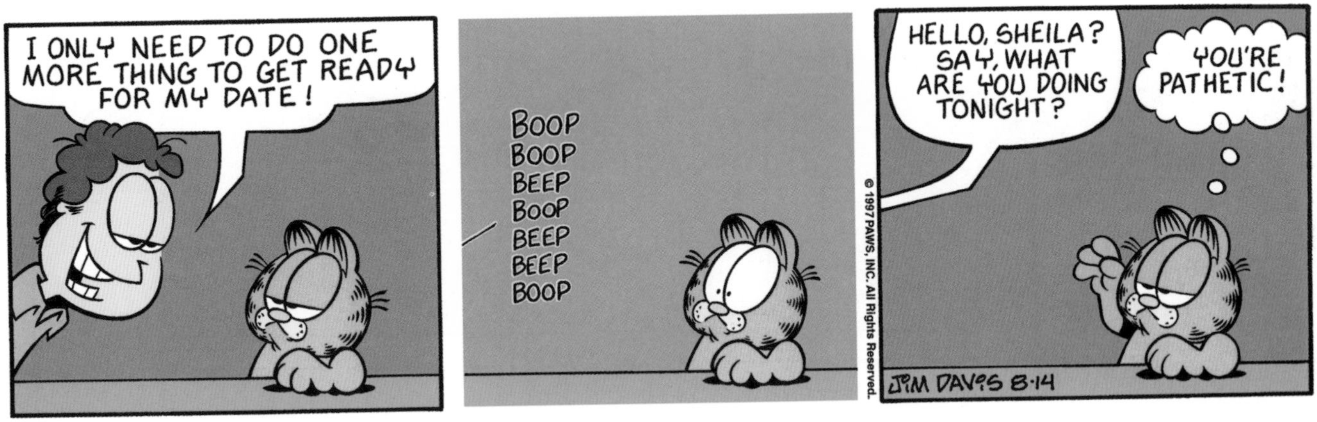
I ONLY NEED TO DO ONE MORE THING TO GET READY FOR MY DATE!
BOOP BOOP BEEP BOOP BEEP BEEP BOOP
HELLO, SHEILA? SAY, WHAT ARE YOU DOING TONIGHT?
YOU'RE PATHETIC!
JIM DAVIS 8·14
© 1997 PAWS, INC. All Rights Reserved.

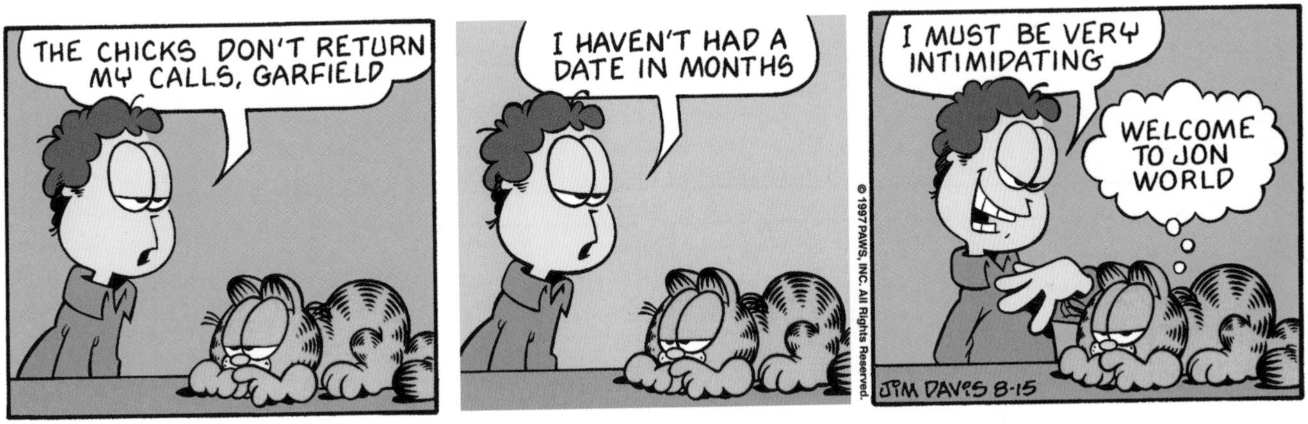
THE CHICKS DON'T RETURN MY CALLS, GARFIELD
I HAVEN'T HAD A DATE IN MONTHS
I MUST BE VERY INTIMIDATING
WELCOME TO JON WORLD
JIM DAVIS 8·15
© 1997 PAWS, INC. All Rights Reserved.

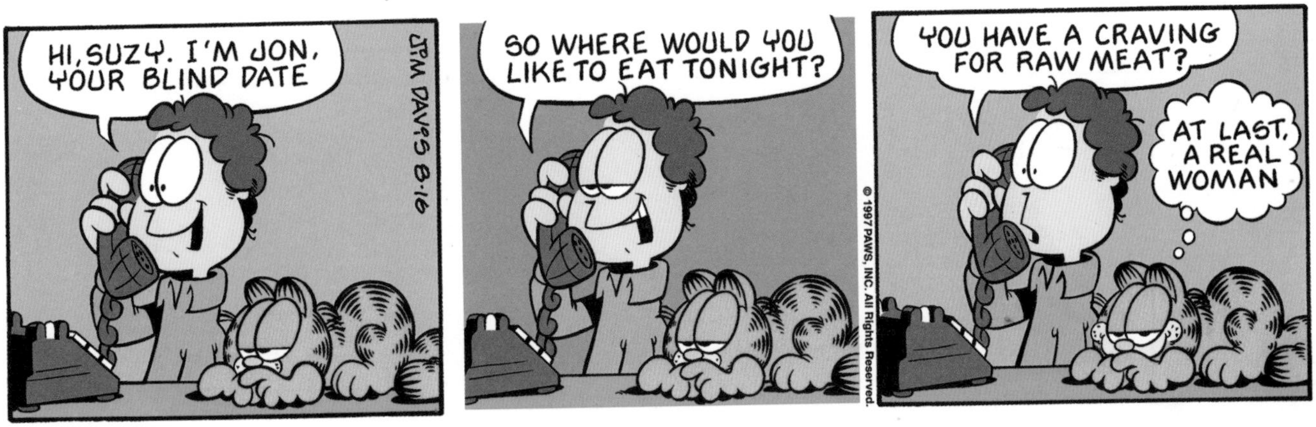
HI, SUZY. I'M JON, YOUR BLIND DATE
JIM DAVIS 8·16
SO WHERE WOULD YOU LIKE TO EAT TONIGHT?
YOU HAVE A CRAVING FOR RAW MEAT?
AT LAST, A REAL WOMAN
© 1997 PAWS, INC. All Rights Reserved.

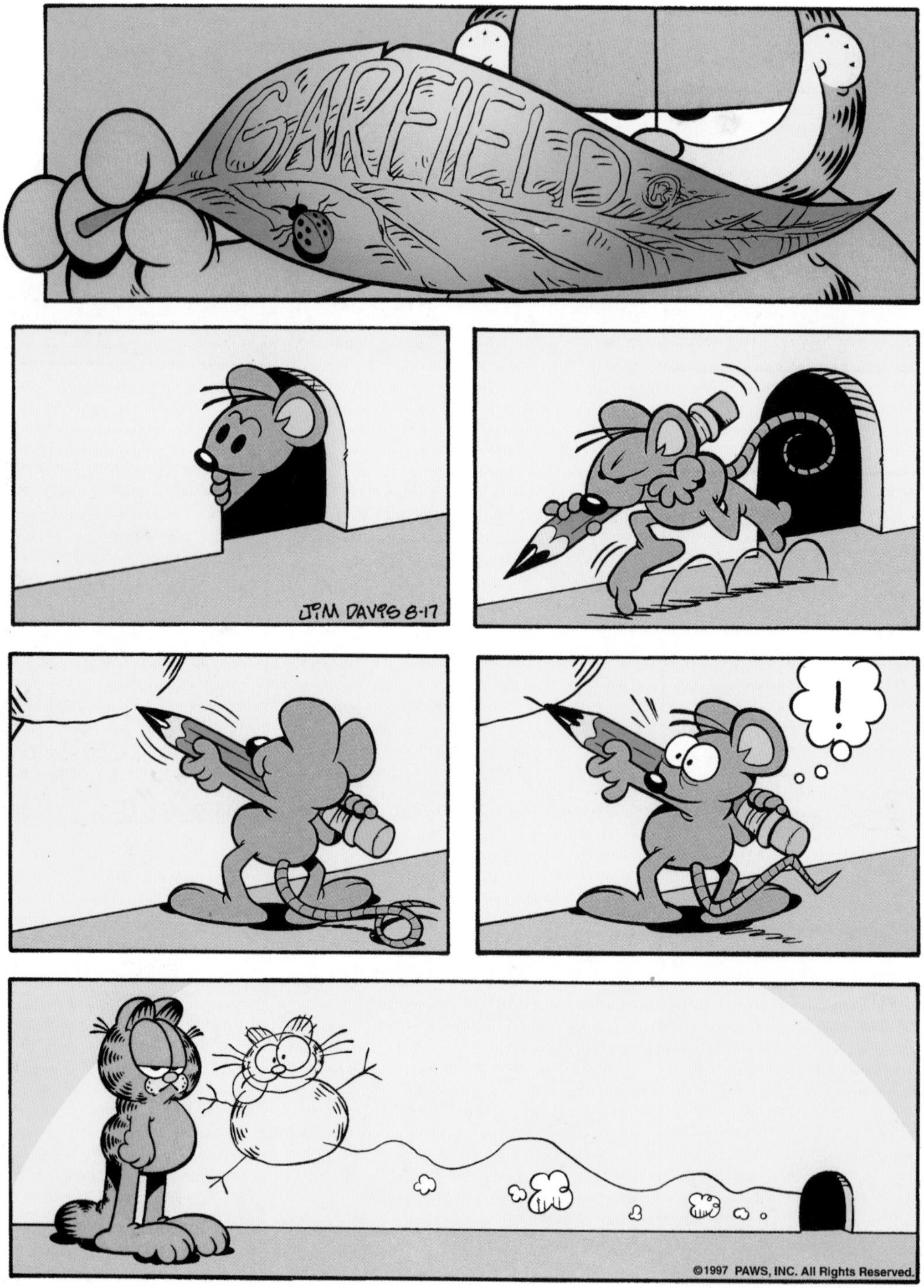
GARFIELD®
JIM DAVIS 8-17
!
©1997 PAWS, INC. All Rights Reserved.

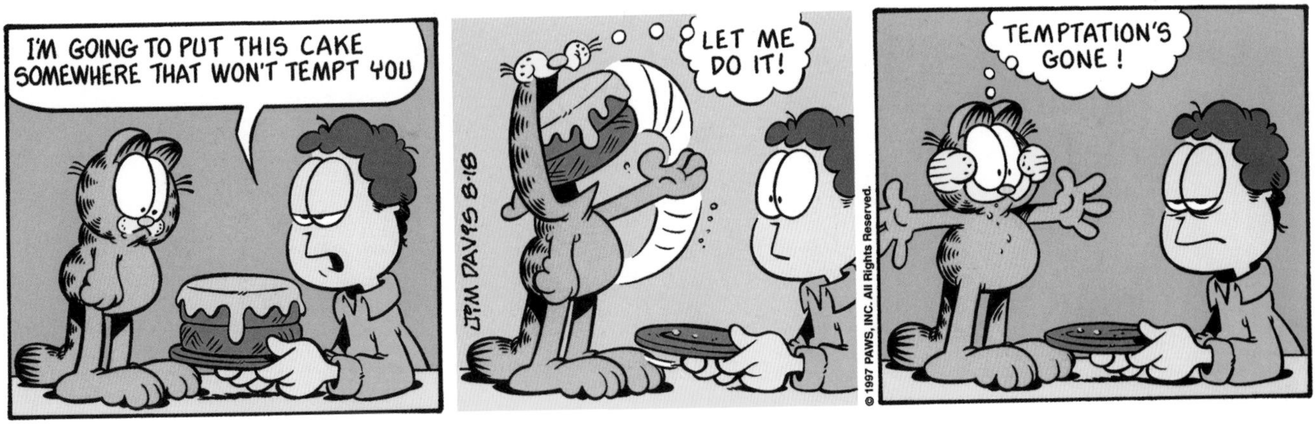
I'M GOING TO PUT THIS CAKE SOMEWHERE THAT WON'T TEMPT YOU
LET ME DO IT!
© 1997 PAWS, INC. All Rights Reserved.
TEMPTATION'S GONE!

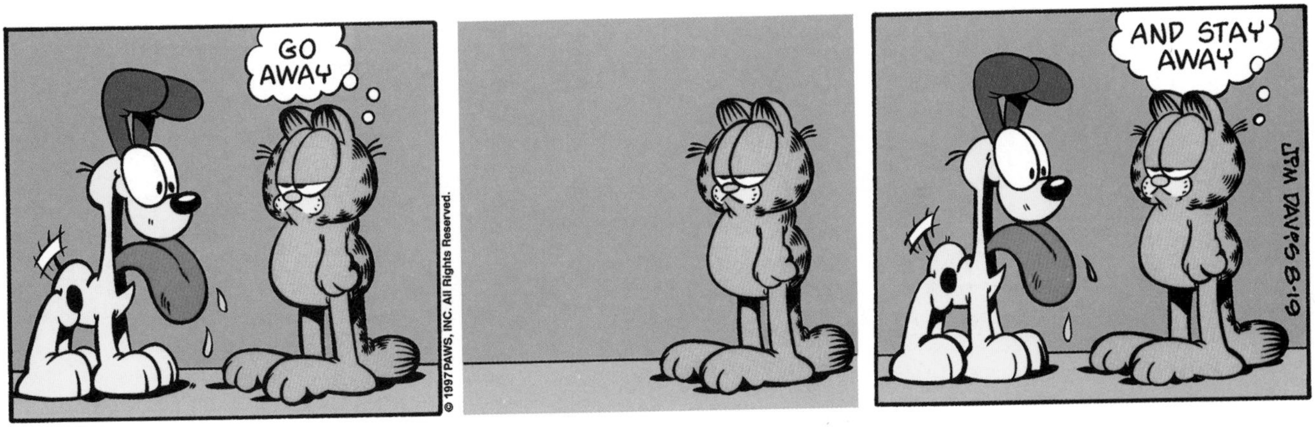
GO AWAY
© 1997 PAWS, INC. All Rights Reserved.
AND STAY AWAY

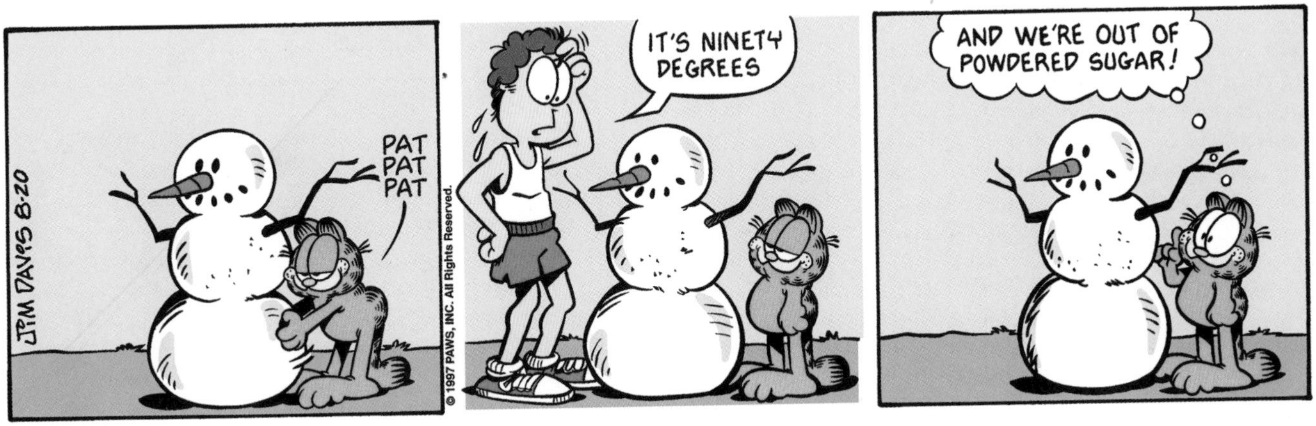
PAT PAT PAT
© 1997 PAWS, INC. All Rights Reserved.
IT'S NINETY DEGREES
AND WE'RE OUT OF POWDERED SUGAR!

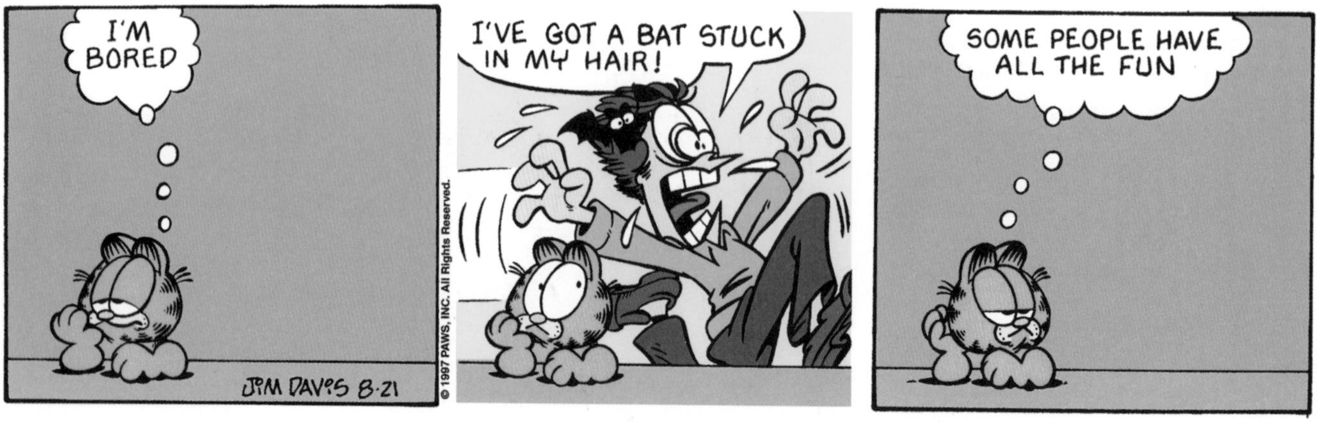
I'M BORED
JIM DAVIS 8-21
© 1997 PAWS, INC. All Rights Reserved.
I'VE GOT A BAT STUCK IN MY HAIR!
SOME PEOPLE HAVE ALL THE FUN

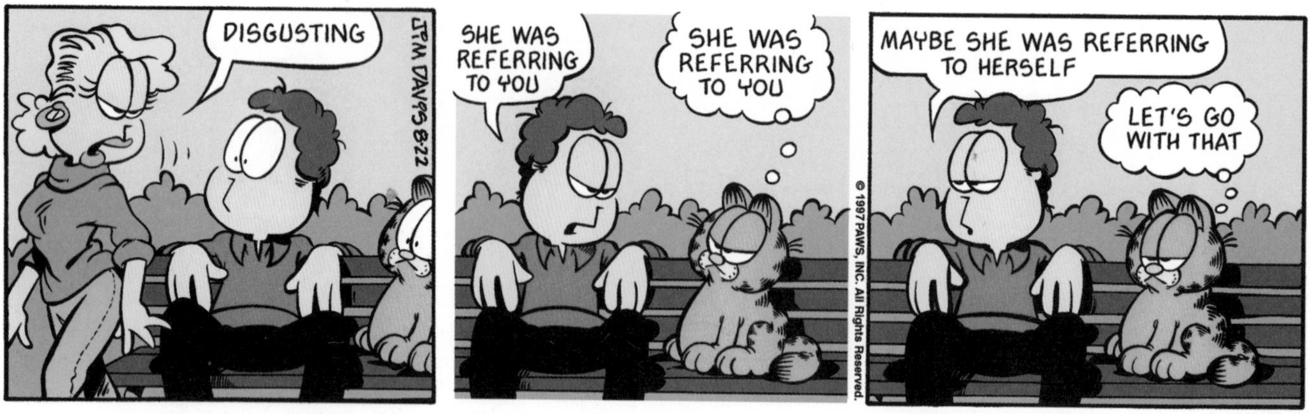
DISGUSTING
JIM DAVIS 8-22
SHE WAS REFERRING TO YOU
SHE WAS REFERRING TO YOU
© 1997 PAWS, INC. All Rights Reserved.
MAYBE SHE WAS REFERRING TO HERSELF
LET'S GO WITH THAT

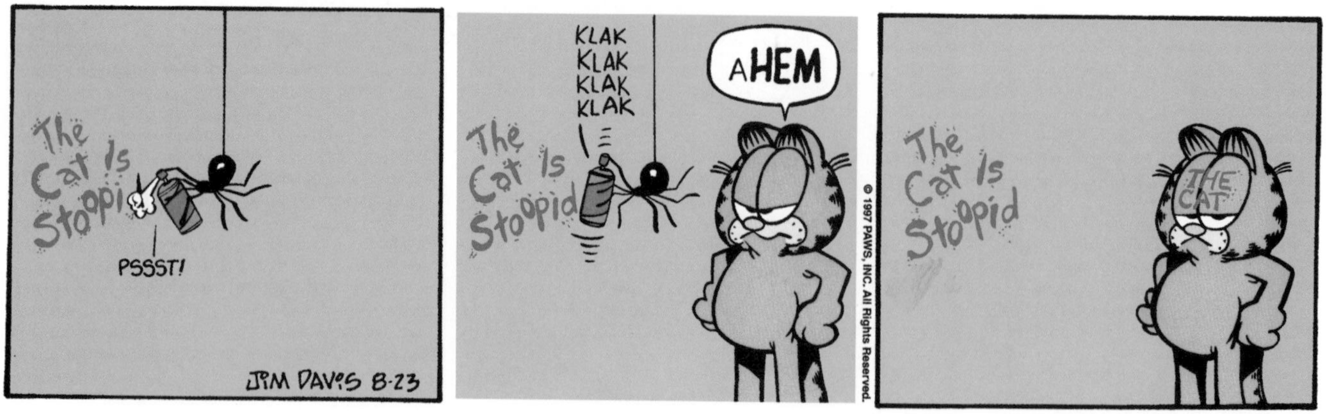
The Cat Is Stoopi
PSSST!
JIM DAVIS 8-23
KLAK KLAK KLAK KLAK
The Cat Is Stoopid
AHEM
© 1997 PAWS, INC. All Rights Reserved.
The Cat Is Stoopid
THE CAT

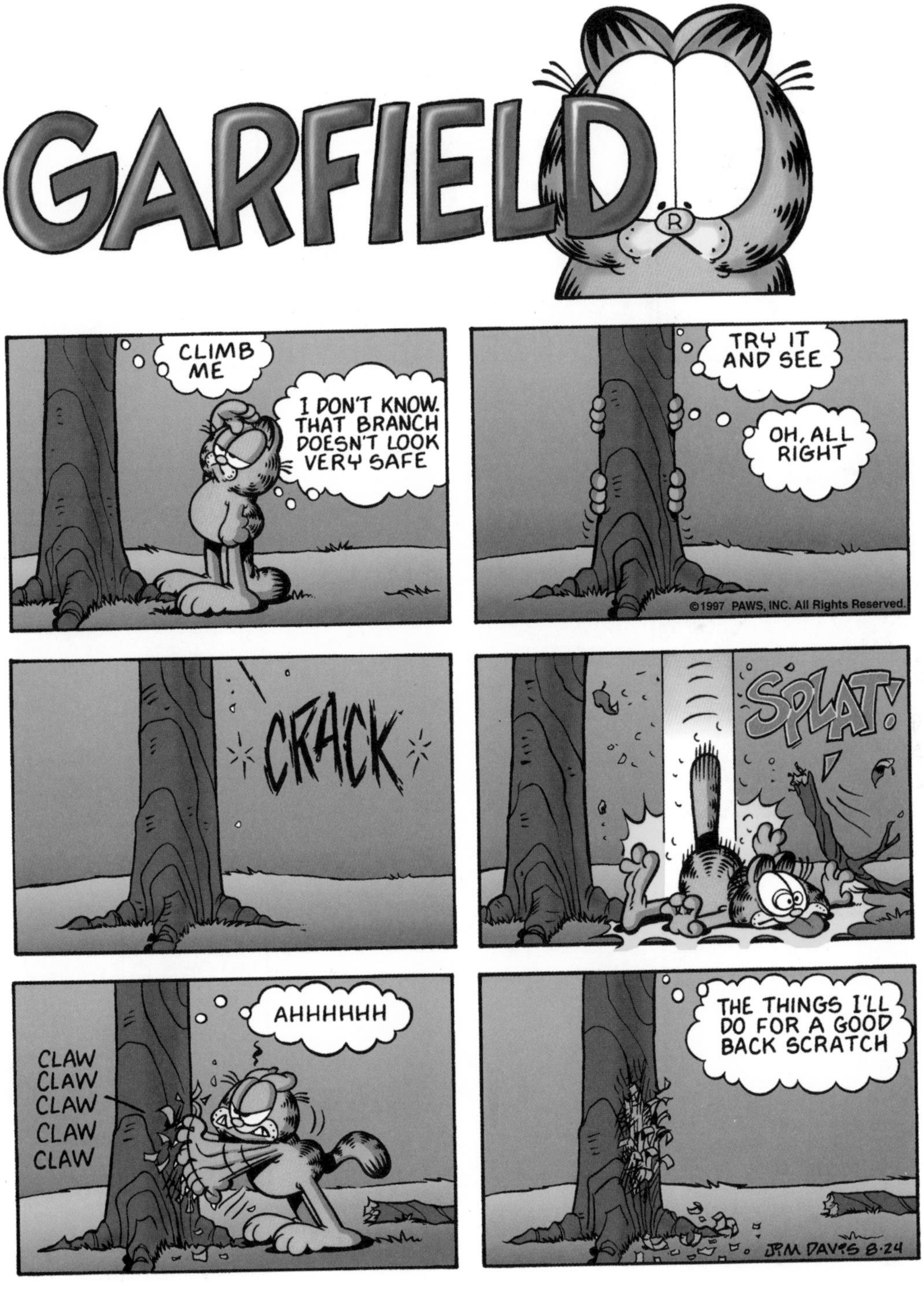
GARFIELD
CLIMB ME
I DON'T KNOW. THAT BRANCH DOESN'T LOOK VERY SAFE
TRY IT AND SEE
OH, ALL RIGHT
©1997 PAWS, INC. All Rights Reserved.
CRACK
SPLAT!
AHHHHHH
CLAW CLAW CLAW CLAW CLAW
THE THINGS I'LL DO FOR A GOOD BACK SCRATCH
JIM DAVIS 8·24

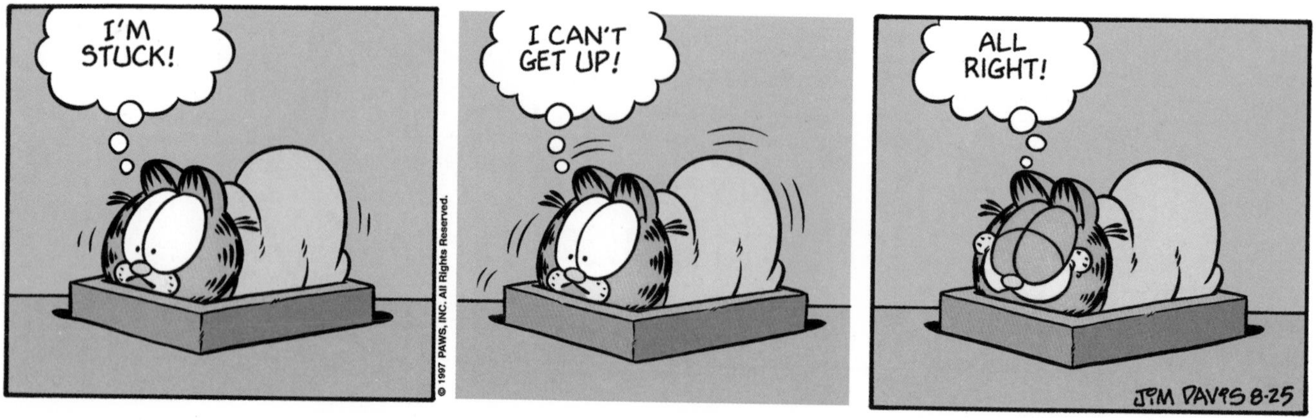
I'M STUCK!
I CAN'T GET UP!
ALL RIGHT!
© 1997 PAWS, INC. All Rights Reserved.
JIM DAVIS 8-25

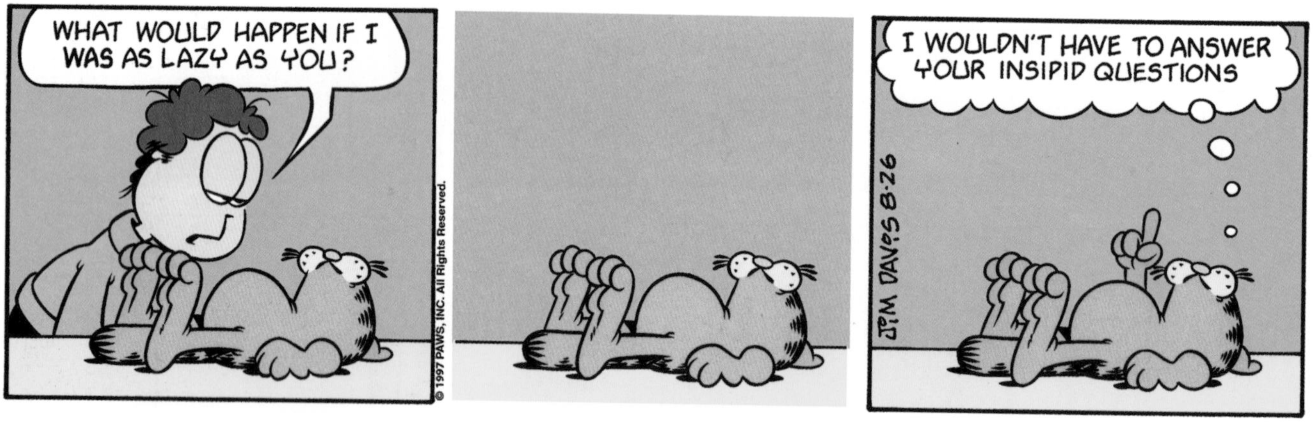
WHAT WOULD HAPPEN IF I WAS AS LAZY AS YOU?
I WOULDN'T HAVE TO ANSWER YOUR INSIPID QUESTIONS
© 1997 PAWS, INC. All Rights Reserved.
JIM DAVIS 8-26

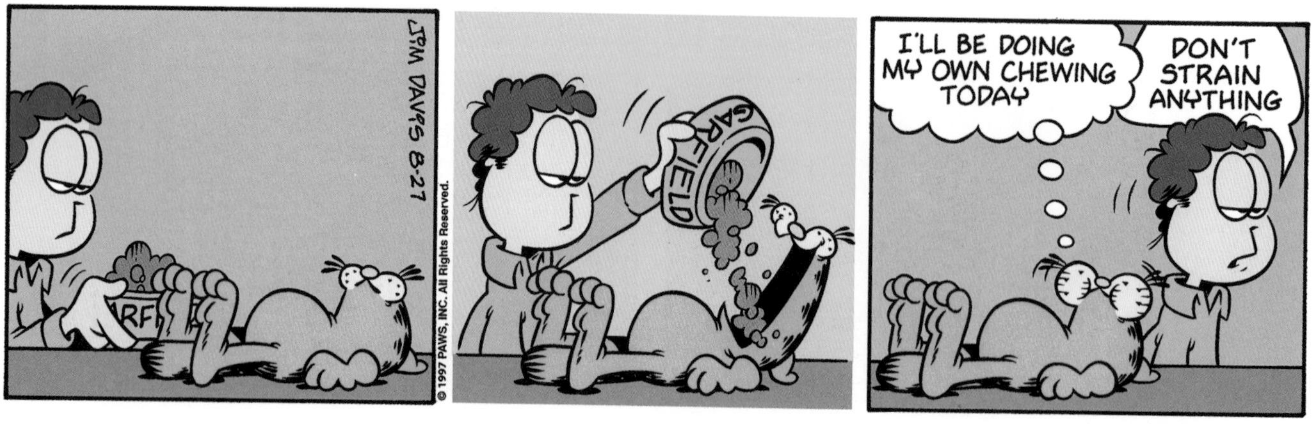
JIM DAVIS 8-27
GARFIELD
I'LL BE DOING MY OWN CHEWING TODAY
DON'T STRAIN ANYTHING
© 1997 PAWS, INC. All Rights Reserved.

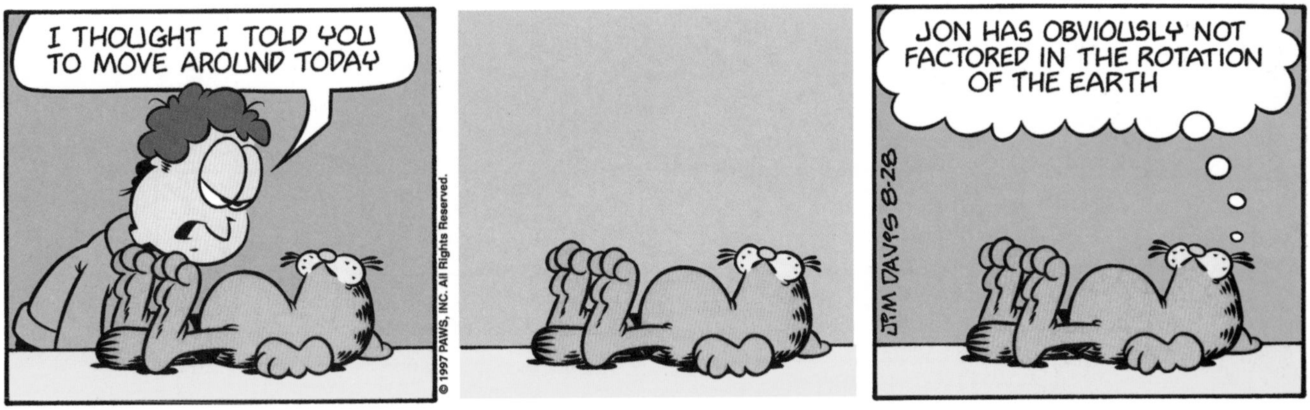
I THOUGHT I TOLD YOU TO MOVE AROUND TODAY
© 1997 PAWS, INC. All Rights Reserved.
JON HAS OBVIOUSLY NOT FACTORED IN THE ROTATION OF THE EARTH
JIM DAVIS 8-28

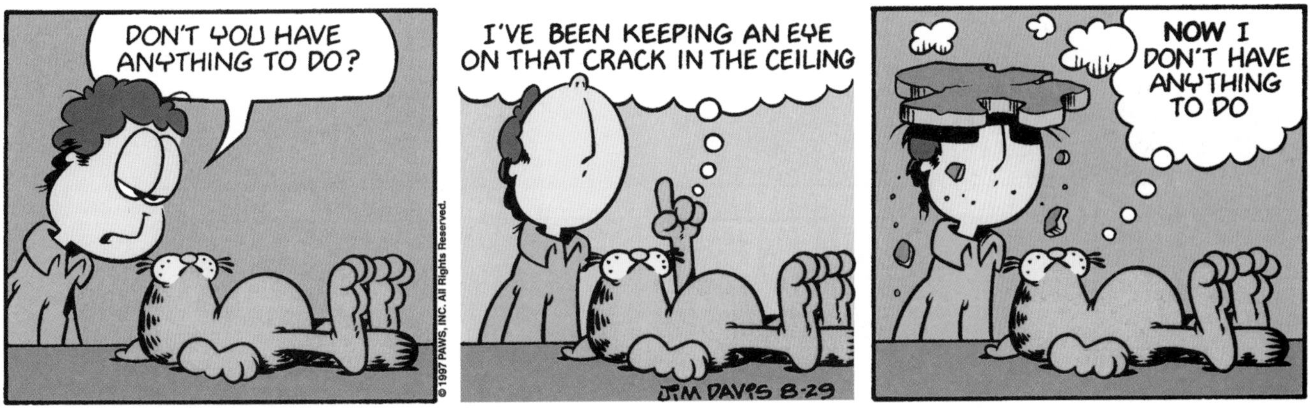
DON'T YOU HAVE ANYTHING TO DO?
© 1997 PAWS, INC. All Rights Reserved.
I'VE BEEN KEEPING AN EYE ON THAT CRACK IN THE CEILING
JIM DAVIS 8-29
NOW I DON'T HAVE ANYTHING TO DO

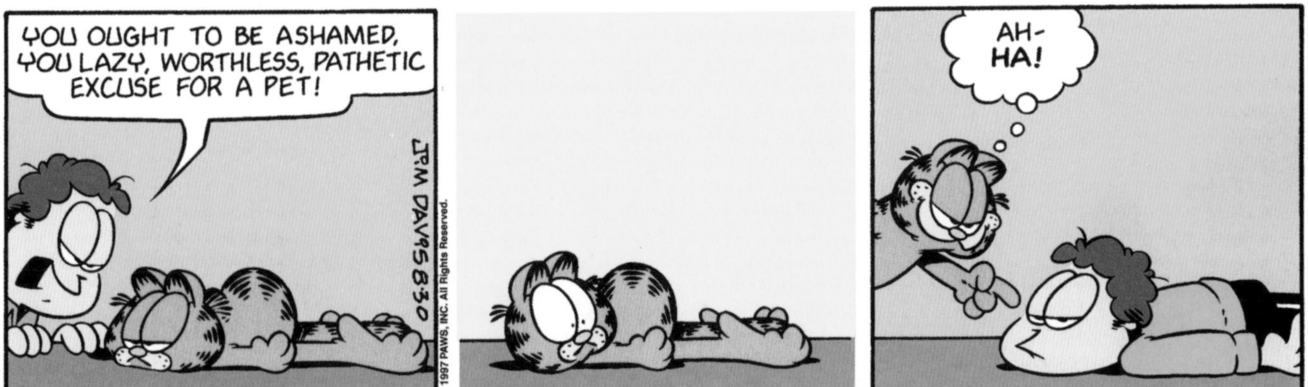
YOU OUGHT TO BE ASHAMED, YOU LAZY, WORTHLESS, PATHETIC EXCUSE FOR A PET!
JIM DAVIS 8-30
© 1997 PAWS, INC. All Rights Reserved.
AH-HA!

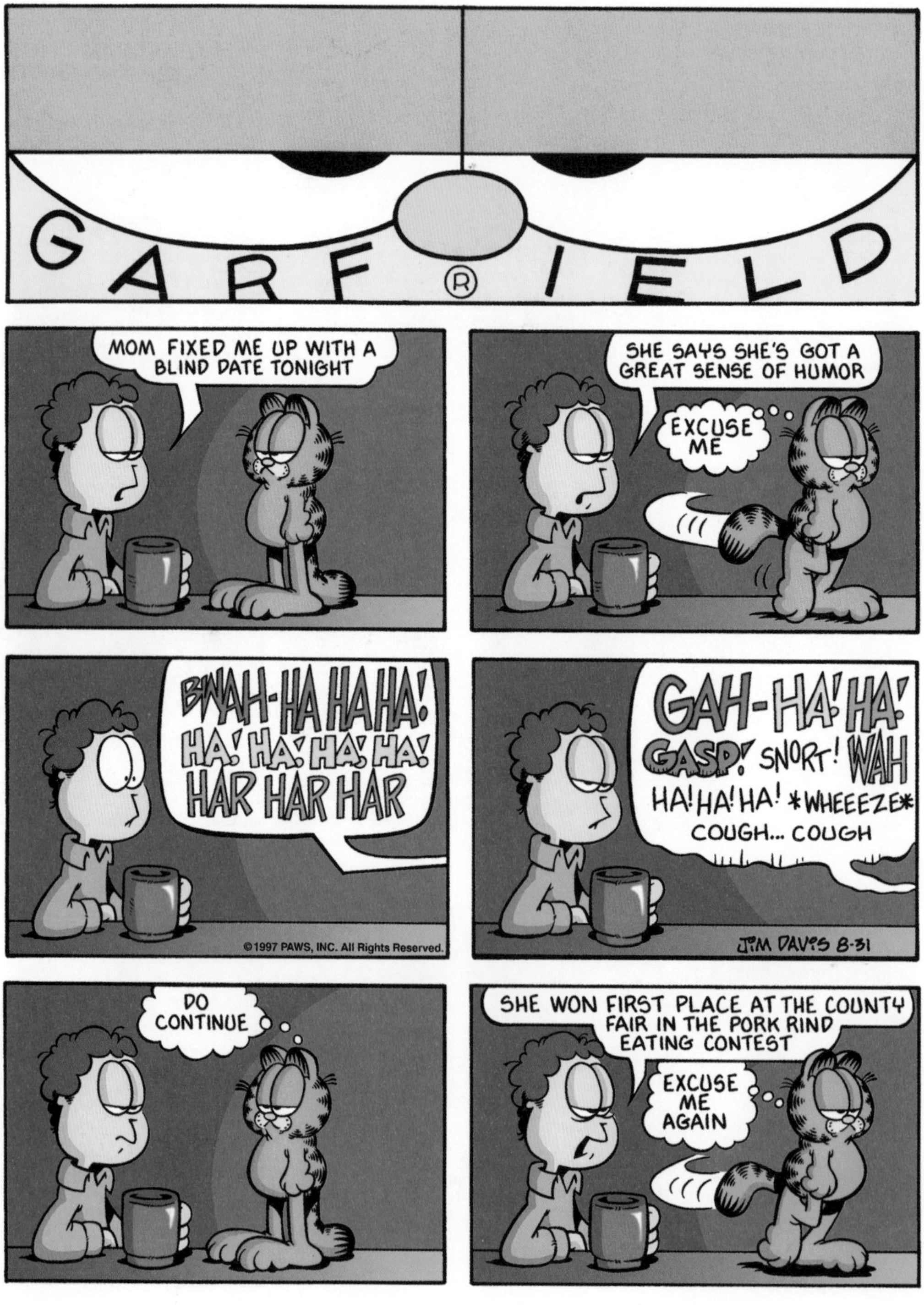
GARFIELD®
MOM FIXED ME UP WITH A BLIND DATE TONIGHT
SHE SAYS SHE'S GOT A GREAT SENSE OF HUMOR
EXCUSE ME
BWAH-HA HAHA! HA! HA! HA! HA! HAR HAR HAR
©1997 PAWS, INC. All Rights Reserved.
GAH-HA! HA! GASP! SNORT! WAH HA! HA! HA! *WHEEEZE* COUGH... COUGH
JIM DAVIS 8-31
DO CONTINUE
SHE WON FIRST PLACE AT THE COUNTY FAIR IN THE PORK RIND EATING CONTEST
EXCUSE ME AGAIN

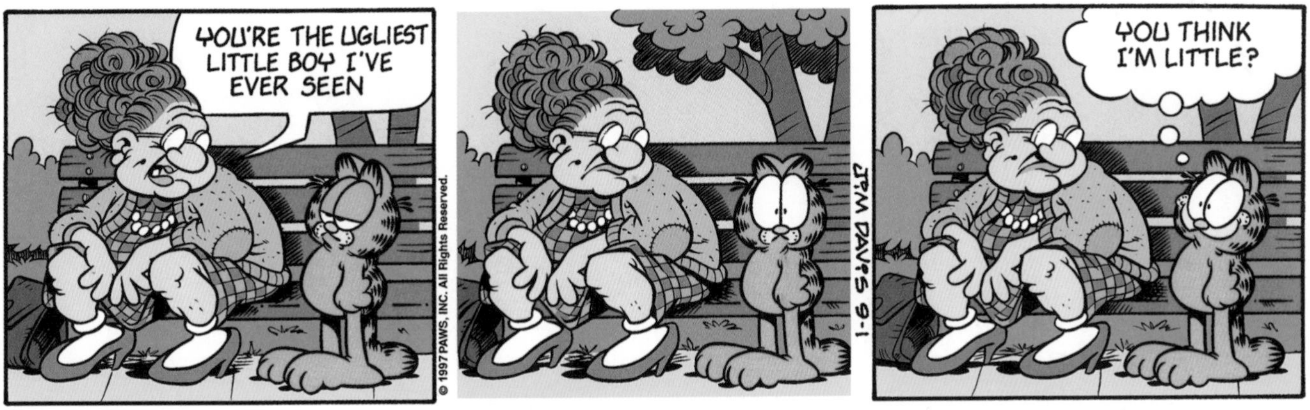
YOU'RE THE UGLIEST LITTLE BOY I'VE EVER SEEN
YOU THINK I'M LITTLE?
© 1997 PAWS, INC. All Rights Reserved.
JIM DAVIS 9-1

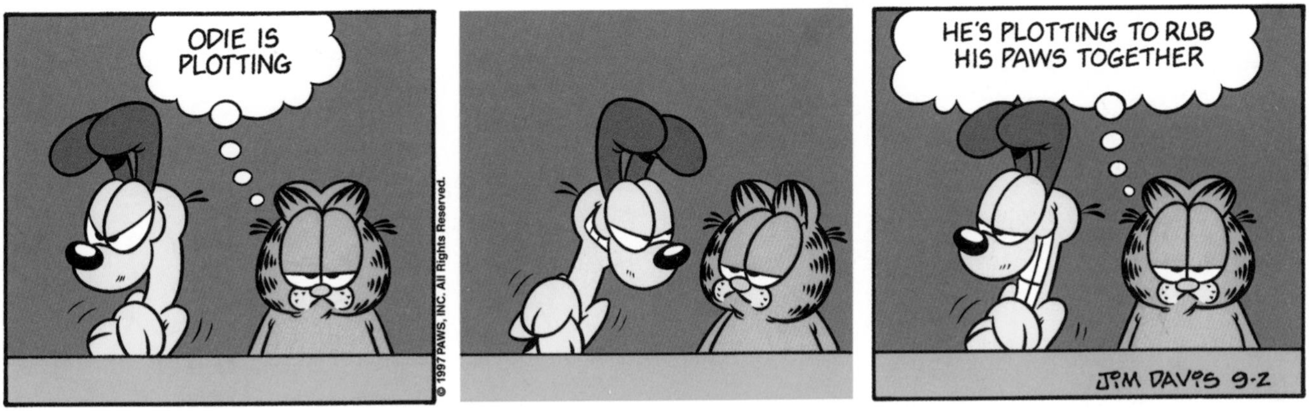
ODIE IS PLOTTING
HE'S PLOTTING TO RUB HIS PAWS TOGETHER
© 1997 PAWS, INC. All Rights Reserved.
JIM DAVIS 9-2

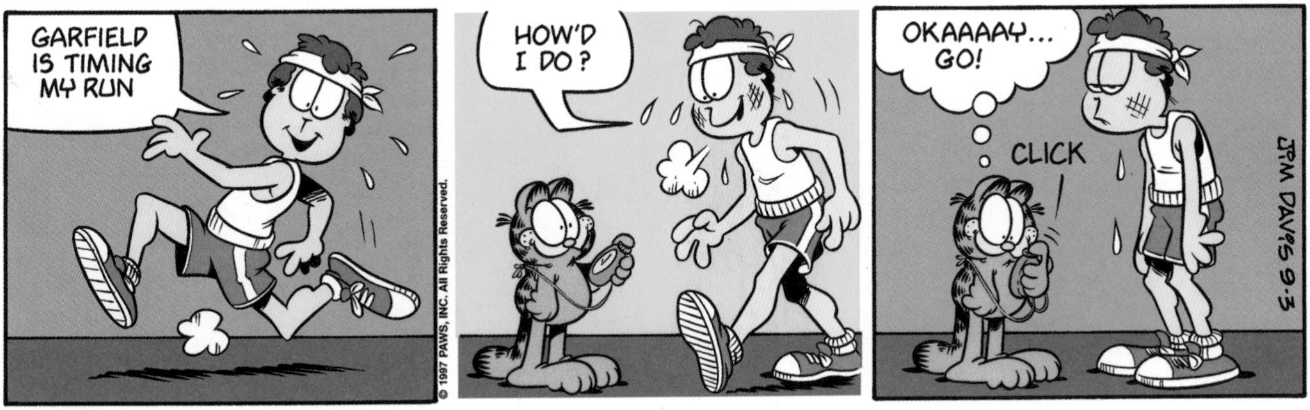
GARFIELD IS TIMING MY RUN
HOW'D I DO?
OKAAAAY... GO!
CLICK
© 1997 PAWS, INC. All Rights Reserved.
JIM DAVIS 9-3

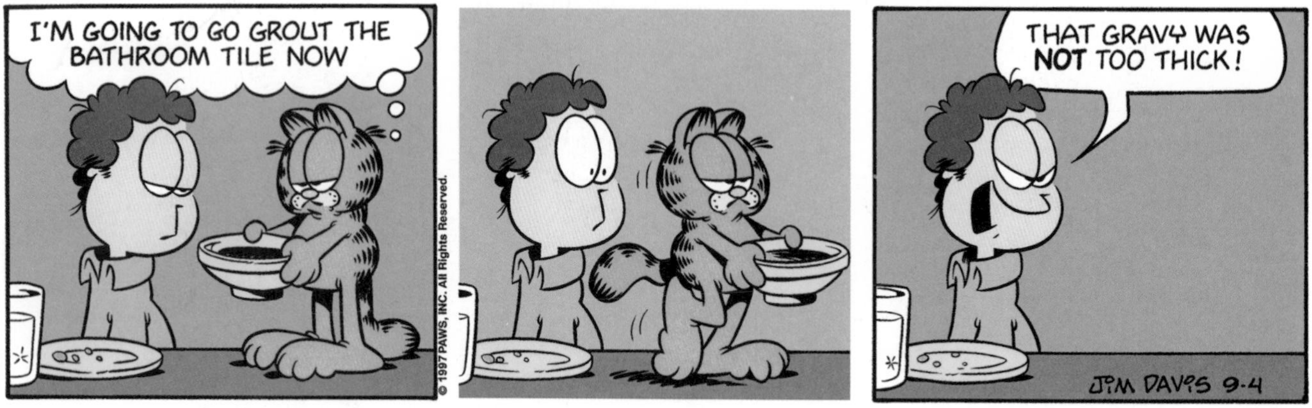
I'M GOING TO GO GROUT THE BATHROOM TILE NOW
© 1997 PAWS, INC. All Rights Reserved.
THAT GRAVY WAS **NOT** TOO THICK!
JIM DAVIS 9-4

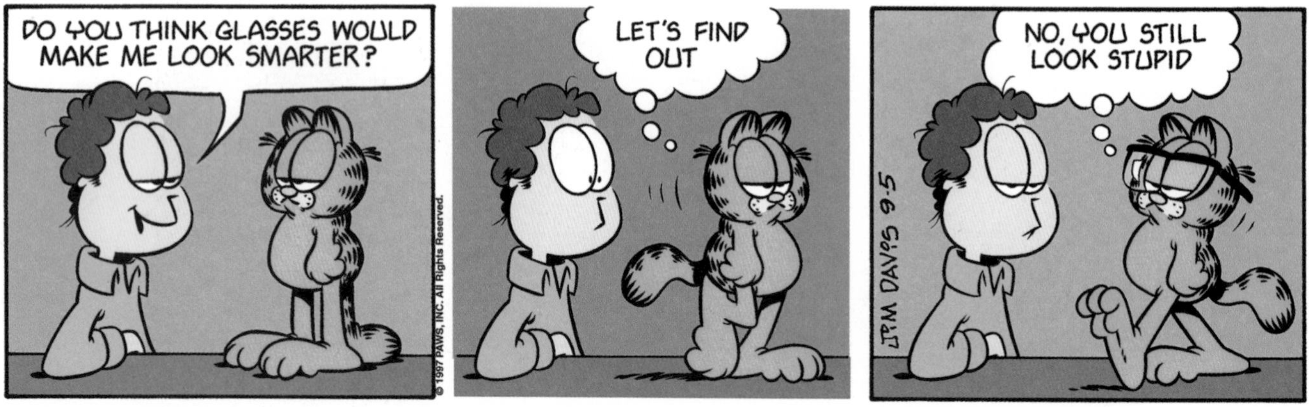
DO YOU THINK GLASSES WOULD MAKE ME LOOK SMARTER?
© 1997 PAWS, INC. All Rights Reserved.
LET'S FIND OUT
JIM DAVIS 9-5
NO, YOU STILL LOOK STUPID

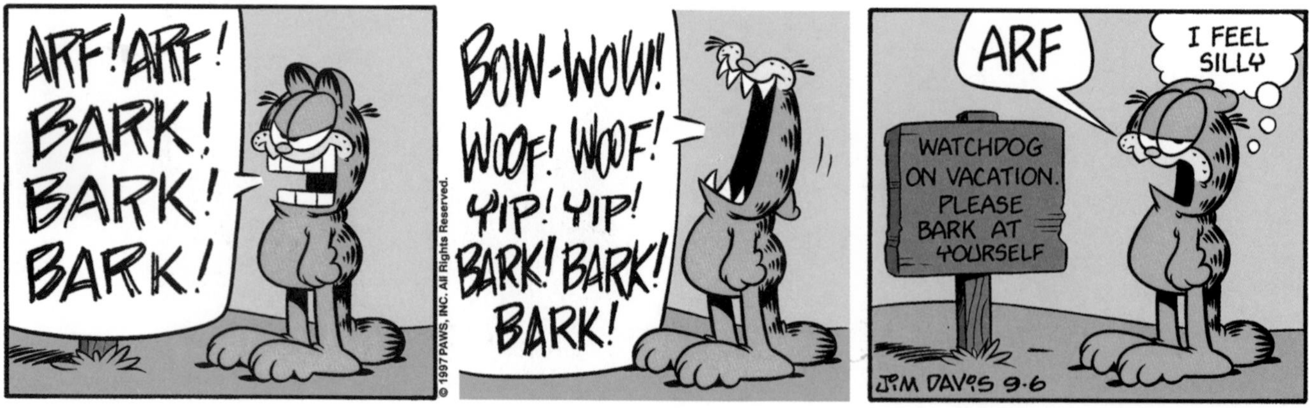
ARF! ARF! BARK! BARK! BARK!
© 1997 PAWS, INC. All Rights Reserved.
BOW-WOW! WOOF! WOOF! YIP! YIP! BARK! BARK! BARK!
ARF
I FEEL SILLY
WATCHDOG ON VACATION. PLEASE BARK AT YOURSELF
JIM DAVIS 9-6

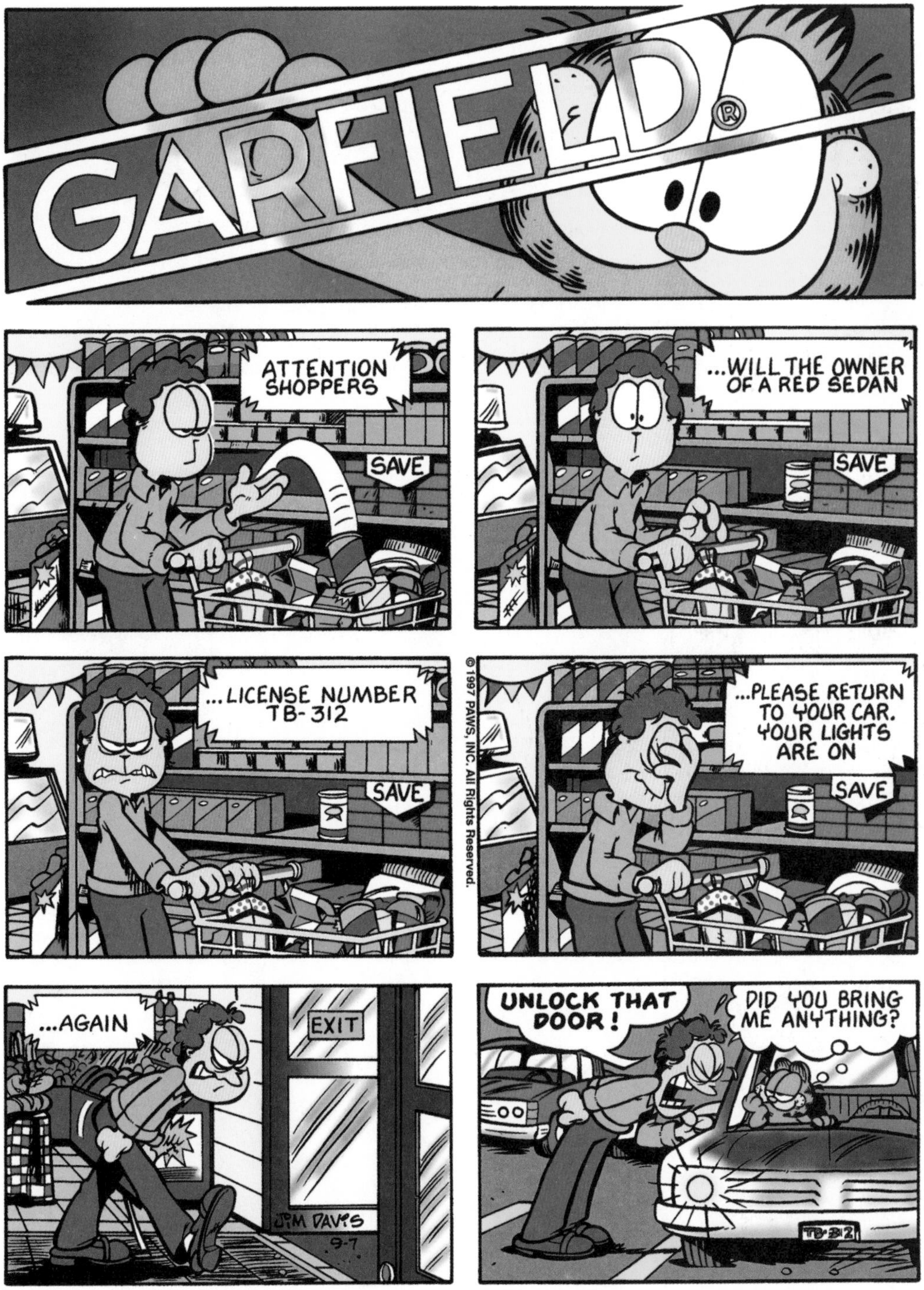
GARFIELD®
ATTENTION SHOPPERS
SAVE
...WILL THE OWNER OF A RED SEDAN
SAVE
...LICENSE NUMBER TB-312
SAVE
...PLEASE RETURN TO YOUR CAR. YOUR LIGHTS ARE ON
SAVE
...AGAIN
EXIT
JIM DAVIS 9-7
UNLOCK THAT DOOR!
DID YOU BRING ME ANYTHING?
TB-312

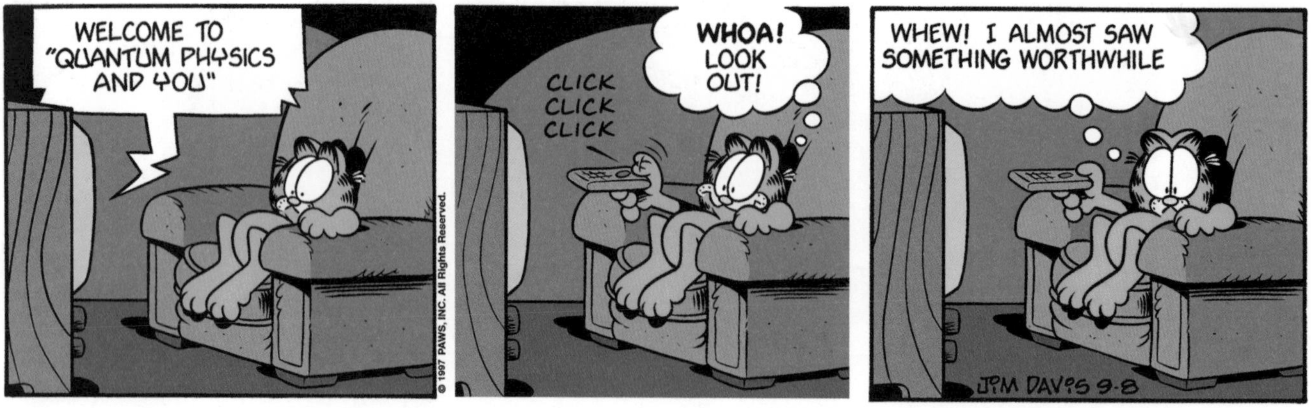
WELCOME TO "QUANTUM PHYSICS AND YOU"
CLICK CLICK CLICK
WHOA! LOOK OUT!
WHEW! I ALMOST SAW SOMETHING WORTHWHILE
JIM DAVIS 9-8

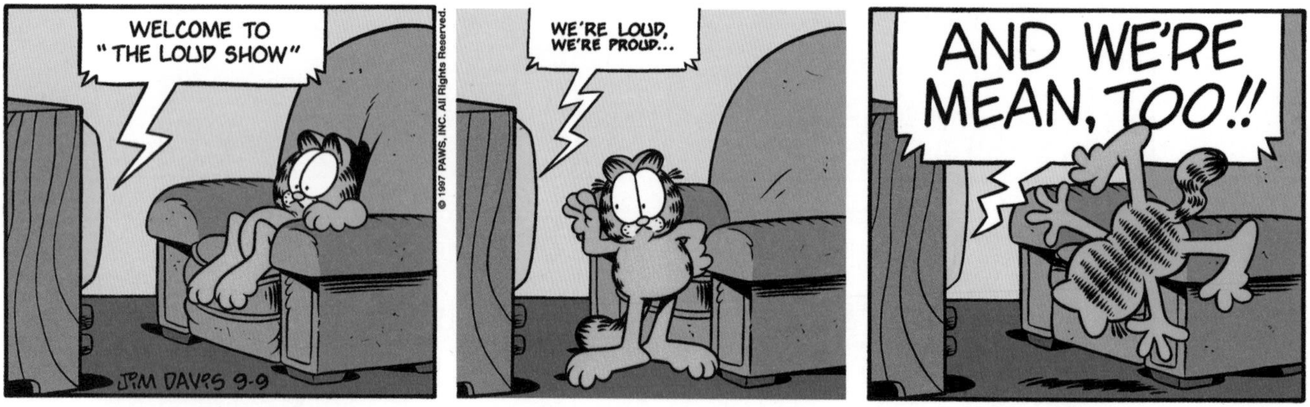
WELCOME TO "THE LOUD SHOW"
JIM DAVIS 9-9
WE'RE LOUD, WE'RE PROUD...
AND WE'RE MEAN, TOO!!

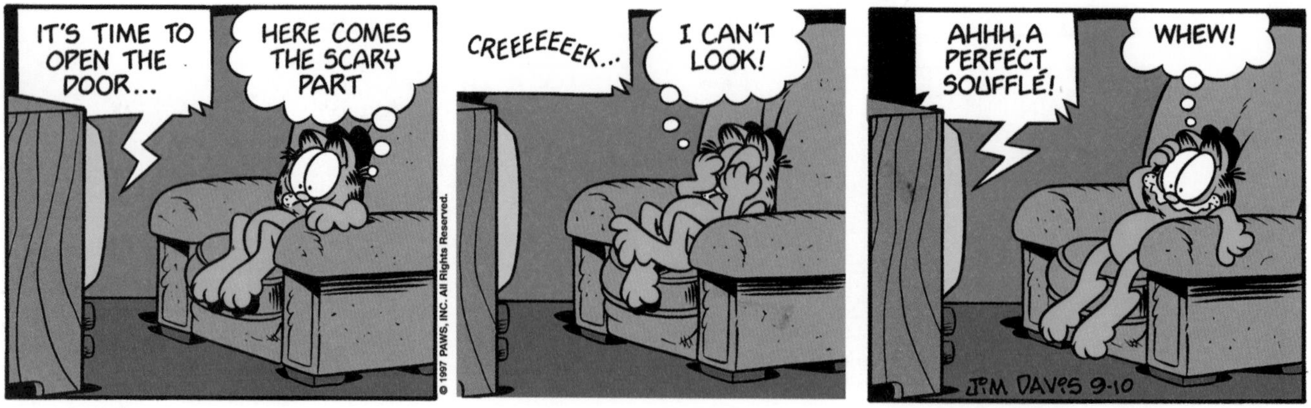
IT'S TIME TO OPEN THE DOOR...
HERE COMES THE SCARY PART
CREEEEEEEEK...
I CAN'T LOOK!
AHHH, A PERFECT SOUFFLÉ!
WHEW!
JIM DAVIS 9-10

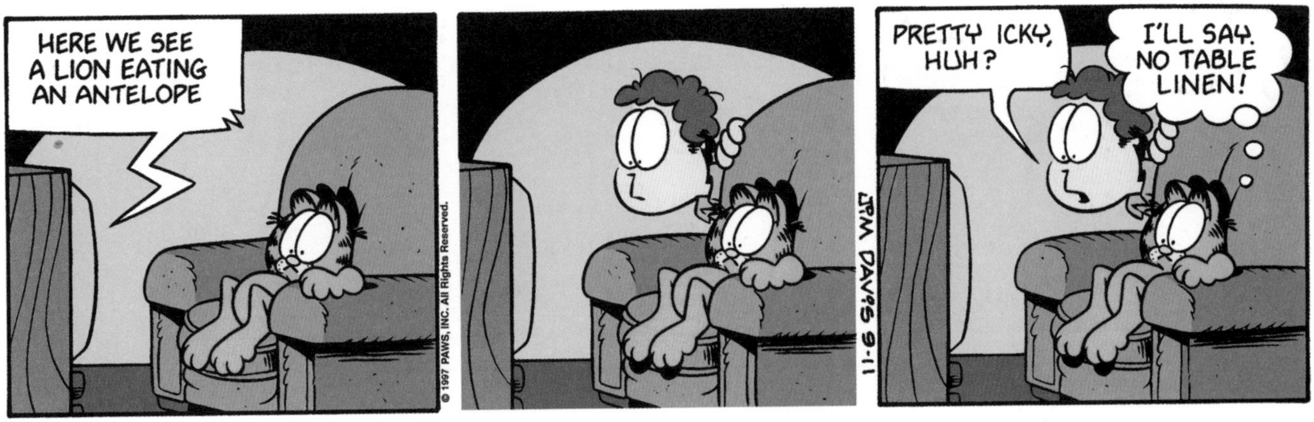
HERE WE SEE A LION EATING AN ANTELOPE
© 1997 PAWS, INC. All Rights Reserved.
JIM DAVIS 9-11
PRETTY ICKY, HUH?
I'LL SAY. NO TABLE LINEN!

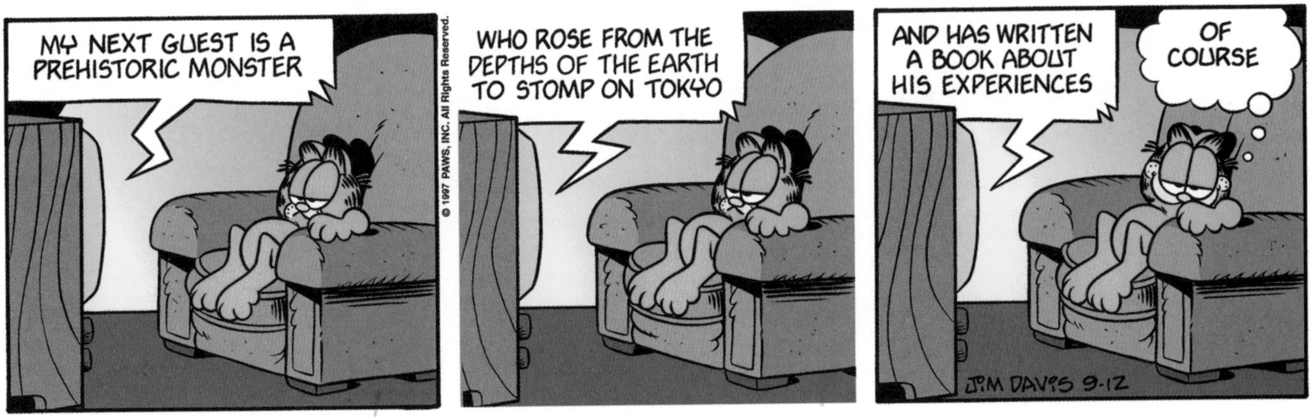
MY NEXT GUEST IS A PREHISTORIC MONSTER
© 1997 PAWS, INC. All Rights Reserved.
WHO ROSE FROM THE DEPTHS OF THE EARTH TO STOMP ON TOKYO
AND HAS WRITTEN A BOOK ABOUT HIS EXPERIENCES
OF COURSE
JIM DAVIS 9-12

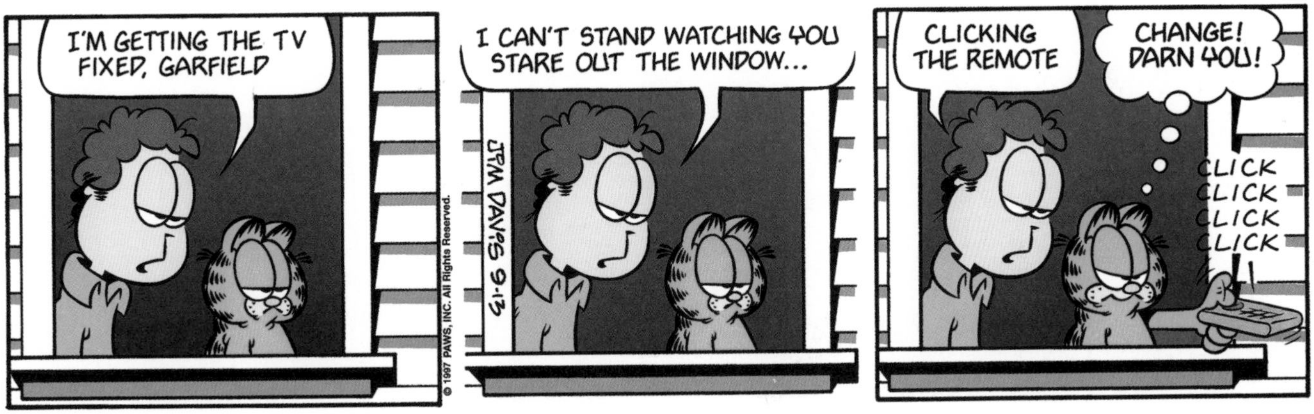
I'M GETTING THE TV FIXED, GARFIELD
© 1997 PAWS, INC. All Rights Reserved.
I CAN'T STAND WATCHING YOU STARE OUT THE WINDOW...
JIM DAVIS 9-13
CLICKING THE REMOTE
CHANGE! DARN YOU!
CLICK
CLICK
CLICK
CLICK

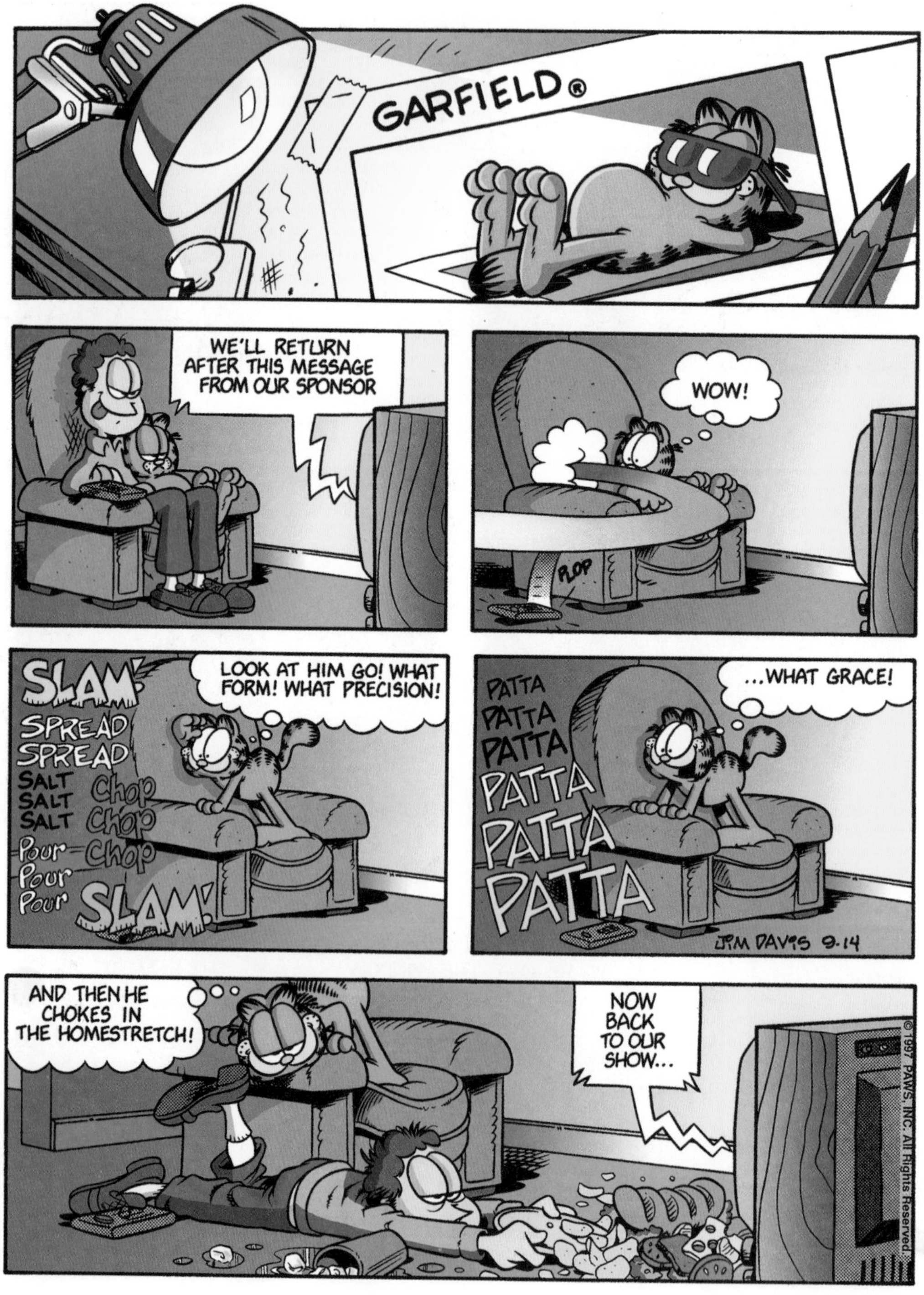
GARFIELD®
WE'LL RETURN AFTER THIS MESSAGE FROM OUR SPONSOR
WOW!
PLOP
SLAM
SPREAD SPREAD
SALT SALT SALT
Chop Chop Chop
Pour Pour Pour
SLAM
LOOK AT HIM GO! WHAT FORM! WHAT PRECISION!
PATTA PATTA PATTA PATTA PATTA PATTA
...WHAT GRACE!
JIM DAVIS 9-14
AND THEN HE CHOKES IN THE HOMESTRETCH!
NOW BACK TO OUR SHOW...
© 1997 PAWS, INC. All Rights Reserved.

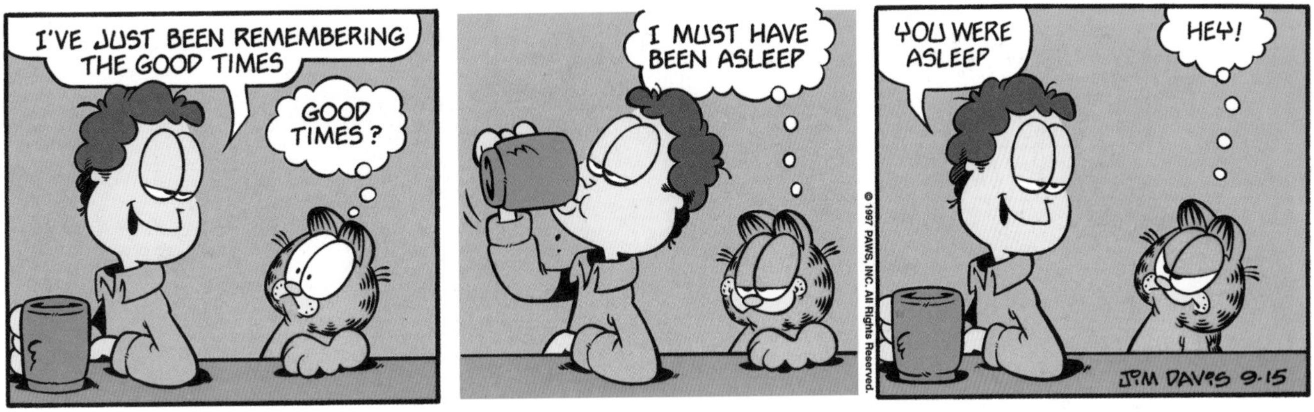
I'VE JUST BEEN REMEMBERING THE GOOD TIMES
GOOD TIMES?
I MUST HAVE BEEN ASLEEP
© 1997 PAWS, INC. All Rights Reserved.
YOU WERE ASLEEP
HEY!
JIM DAVIS 9-15

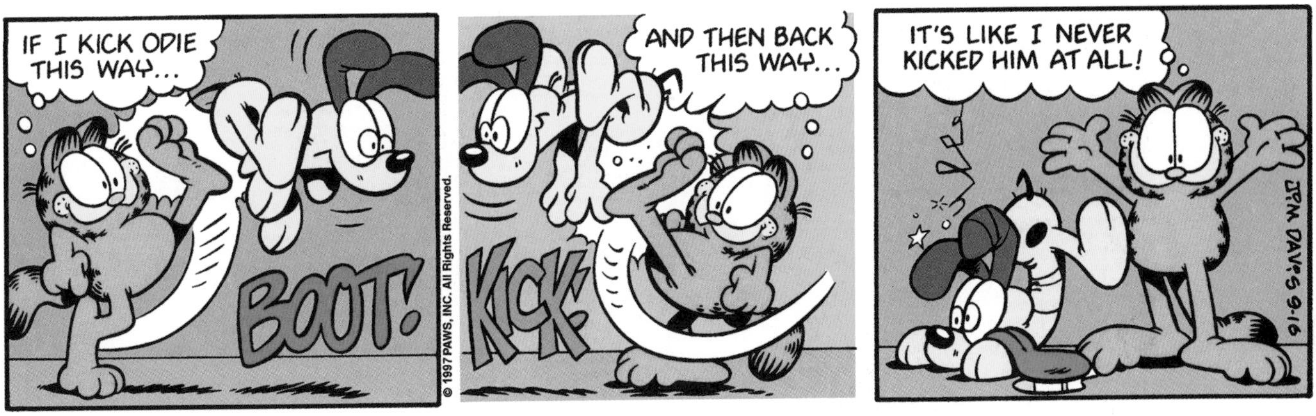
IF I KICK ODIE THIS WAY...
BOOT!
© 1997 PAWS, INC. All Rights Reserved.
KICK
AND THEN BACK THIS WAY...
IT'S LIKE I NEVER KICKED HIM AT ALL!
JIM DAVIS 9-16

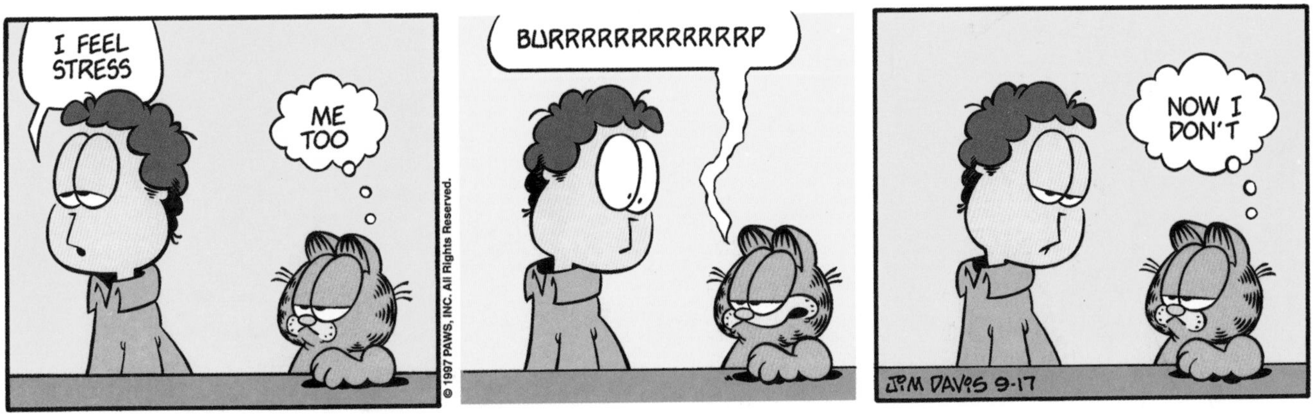
I FEEL STRESS
ME TOO
© 1997 PAWS, INC. All Rights Reserved.
BURRRRRRRRRRRRP
NOW I DON'T
JIM DAVIS 9-17

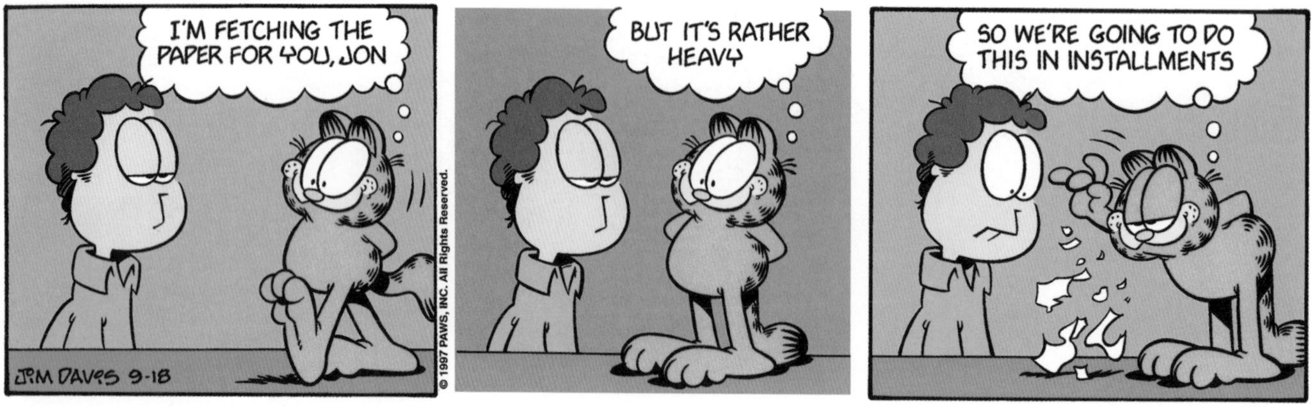
I'M FETCHING THE PAPER FOR YOU, JON
JIM DAVIS 9-18
BUT IT'S RATHER HEAVY
SO WE'RE GOING TO DO THIS IN INSTALLMENTS

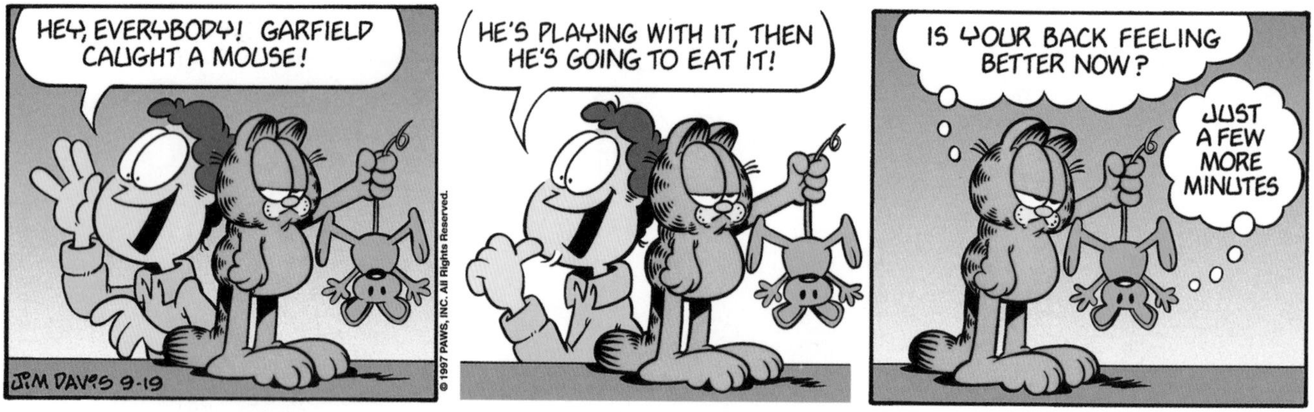
HEY, EVERYBODY! GARFIELD CAUGHT A MOUSE!
JIM DAVIS 9-19
HE'S PLAYING WITH IT, THEN HE'S GOING TO EAT IT!
IS YOUR BACK FEELING BETTER NOW?
JUST A FEW MORE MINUTES

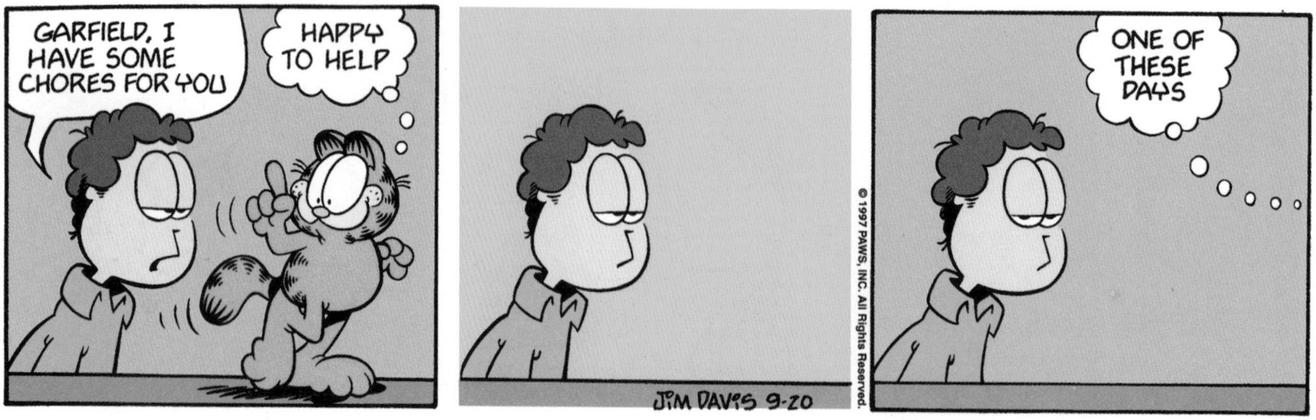
GARFIELD, I HAVE SOME CHORES FOR YOU
HAPPY TO HELP
JIM DAVIS 9-20
ONE OF THESE DAYS

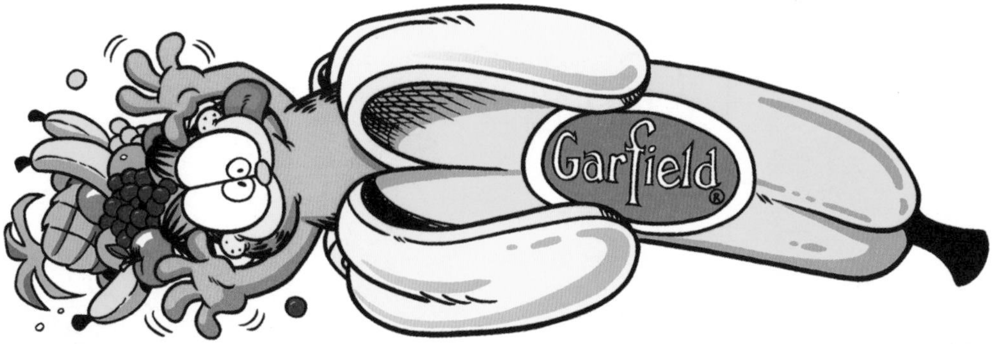

Garfield®

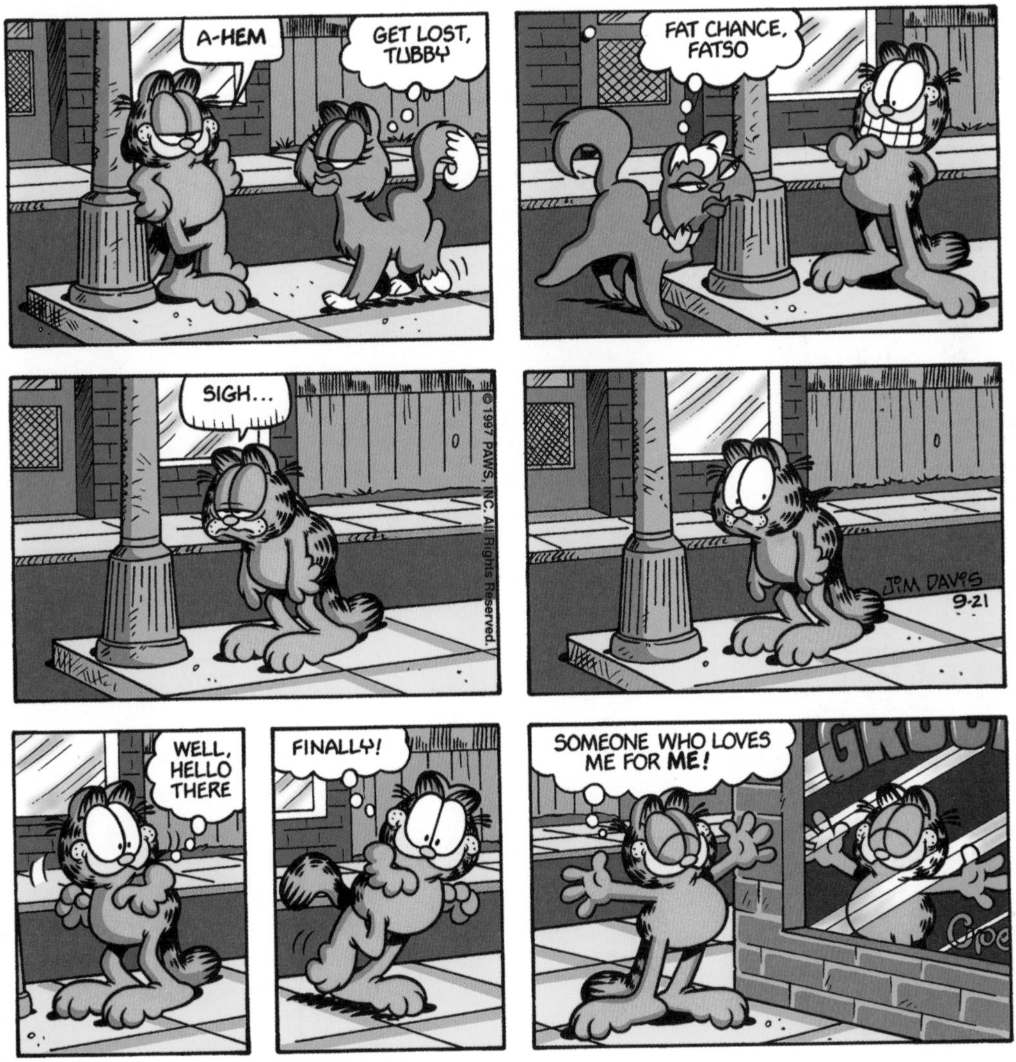

A-HEM
GET LOST, TUBBY
FAT CHANCE, FATSO
SIGH...
© 1997 PAWS, INC. All Rights Reserved.
JIM DAVIS 9-21
WELL, HELLO THERE
FINALLY!
SOMEONE WHO LOVES ME FOR **ME**!

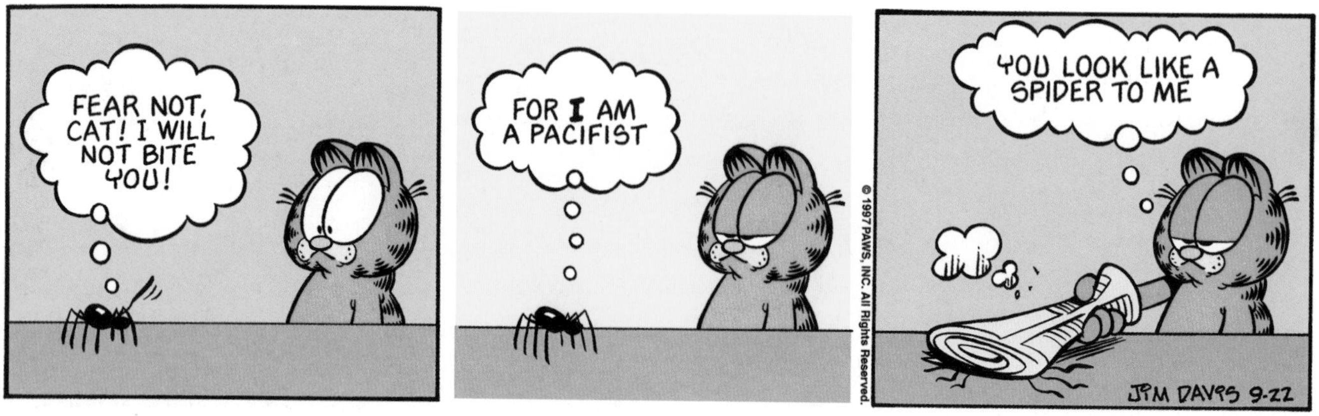
FEAR NOT, CAT! I WILL NOT BITE YOU!
FOR I AM A PACIFIST
YOU LOOK LIKE A SPIDER TO ME
© 1997 PAWS, INC. All Rights Reserved.
JIM DAVIS 9-22

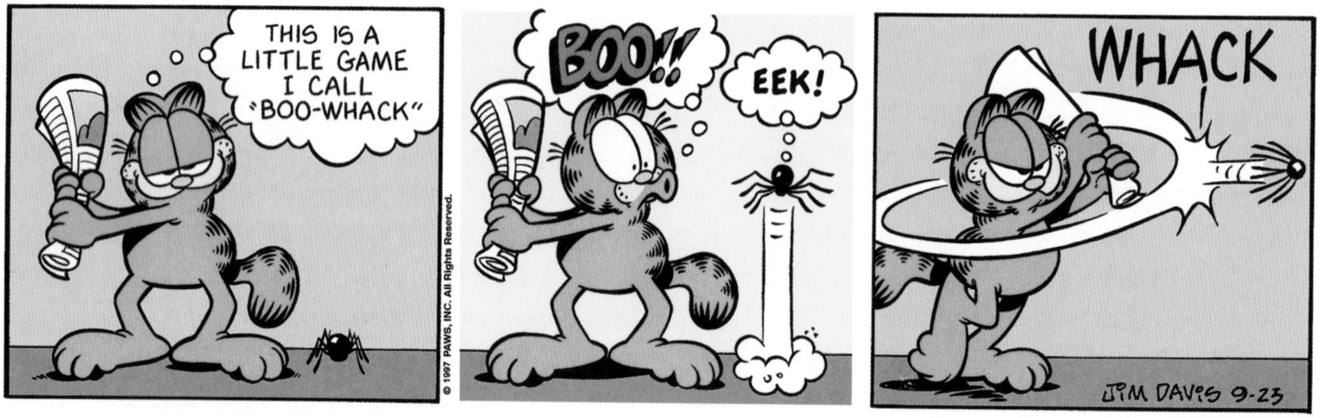
THIS IS A LITTLE GAME I CALL "BOO-WHACK"
© 1997 PAWS, INC. All Rights Reserved.
BOO!!
EEK!
WHACK
JIM DAVIS 9-23

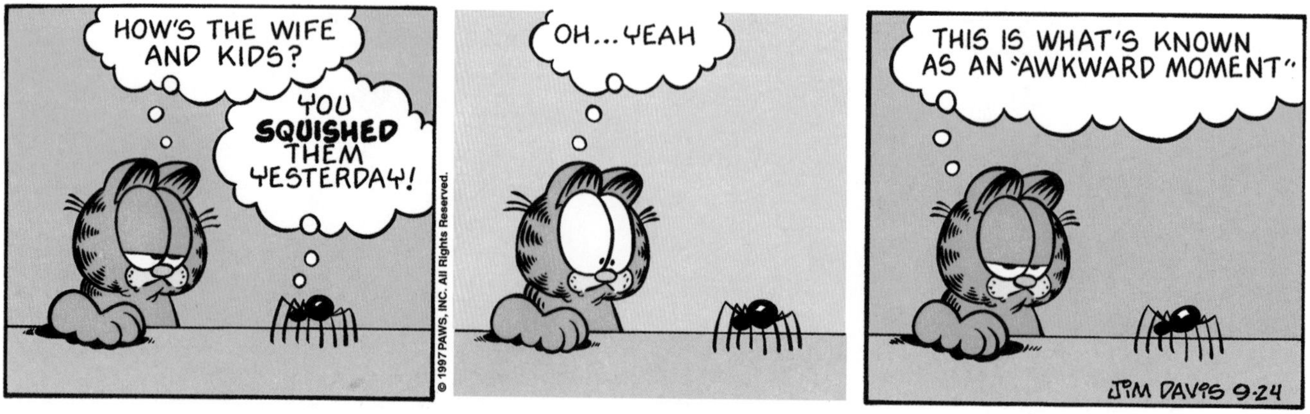
HOW'S THE WIFE AND KIDS?
YOU SQUISHED THEM YESTERDAY!
© 1997 PAWS, INC. All Rights Reserved.
OH...YEAH
THIS IS WHAT'S KNOWN AS AN "AWKWARD MOMENT"
JIM DAVIS 9-24

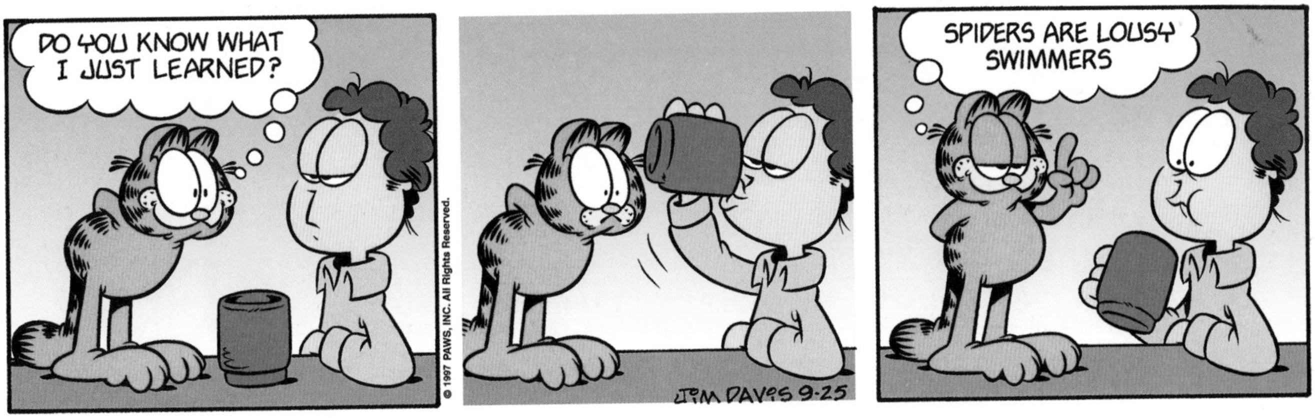
DO YOU KNOW WHAT I JUST LEARNED?
© 1997 PAWS, INC. All Rights Reserved.
JIM DAVIS 9-25
SPIDERS ARE LOUSY SWIMMERS

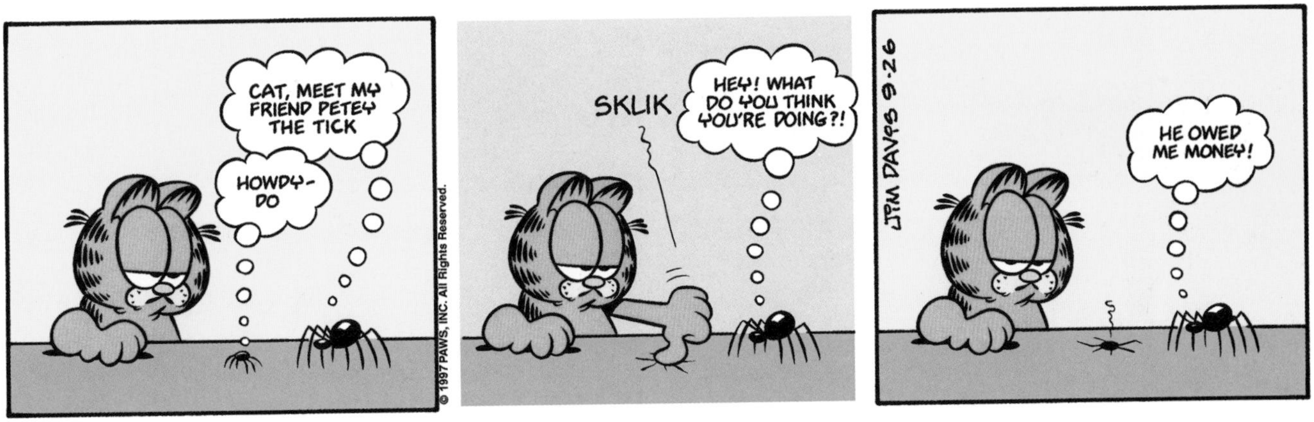
CAT, MEET MY FRIEND PETEY THE TICK
HOWDY-DO
© 1997 PAWS, INC. All Rights Reserved.
SKLIK
HEY! WHAT DO YOU THINK YOU'RE DOING?!
JIM DAVIS 9-26
HE OWED ME MONEY!

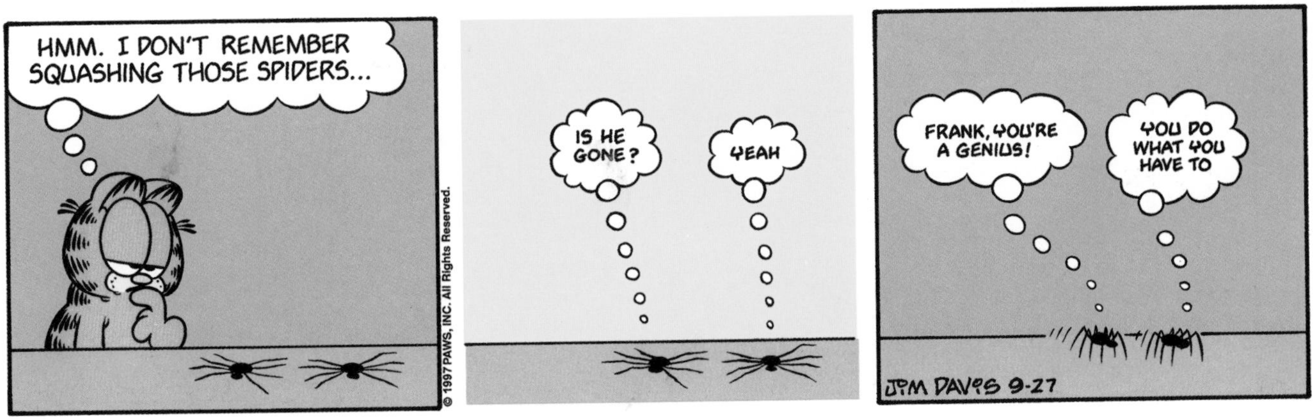
HMM. I DON'T REMEMBER SQUASHING THOSE SPIDERS...
© 1997 PAWS, INC. All Rights Reserved.
IS HE GONE?
YEAH
FRANK, YOU'RE A GENIUS!
YOU DO WHAT YOU HAVE TO
JIM DAVIS 9-27

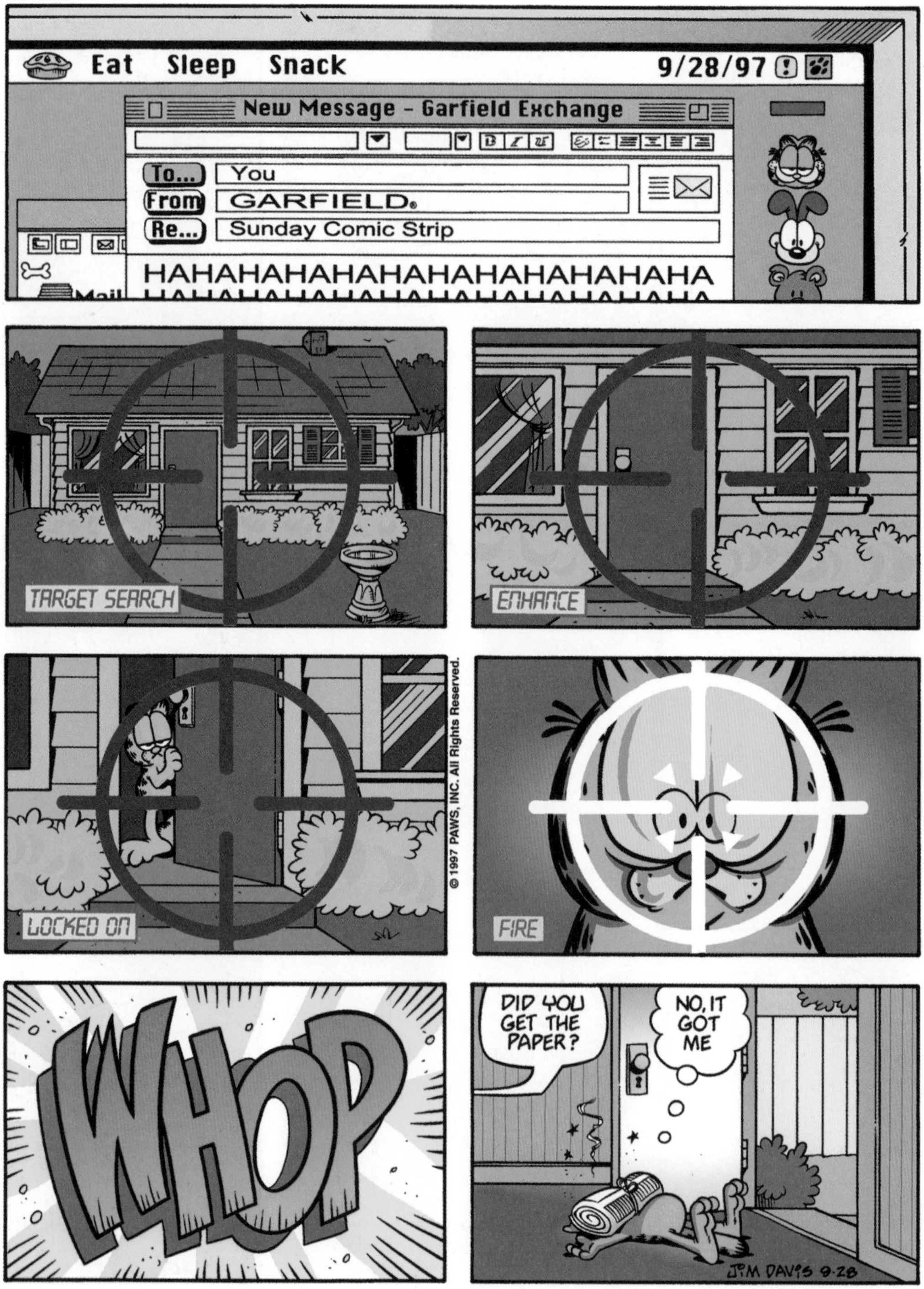
Eat
Sleep
Snack
9/28/97
New Message - Garfield Exchange
To...
You
From
GARFIELD®
Re...
Sunday Comic Strip
HAHAHAHAHAHAHAHAHAHAHAHAHA
TARGET SEARCH
ENHANCE
LOCKED ON
FIRE
WHOP
DID YOU GET THE PAPER?
NO, IT GOT ME
JIM DAVIS 9-28

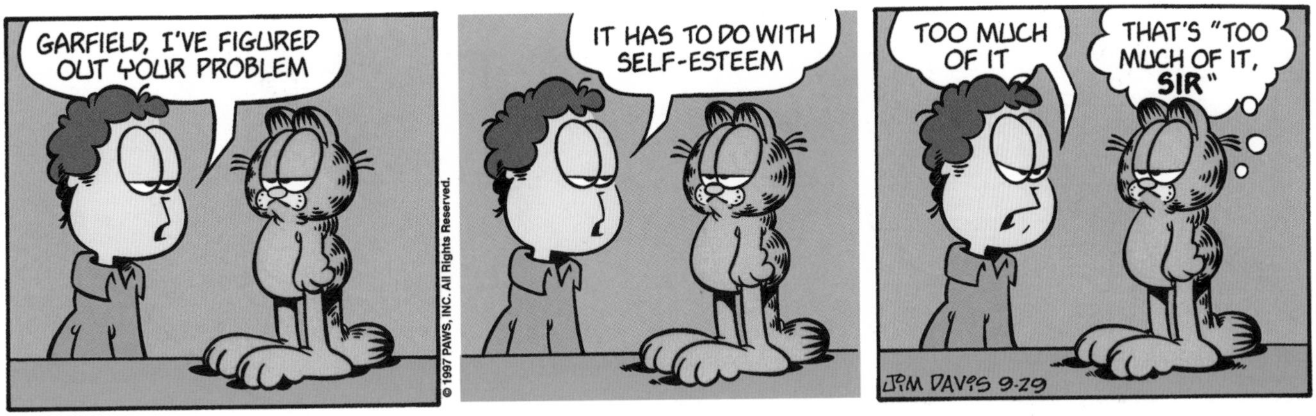
GARFIELD, I'VE FIGURED OUT YOUR PROBLEM
© 1997 PAWS, INC. All Rights Reserved.
IT HAS TO DO WITH SELF-ESTEEM
TOO MUCH OF IT
THAT'S "TOO MUCH OF IT, SIR"
JIM DAVIS 9-29

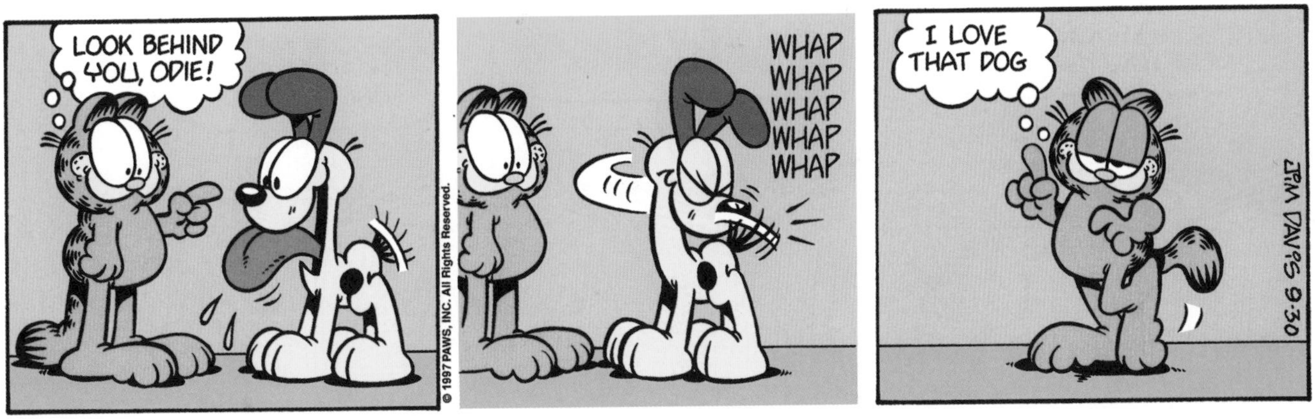
LOOK BEHIND YOU, ODIE!
© 1997 PAWS, INC. All Rights Reserved.
WHAP WHAP WHAP WHAP WHAP
I LOVE THAT DOG
JIM DAVIS 9-30

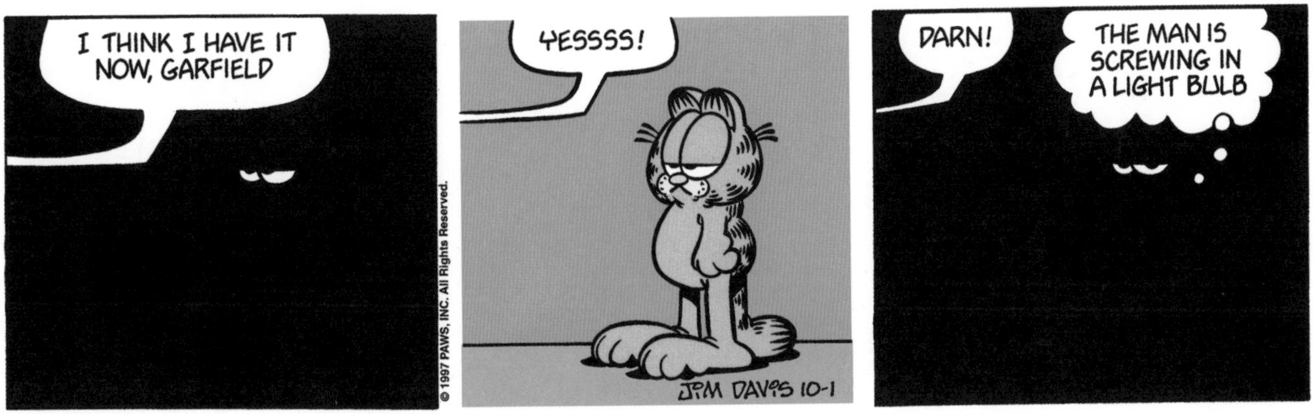
I THINK I HAVE IT NOW, GARFIELD
© 1997 PAWS, INC. All Rights Reserved.
YESSSS!
JIM DAVIS 10-1
DARN!
THE MAN IS SCREWING IN A LIGHT BULB

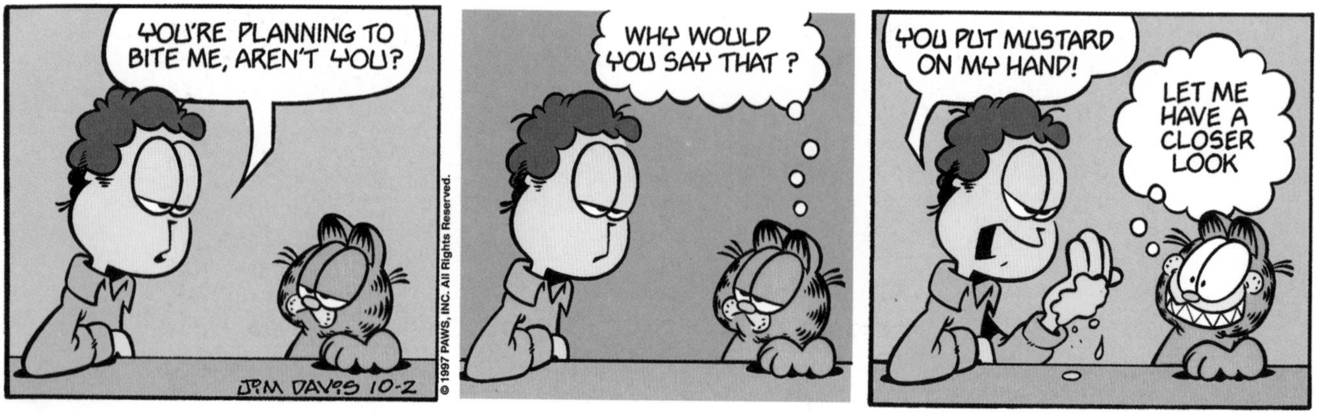
YOU'RE PLANNING TO BITE ME, AREN'T YOU?
WHY WOULD YOU SAY THAT ?
YOU PUT MUSTARD ON MY HAND!
LET ME HAVE A CLOSER LOOK
JIM DAVIS 10-2

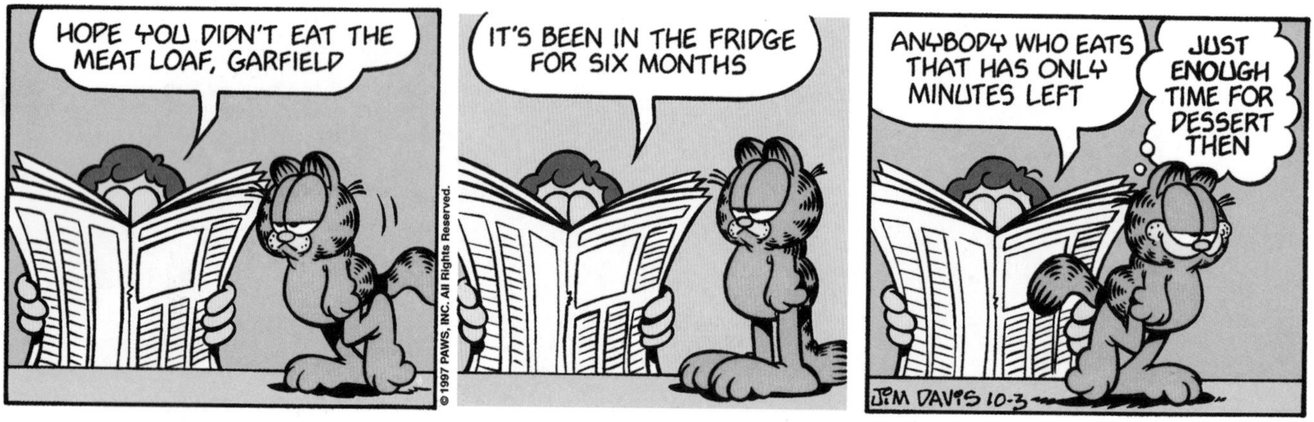
HOPE YOU DIDN'T EAT THE MEAT LOAF, GARFIELD
IT'S BEEN IN THE FRIDGE FOR SIX MONTHS
ANYBODY WHO EATS THAT HAS ONLY MINUTES LEFT
JUST ENOUGH TIME FOR DESSERT THEN
JIM DAVIS 10-3

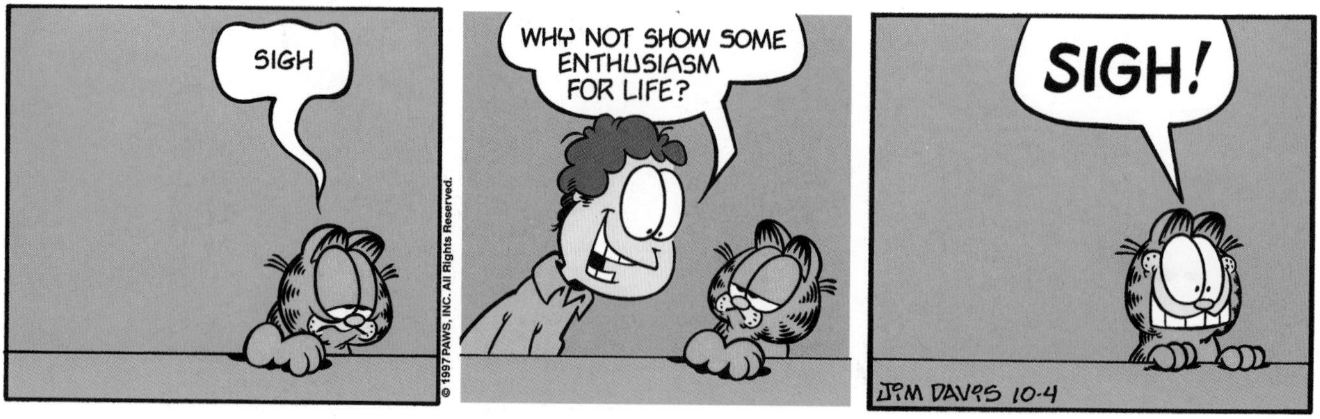
SIGH
WHY NOT SHOW SOME ENTHUSIASM FOR LIFE?
SIGH!
JIM DAVIS 10-4

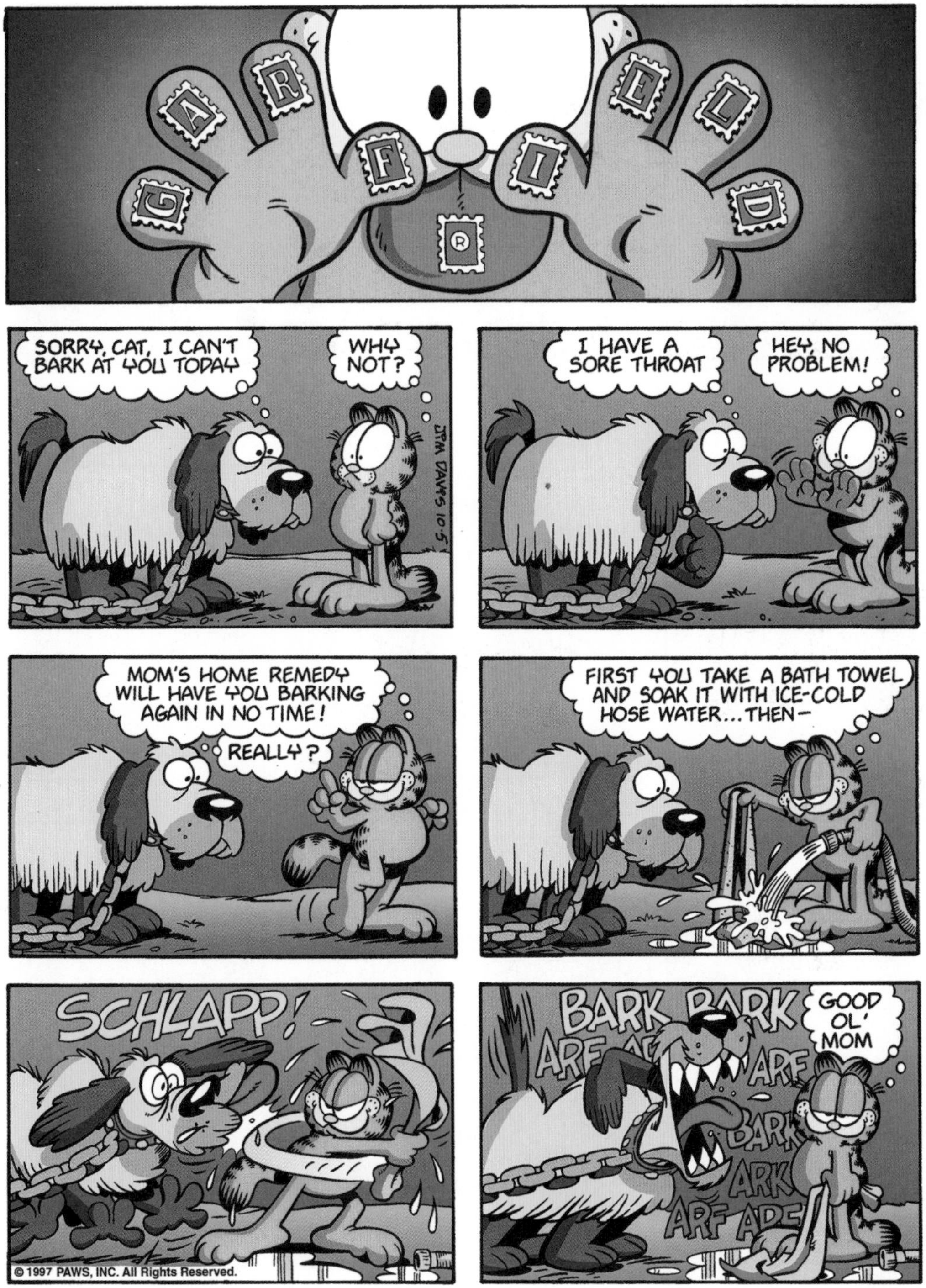
GARFIELD
SORRY, CAT, I CAN'T BARK AT YOU TODAY
WHY NOT?
JIM DAVIS 10-5
I HAVE A SORE THROAT
HEY, NO PROBLEM!
MOM'S HOME REMEDY WILL HAVE YOU BARKING AGAIN IN NO TIME!
REALLY?
FIRST YOU TAKE A BATH TOWEL AND SOAK IT WITH ICE-COLD HOSE WATER... THEN—
SCHLAPP!
BARK
ARF
ARF
BARK
ARK
ARF
GOOD OL' MOM

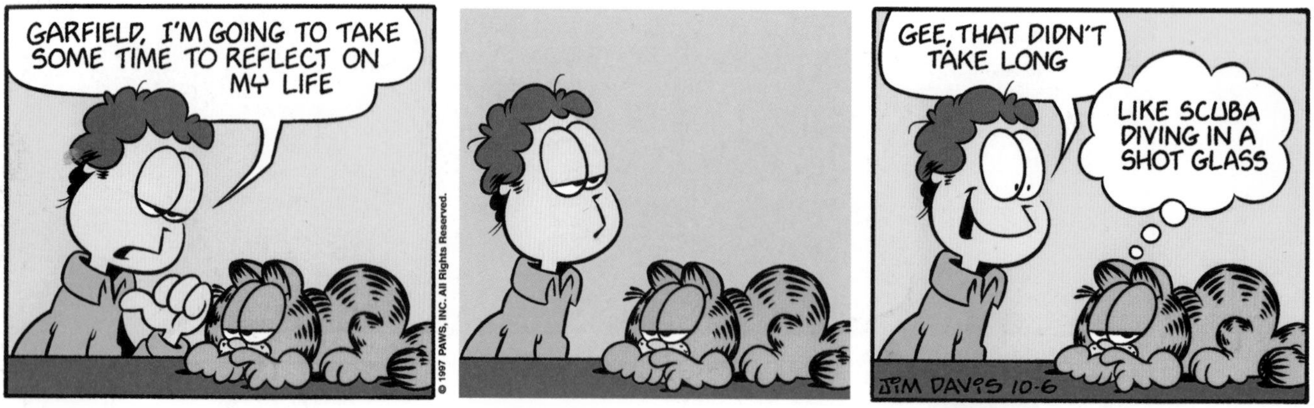
GARFIELD, I'M GOING TO TAKE SOME TIME TO REFLECT ON MY LIFE
© 1997 PAWS, INC. All Rights Reserved.
GEE, THAT DIDN'T TAKE LONG
LIKE SCUBA DIVING IN A SHOT GLASS
JIM DAVIS 10-6

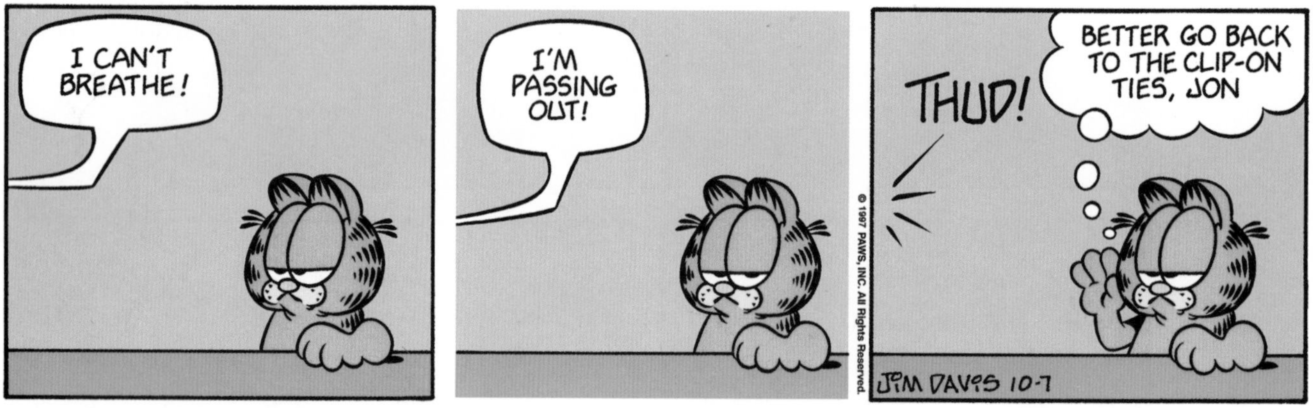
I CAN'T BREATHE!
I'M PASSING OUT!
THUD!
BETTER GO BACK TO THE CLIP-ON TIES, JON
© 1997 PAWS, INC. All Rights Reserved.
JIM DAVIS 10-7

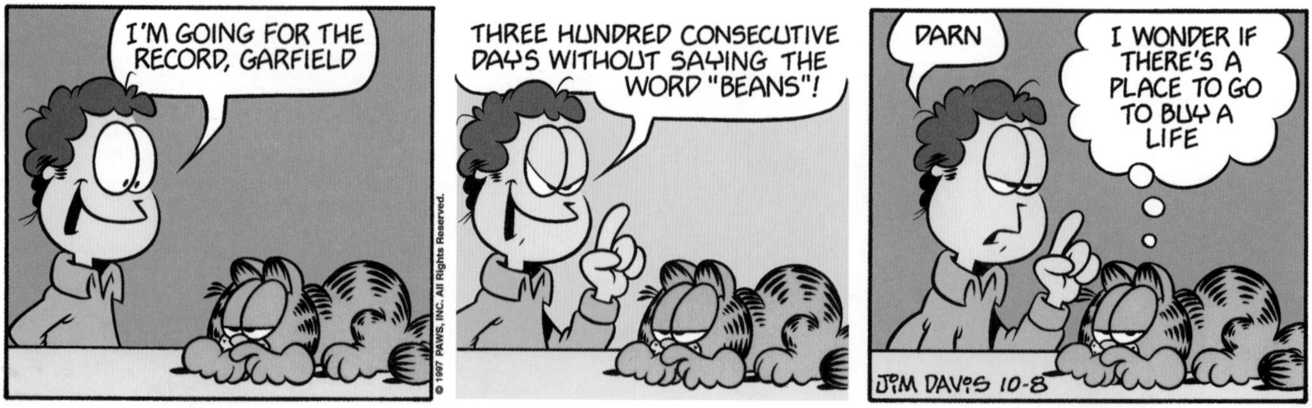
I'M GOING FOR THE RECORD, GARFIELD
© 1997 PAWS, INC. All Rights Reserved.
THREE HUNDRED CONSECUTIVE DAYS WITHOUT SAYING THE WORD "BEANS"!
DARN
I WONDER IF THERE'S A PLACE TO GO TO BUY A LIFE
JIM DAVIS 10-8

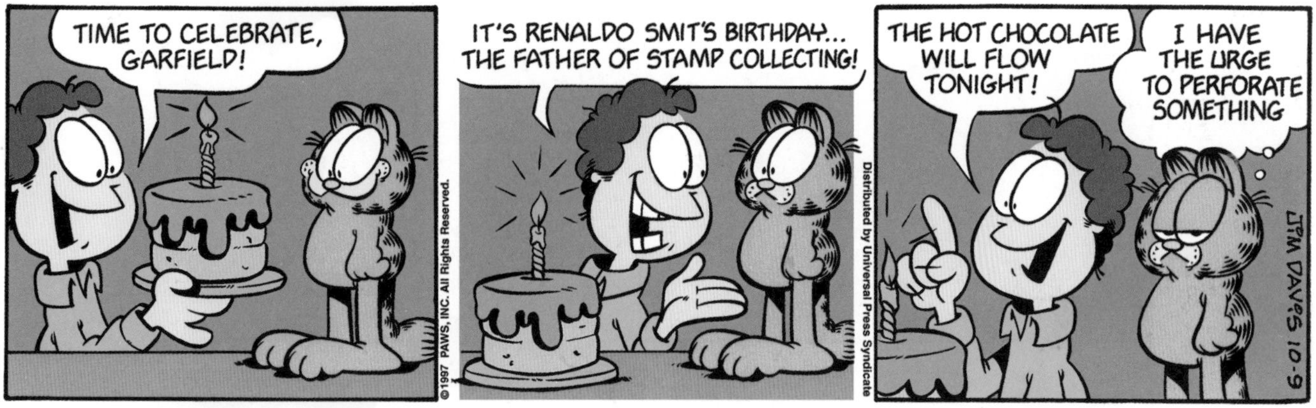
TIME TO CELEBRATE, GARFIELD!
© 1997 PAWS, INC. All Rights Reserved.
IT'S RENALDO SMIT'S BIRTHDAY... THE FATHER OF STAMP COLLECTING!
Distributed by Universal Press Syndicate
THE HOT CHOCOLATE WILL FLOW TONIGHT!
I HAVE THE URGE TO PERFORATE SOMETHING
JIM DAVIS 10-9

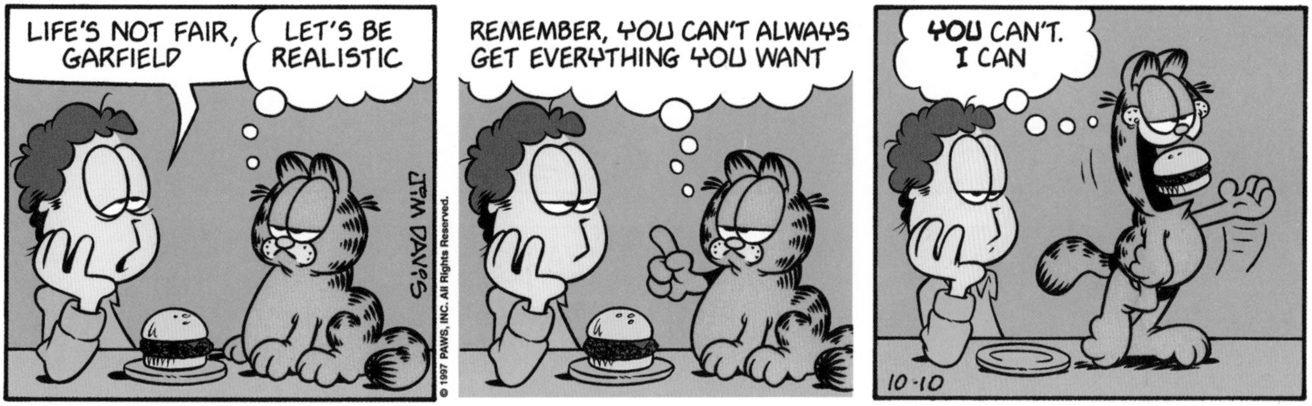
LIFE'S NOT FAIR, GARFIELD
LET'S BE REALISTIC
JIM DAVIS
© 1997 PAWS, INC. All Rights Reserved.
REMEMBER, YOU CAN'T ALWAYS GET EVERYTHING YOU WANT
YOU CAN'T. I CAN
10-10

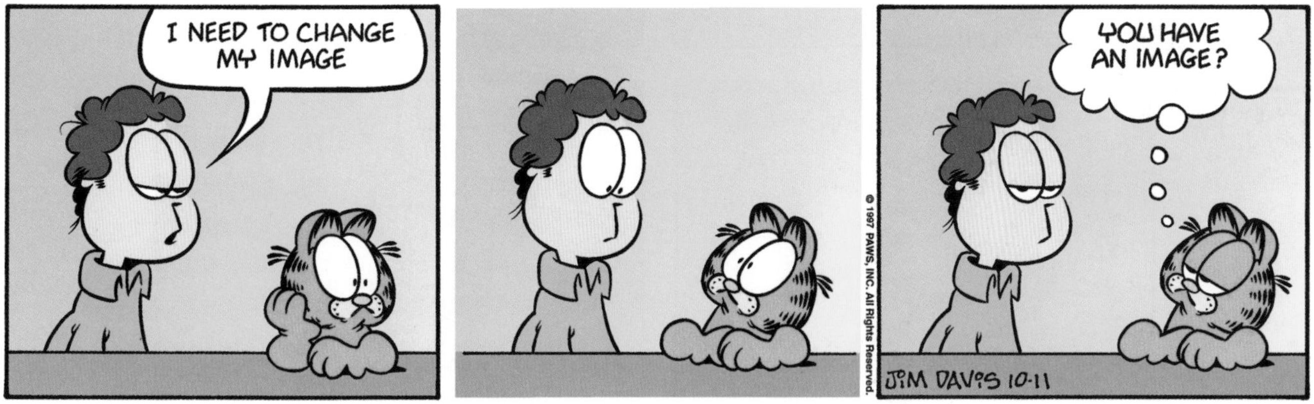
I NEED TO CHANGE MY IMAGE
© 1997 PAWS, INC. All Rights Reserved.
YOU HAVE AN IMAGE?
JIM DAVIS 10-11

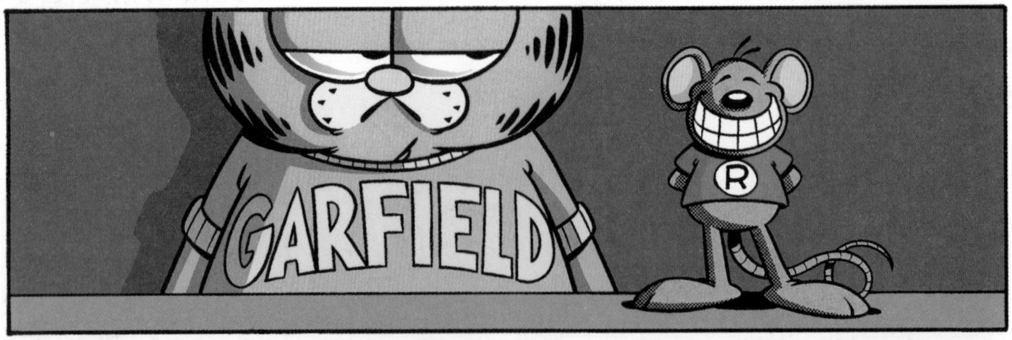
GARFIELD
R

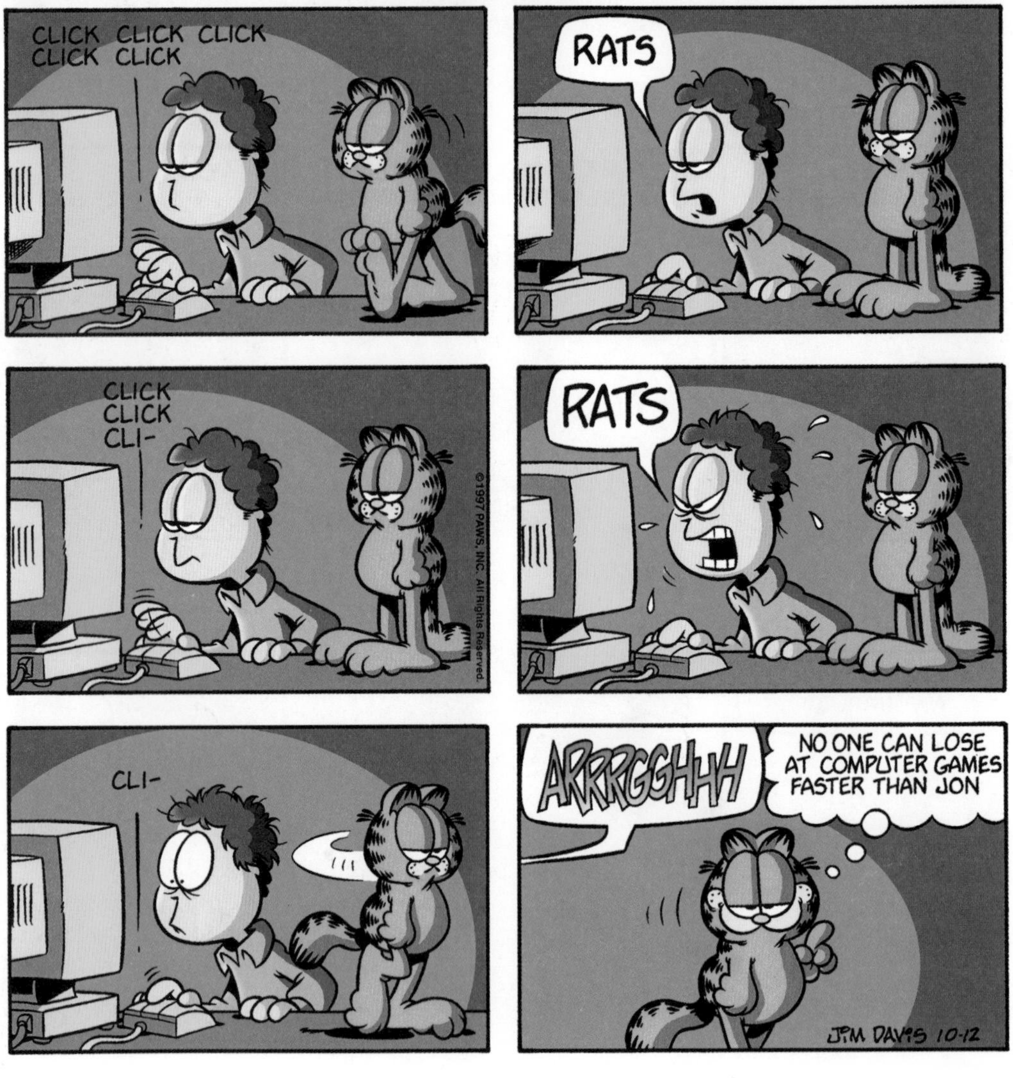
CLICK CLICK CLICK
CLICK CLICK
RATS
CLICK
CLICK
CLI-
©1997 PAWS, INC. All Rights Reserved.
RATS
CLI-
ARRRGGHHH
NO ONE CAN LOSE
AT COMPUTER GAMES
FASTER THAN JON
JIM DAVIS 10-12

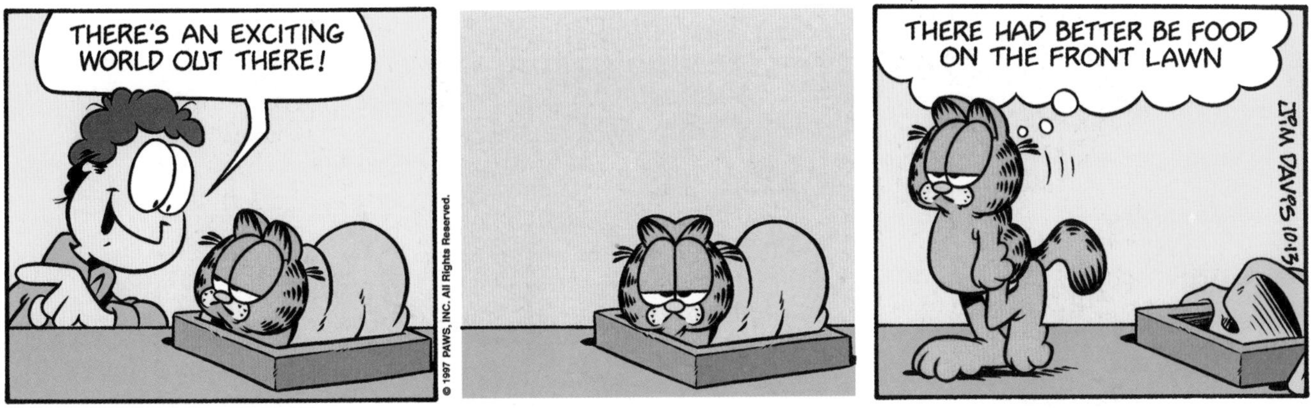
THERE'S AN EXCITING WORLD OUT THERE!
© 1997 PAWS, INC. All Rights Reserved.
THERE HAD BETTER BE FOOD ON THE FRONT LAWN
JIM DAVIS 10-13

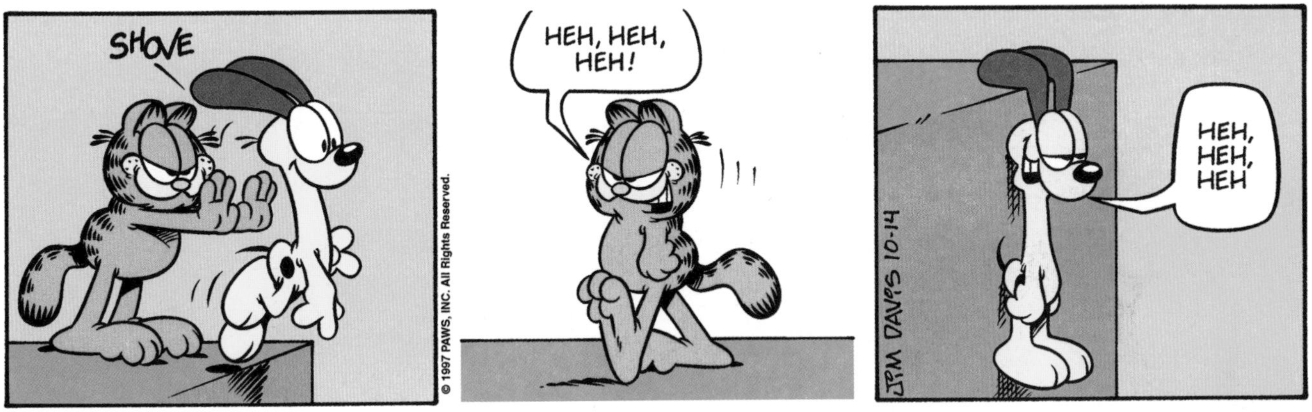
SHOVE
© 1997 PAWS, INC. All Rights Reserved.
HEH, HEH, HEH!
HEH, HEH, HEH
JIM DAVIS 10-14

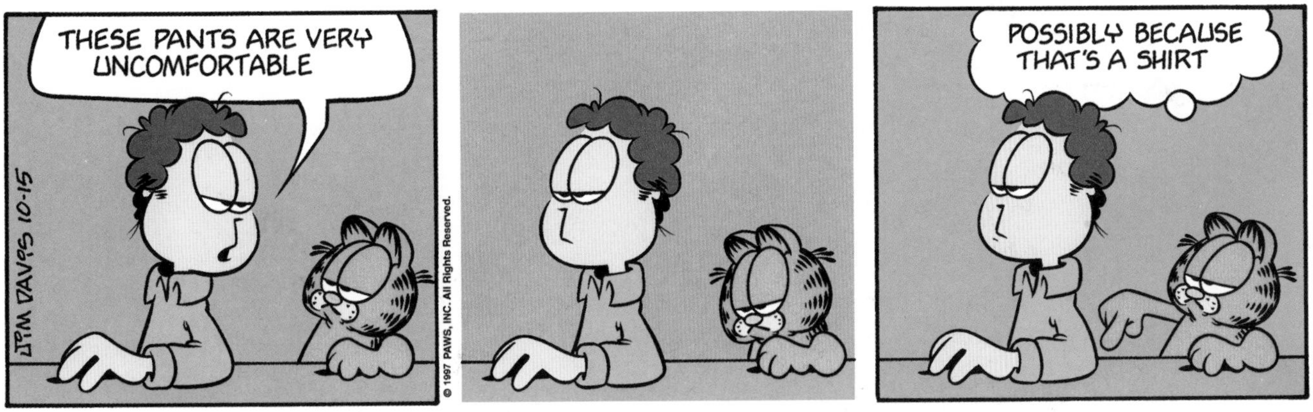
THESE PANTS ARE VERY UNCOMFORTABLE
JIM DAVIS 10-15
© 1997 PAWS, INC. All Rights Reserved.
POSSIBLY BECAUSE THAT'S A SHIRT

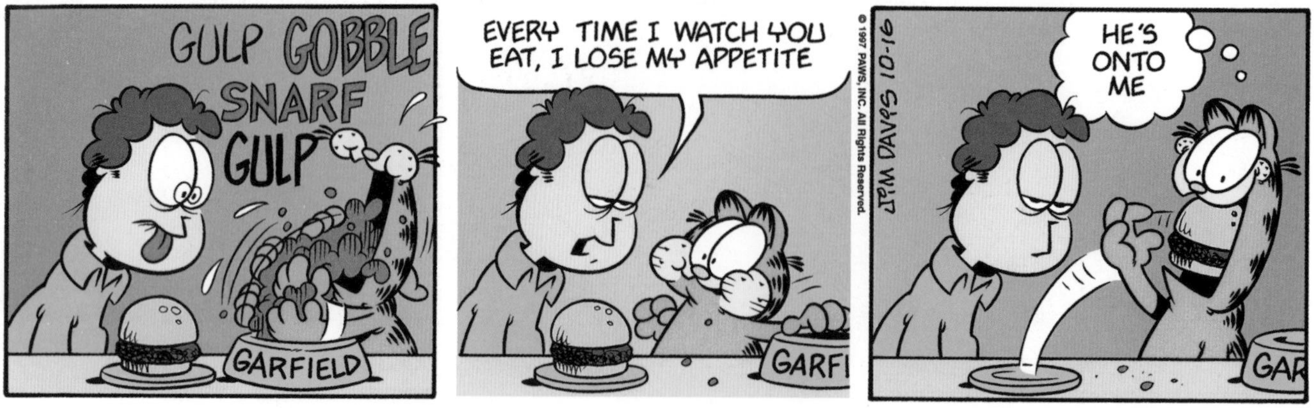
GULP GOBBLE SNARF GULP
GARFIELD
EVERY TIME I WATCH YOU EAT, I LOSE MY APPETITE
GARFI
© 1997 PAWS, INC. All Rights Reserved.
JIM DAVIS 10-16
HE'S ONTO ME
GAR

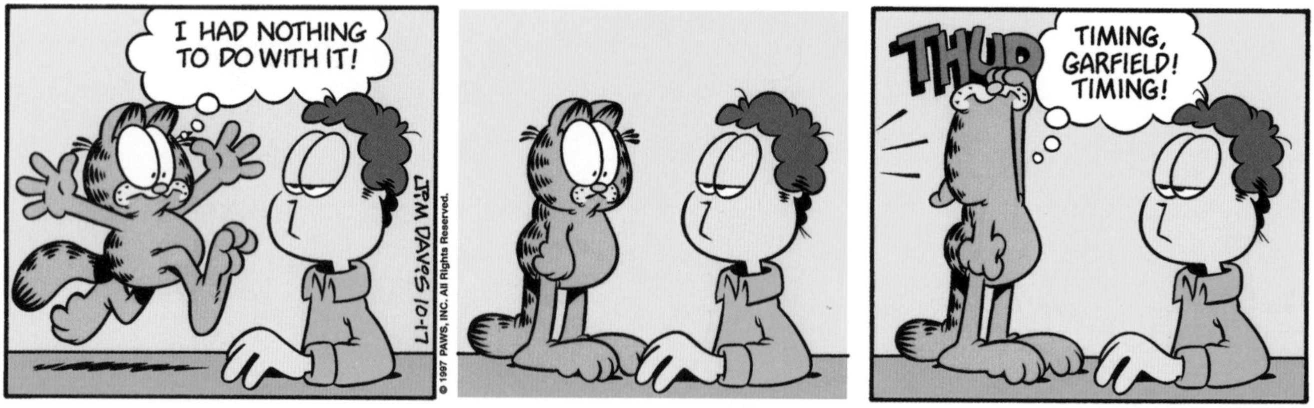
I HAD NOTHING TO DO WITH IT!
JIM DAVIS 10-17
© 1997 PAWS, INC. All Rights Reserved.
THUD
TIMING, GARFIELD! TIMING!

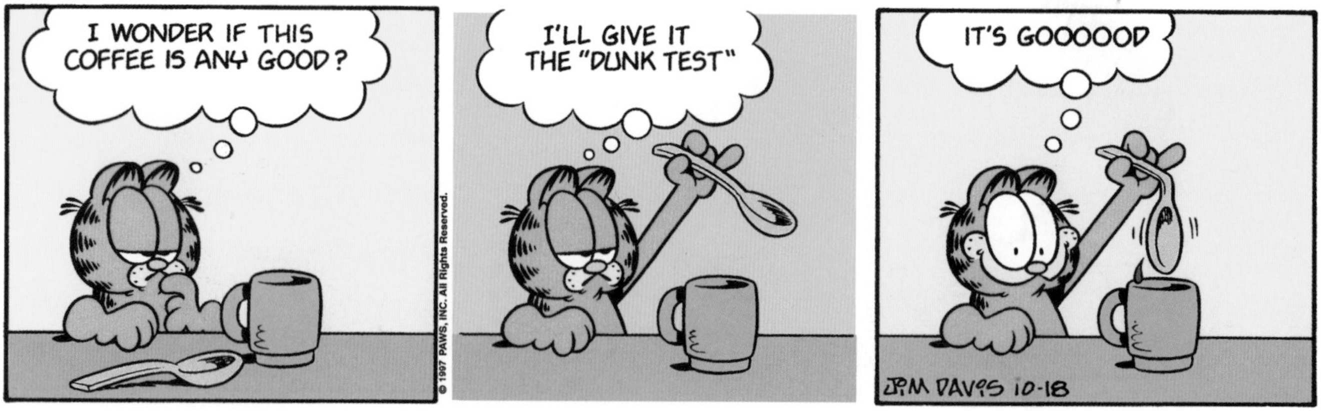
I WONDER IF THIS COFFEE IS ANY GOOD?
© 1997 PAWS, INC. All Rights Reserved.
I'LL GIVE IT THE "DUNK TEST"
IT'S GOOOOOD
JIM DAVIS 10-18

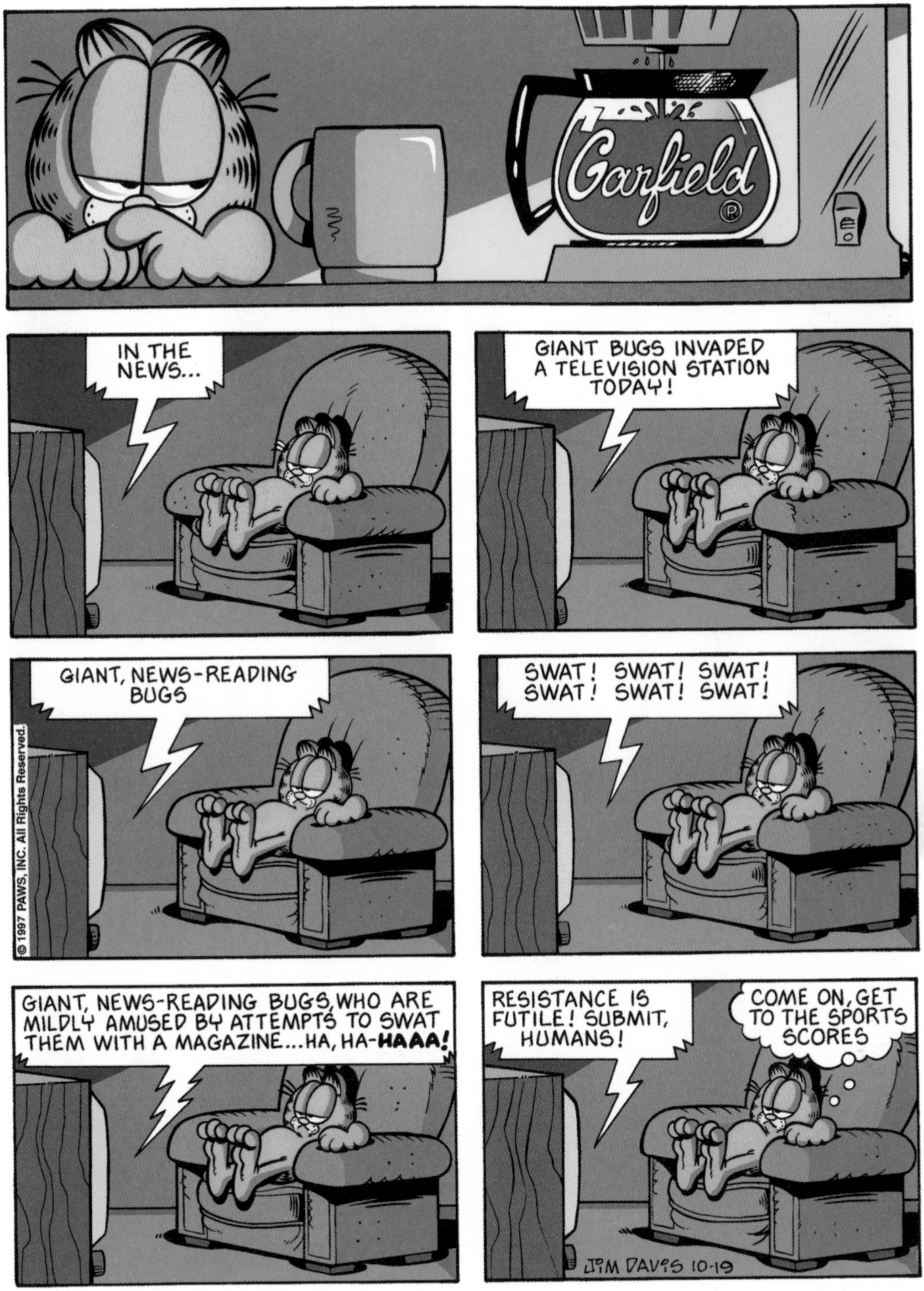
Garfield
IN THE NEWS...
GIANT BUGS INVADED A TELEVISION STATION TODAY!
GIANT, NEWS-READING BUGS
SWAT! SWAT! SWAT! SWAT! SWAT! SWAT!
GIANT, NEWS-READING BUGS, WHO ARE MILDLY AMUSED BY ATTEMPTS TO SWAT THEM WITH A MAGAZINE...HA, HA-HAAA!
RESISTANCE IS FUTILE! SUBMIT, HUMANS!
COME ON, GET TO THE SPORTS SCORES
JIM DAVIS 10-19

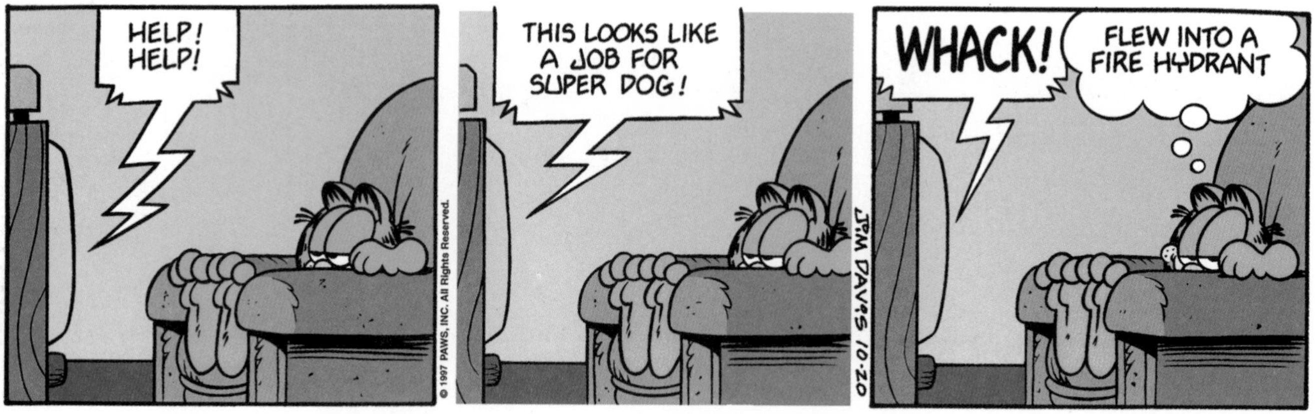
HELP! HELP!
THIS LOOKS LIKE A JOB FOR SUPER DOG!
JIM DAVIS 10-20
WHACK!
FLEW INTO A FIRE HYDRANT

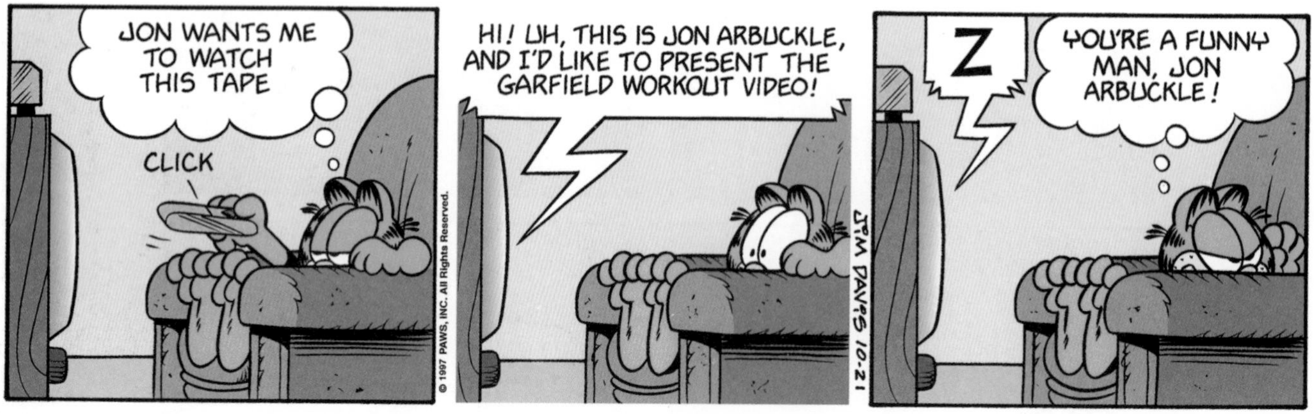
JON WANTS ME TO WATCH THIS TAPE
CLICK
HI! UH, THIS IS JON ARBUCKLE, AND I'D LIKE TO PRESENT THE GARFIELD WORKOUT VIDEO!
JIM DAVIS 10-21
Z
YOU'RE A FUNNY MAN, JON ARBUCKLE!

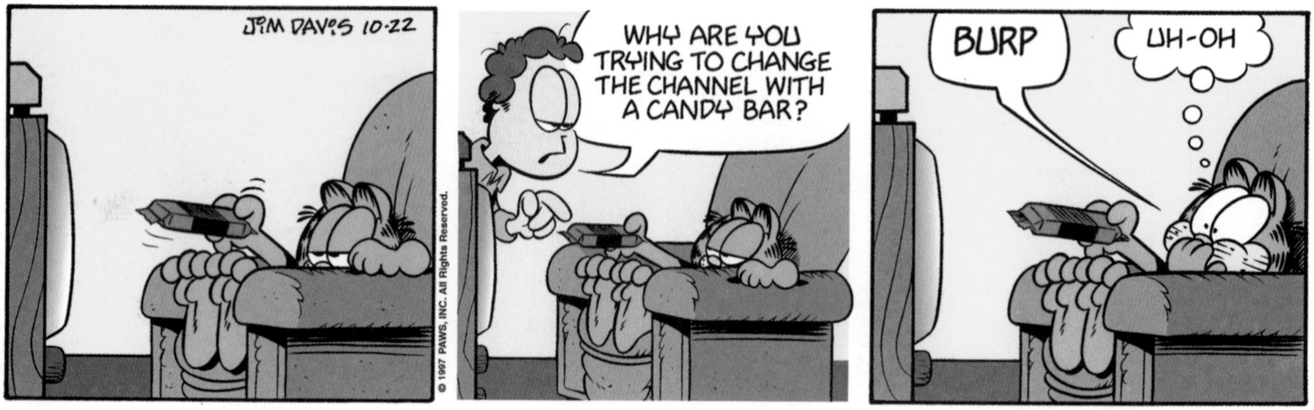
JIM DAVIS 10-22
WHY ARE YOU TRYING TO CHANGE THE CHANNEL WITH A CANDY BAR?
BURP
UH-OH

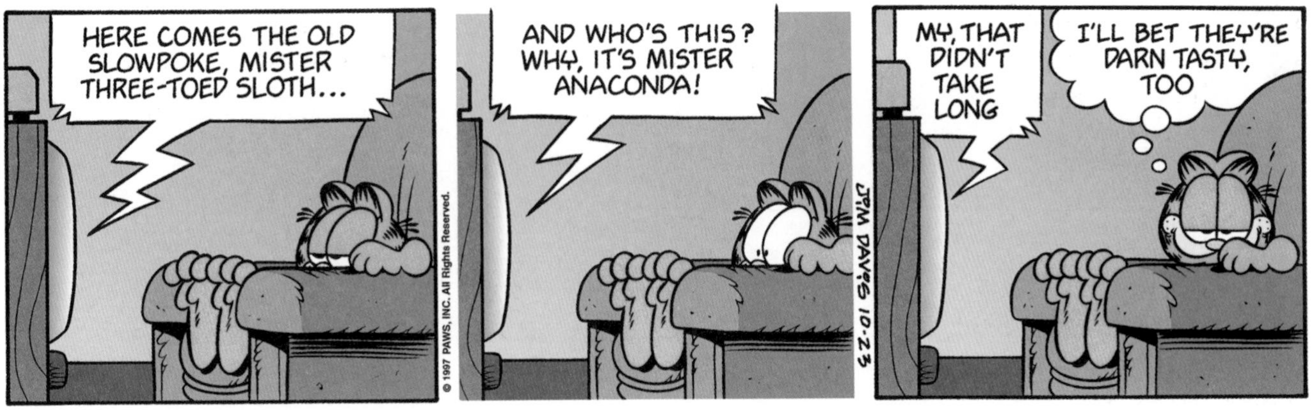
HERE COMES THE OLD SLOWPOKE, MISTER THREE-TOED SLOTH...
© 1997 PAWS, INC. All Rights Reserved.
AND WHO'S THIS? WHY, IT'S MISTER ANACONDA!
JIM DAVIS 10-23
MY, THAT DIDN'T TAKE LONG
I'LL BET THEY'RE DARN TASTY, TOO

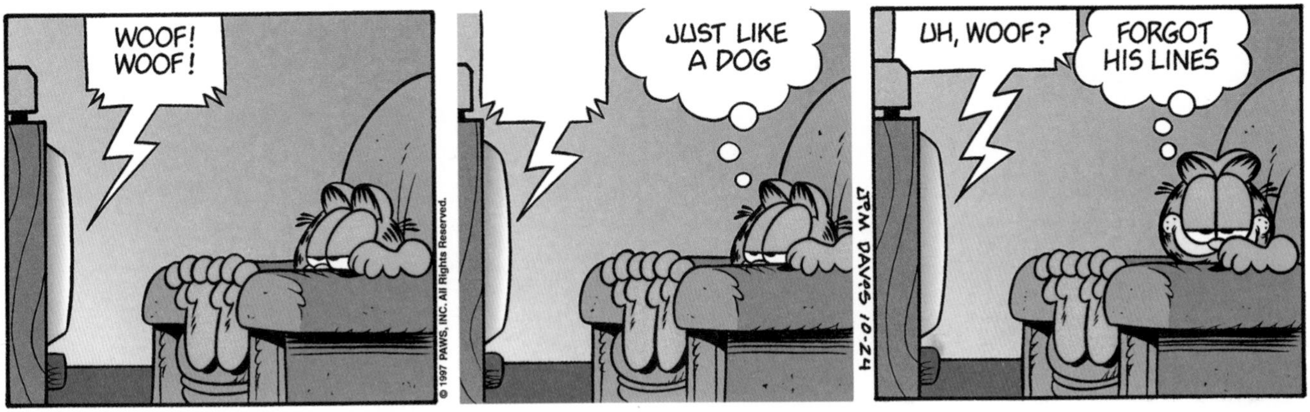
WOOF! WOOF!
© 1997 PAWS, INC. All Rights Reserved.
JUST LIKE A DOG
JIM DAVIS 10-24
UH, WOOF?
FORGOT HIS LINES

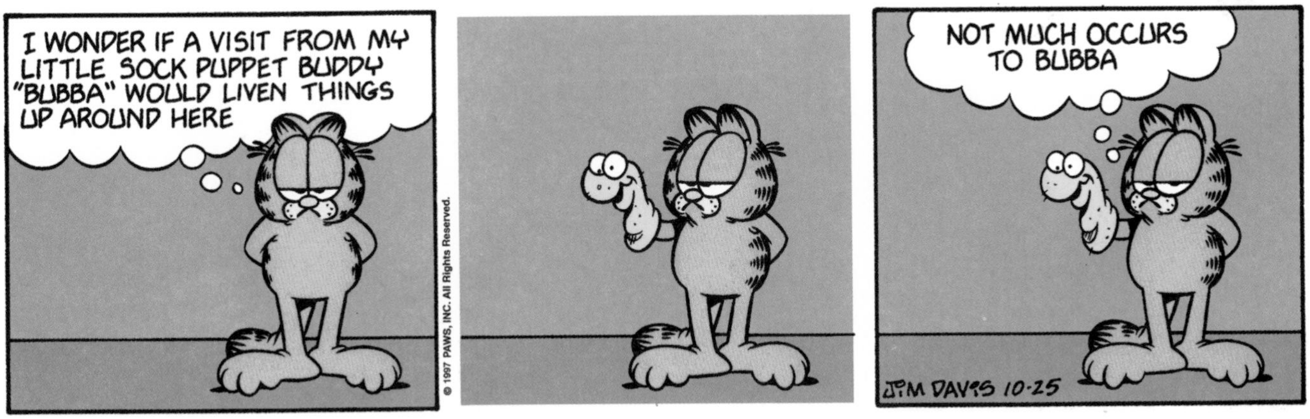
I WONDER IF A VISIT FROM MY LITTLE SOCK PUPPET BUDDY "BUBBA" WOULD LIVEN THINGS UP AROUND HERE
© 1997 PAWS, INC. All Rights Reserved.
NOT MUCH OCCURS TO BUBBA
JIM DAVIS 10-25

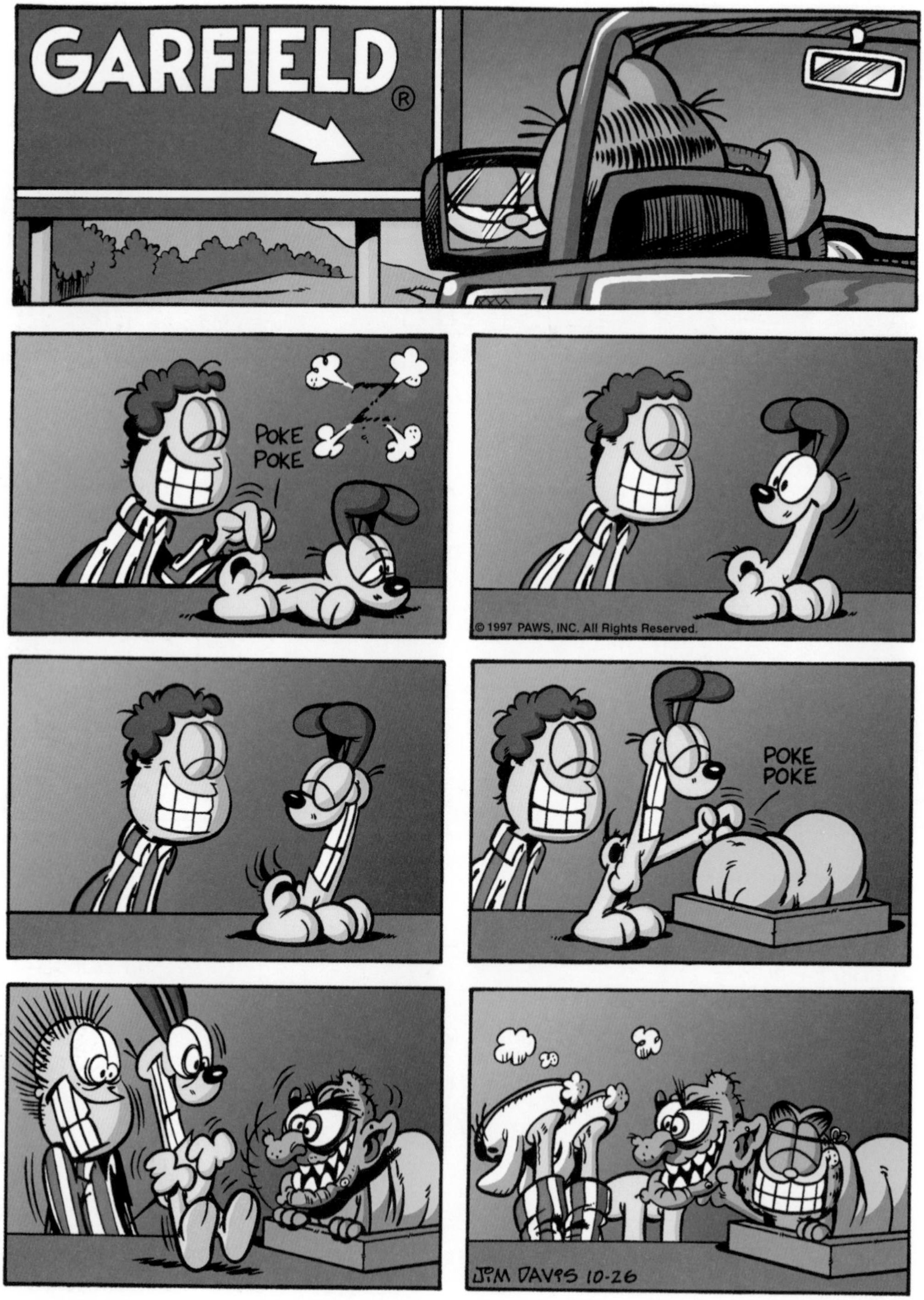
GARFIELD®
POKE POKE
© 1997 PAWS, INC. All Rights Reserved.
POKE POKE
JIM DAVIS 10-26

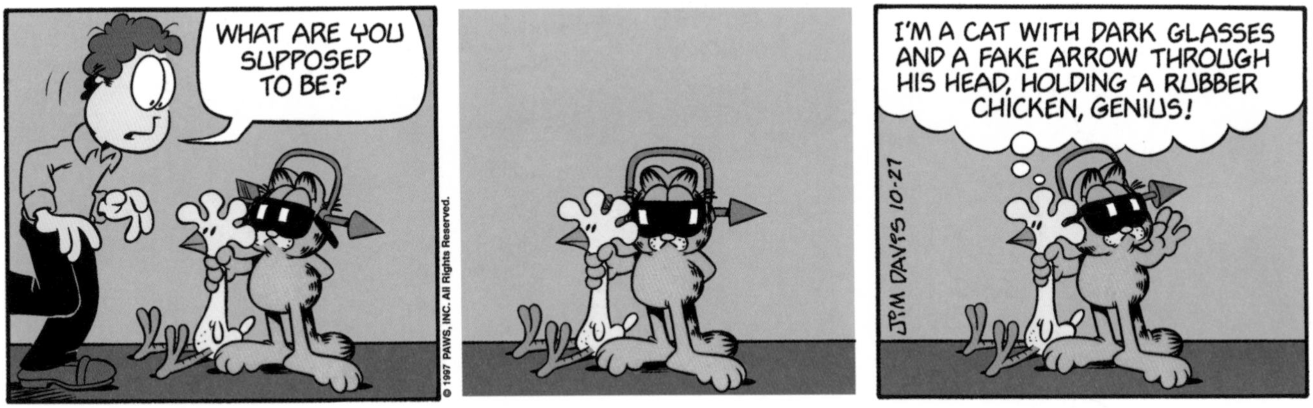
WHAT ARE YOU SUPPOSED TO BE?
I'M A CAT WITH DARK GLASSES AND A FAKE ARROW THROUGH HIS HEAD, HOLDING A RUBBER CHICKEN, GENIUS!
JIM DAVIS 10-27
© 1997 PAWS, INC. All Rights Reserved.

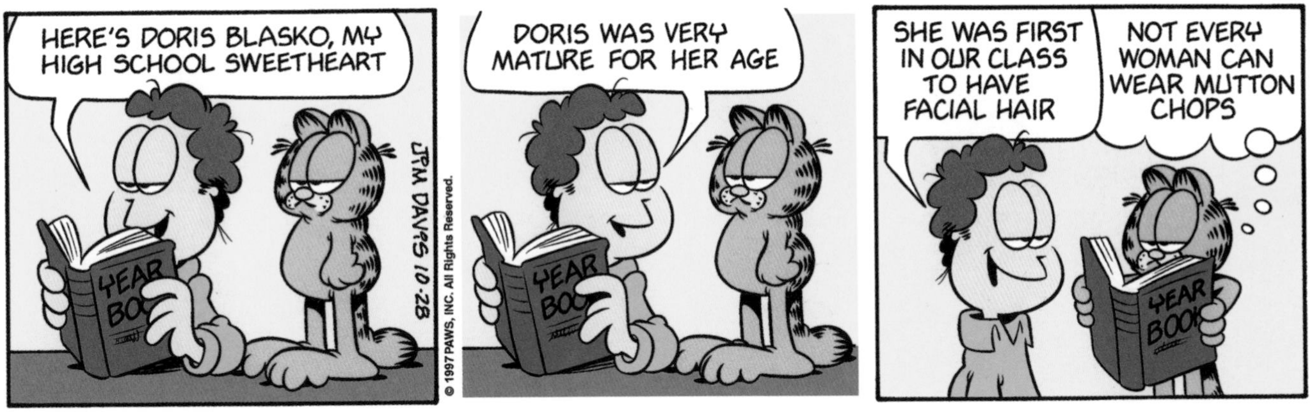
HERE'S DORIS BLASKO, MY HIGH SCHOOL SWEETHEART
YEAR BOOK
JIM DAVIS 10-28
© 1997 PAWS, INC. All Rights Reserved.
DORIS WAS VERY MATURE FOR HER AGE
SHE WAS FIRST IN OUR CLASS TO HAVE FACIAL HAIR
NOT EVERY WOMAN CAN WEAR MUTTON CHOPS

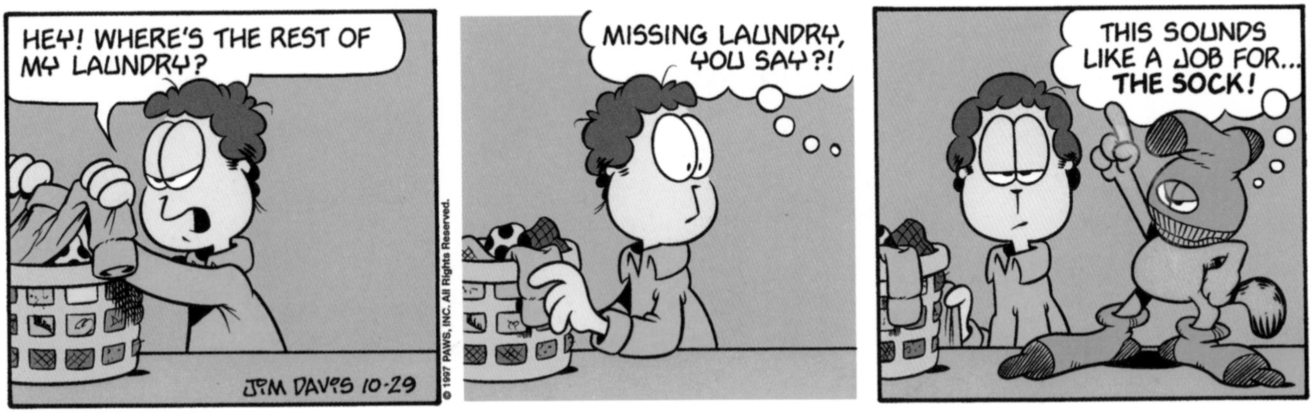
HEY! WHERE'S THE REST OF MY LAUNDRY?
JIM DAVIS 10-29
© 1997 PAWS, INC. All Rights Reserved.
MISSING LAUNDRY, YOU SAY?!
THIS SOUNDS LIKE A JOB FOR... THE SOCK!

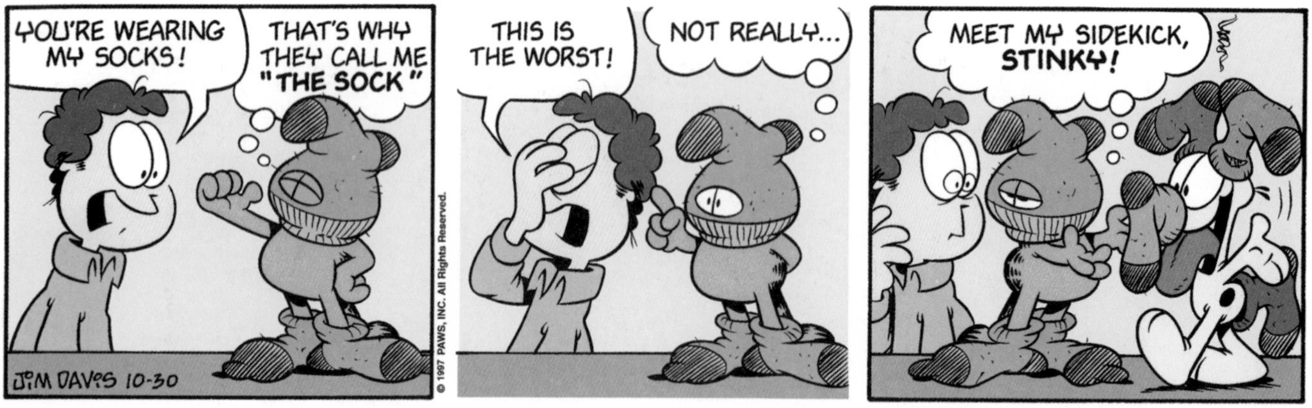
YOU'RE WEARING MY SOCKS!
THAT'S WHY THEY CALL ME "THE SOCK"
THIS IS THE WORST!
NOT REALLY...
MEET MY SIDEKICK, STINKY!
JIM DAVIS 10-30
© 1997 PAWS, INC. All Rights Reserved.

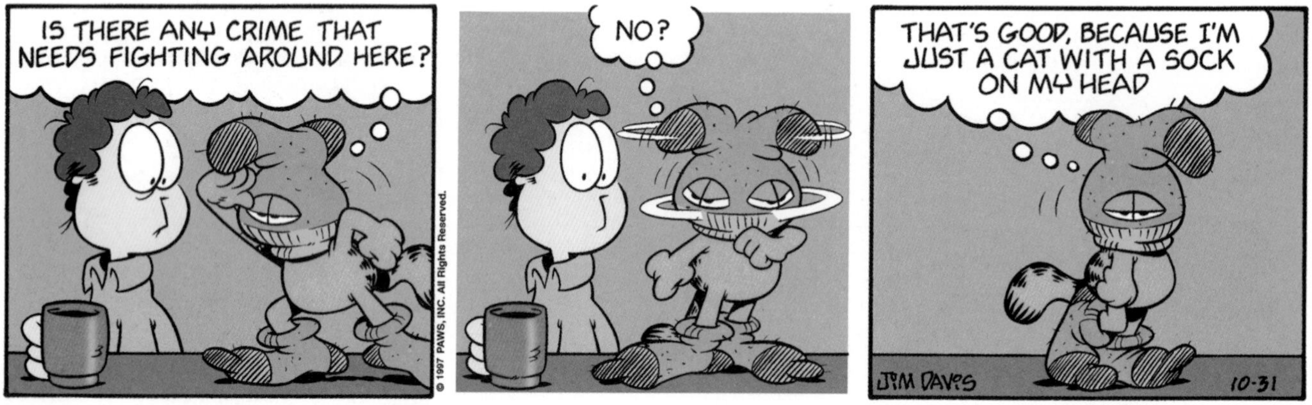
IS THERE ANY CRIME THAT NEEDS FIGHTING AROUND HERE?
NO?
THAT'S GOOD, BECAUSE I'M JUST A CAT WITH A SOCK ON MY HEAD
JIM DAVIS 10-31
© 1997 PAWS, INC. All Rights Reserved.

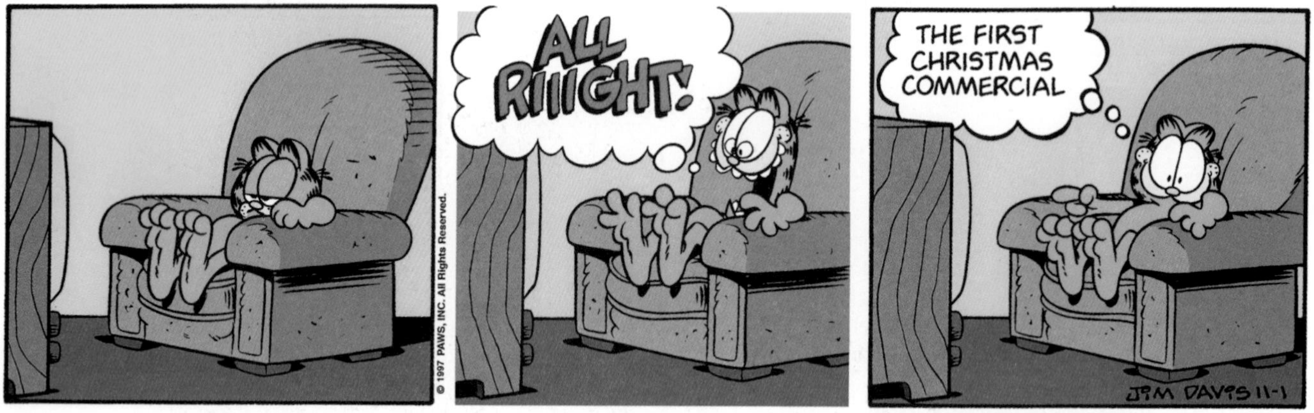
ALL RIIIGHT!
THE FIRST CHRISTMAS COMMERCIAL
JIM DAVIS 11-1
© 1997 PAWS, INC. All Rights Reserved.

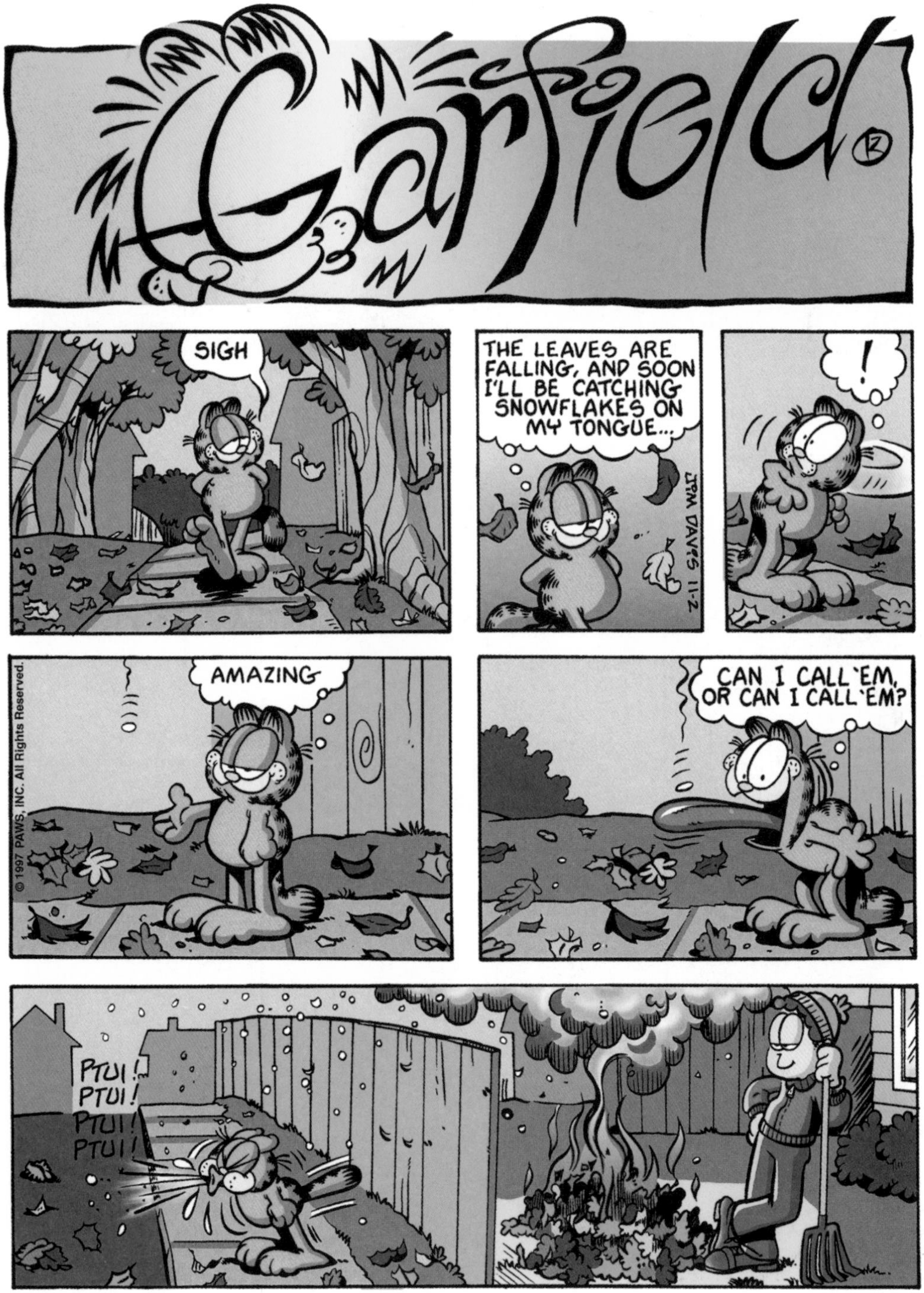
Garfield
SIGH
THE LEAVES ARE FALLING, AND SOON I'LL BE CATCHING SNOWFLAKES ON MY TONGUE...
JIM DAVIS 11-2
!
© 1997 PAWS, INC. All Rights Reserved.
AMAZING
CAN I CALL 'EM, OR CAN I CALL 'EM?
PTUI! PTUI! PTUI! PTUI!

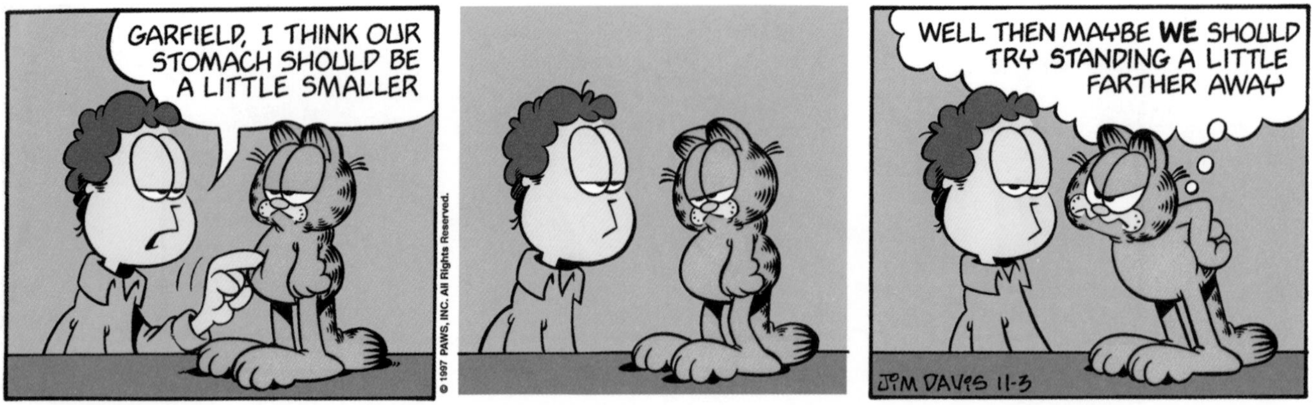
GARFIELD, I THINK OUR STOMACH SHOULD BE A LITTLE SMALLER
© 1997 PAWS, INC. All Rights Reserved.
WELL THEN MAYBE **WE** SHOULD TRY STANDING A LITTLE FARTHER AWAY
JIM DAVIS 11-3

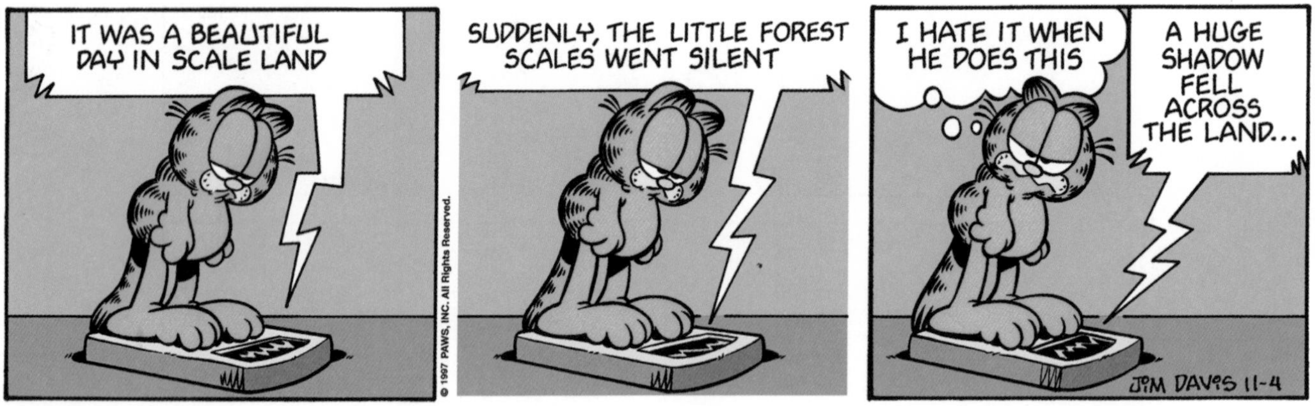
IT WAS A BEAUTIFUL DAY IN SCALE LAND
© 1997 PAWS, INC. All Rights Reserved.
SUDDENLY, THE LITTLE FOREST SCALES WENT SILENT
I HATE IT WHEN HE DOES THIS
A HUGE SHADOW FELL ACROSS THE LAND...
JIM DAVIS 11-4

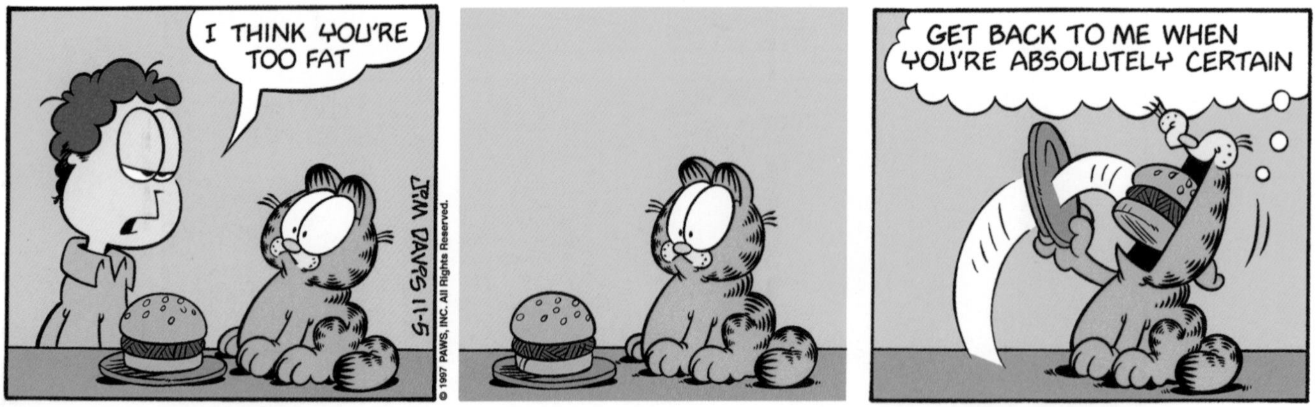
I THINK YOU'RE TOO FAT
JIM DAVIS 11-5
© 1997 PAWS, INC. All Rights Reserved.
GET BACK TO ME WHEN YOU'RE ABSOLUTELY CERTAIN

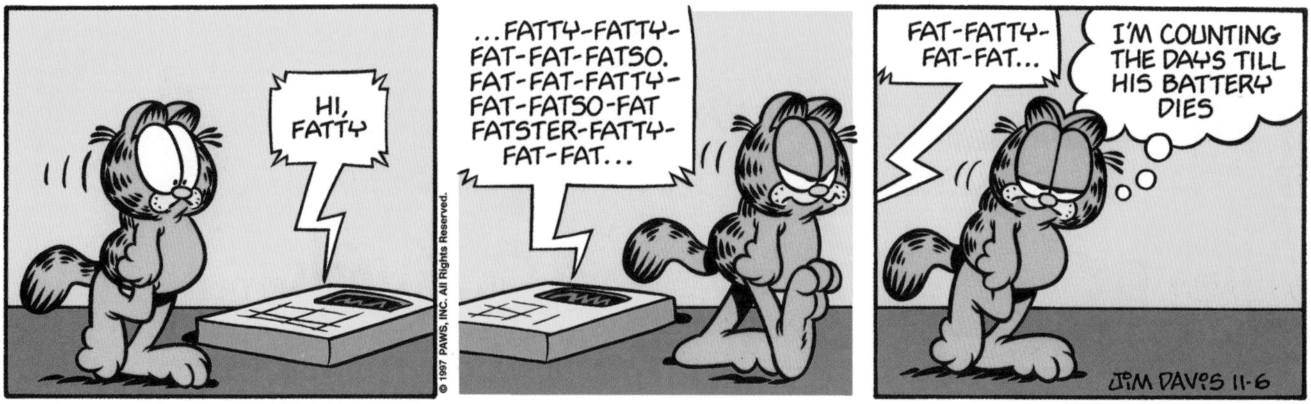
HI, FATTY
© 1997 PAWS, INC. All Rights Reserved.
...FATTY-FATTY-FAT-FAT-FATSO. FAT-FAT-FATTY-FAT-FATSO-FAT FATSTER-FATTY-FAT-FAT...
FAT-FATTY-FAT-FAT...
I'M COUNTING THE DAYS TILL HIS BATTERY DIES
JIM DAVIS 11-6

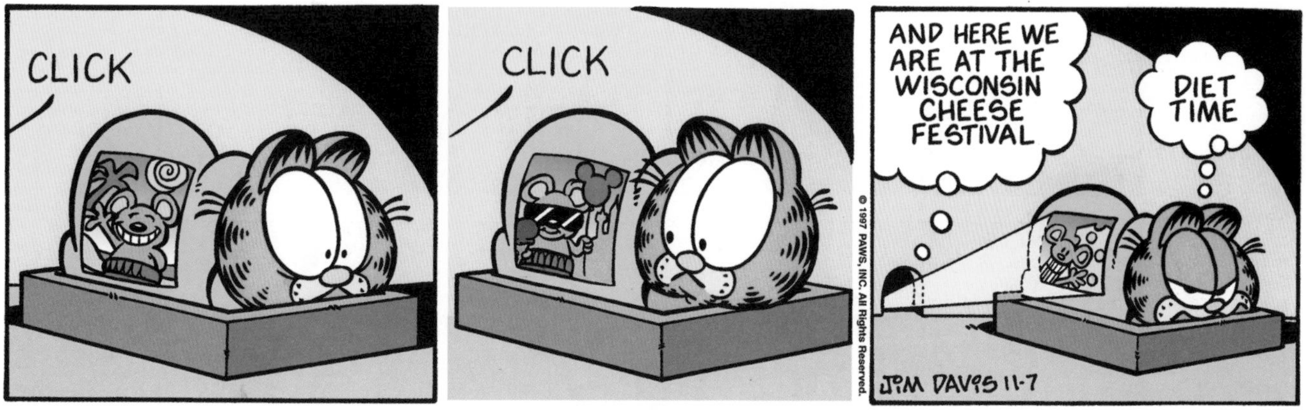
CLICK
CLICK
© 1997 PAWS, INC. All Rights Reserved.
AND HERE WE ARE AT THE WISCONSIN CHEESE FESTIVAL
DIET TIME
JIM DAVIS 11-7

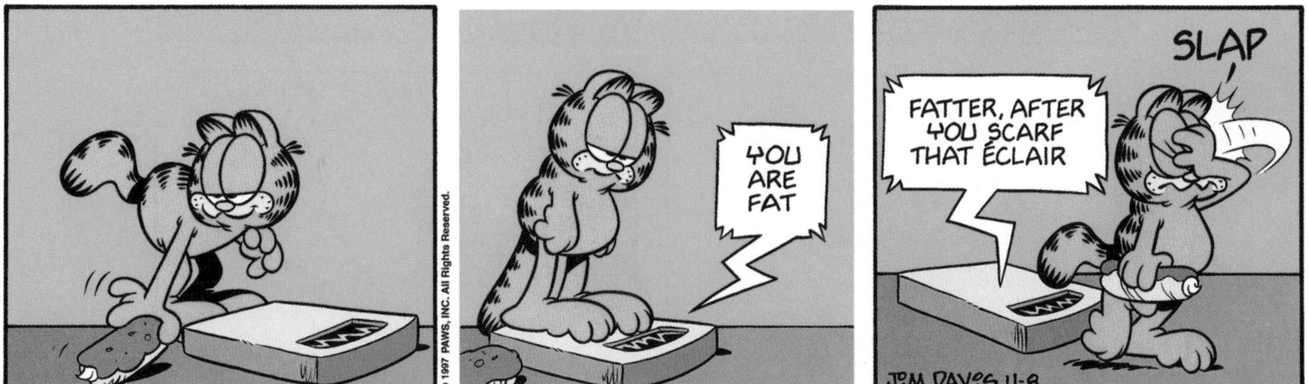
© 1997 PAWS, INC. All Rights Reserved.
YOU ARE FAT
FATTER, AFTER YOU SCARF THAT ÉCLAIR
SLAP
JIM DAVIS 11-8

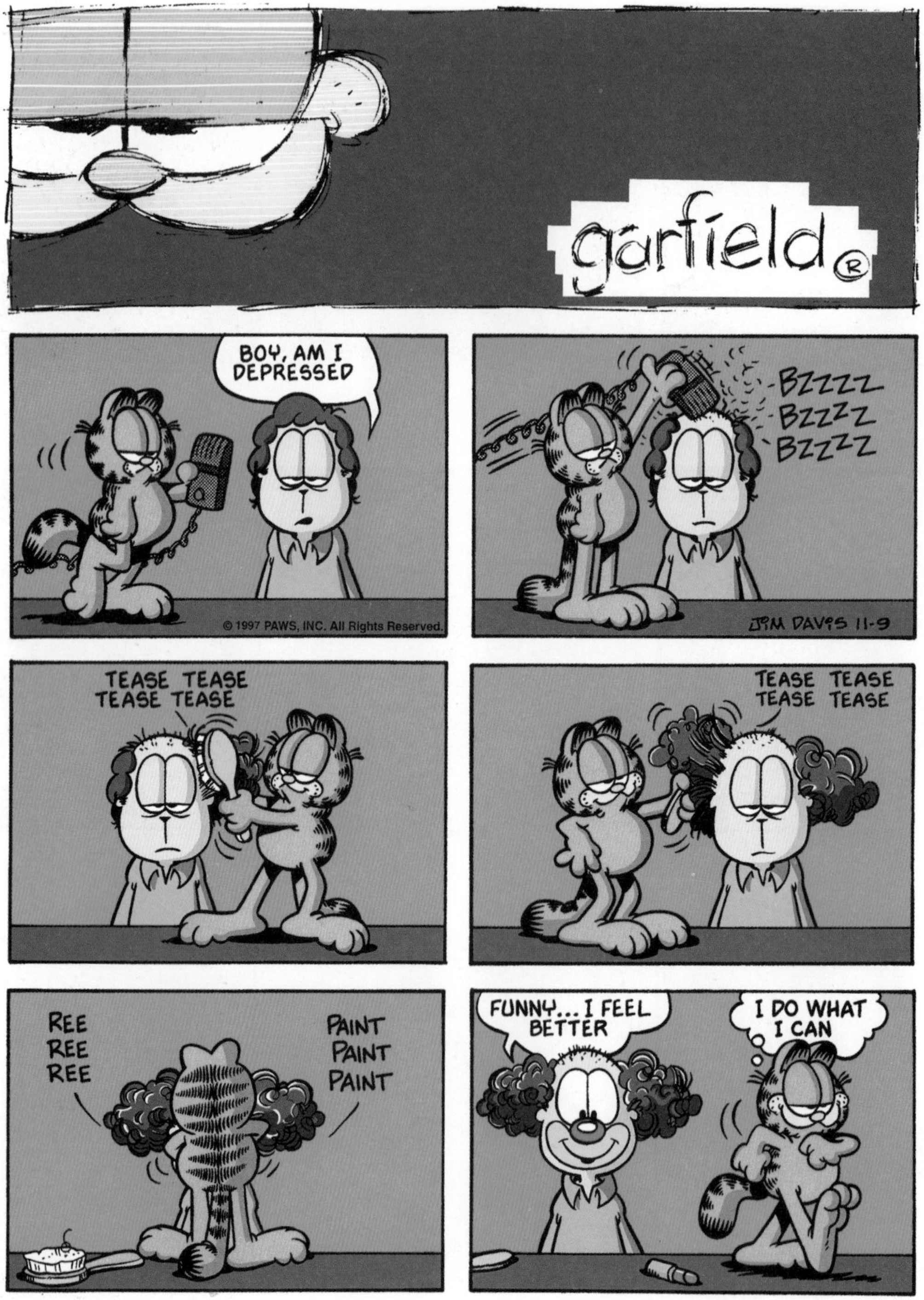
garfield ®
BOY, AM I DEPRESSED
© 1997 PAWS, INC. All Rights Reserved.
BZZZZ BZZZZ BZZZZ
JIM DAVIS 11-9
TEASE TEASE TEASE TEASE
TEASE TEASE TEASE TEASE
REE REE REE
PAINT PAINT PAINT
FUNNY... I FEEL BETTER
I DO WHAT I CAN

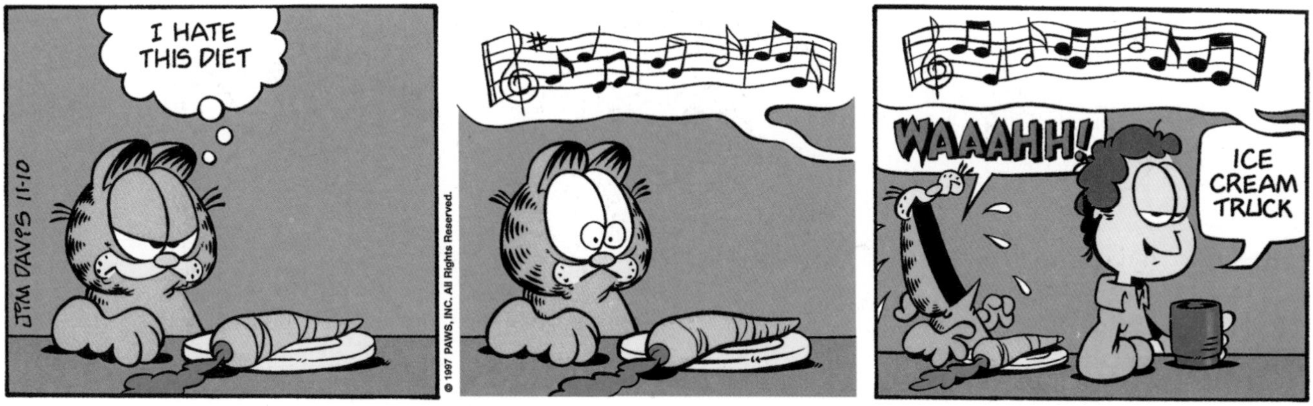
I HATE THIS DIET
JIM DAVIS 11-10
© 1997 PAWS, INC. All Rights Reserved.
WAAAHH!
ICE CREAM TRUCK

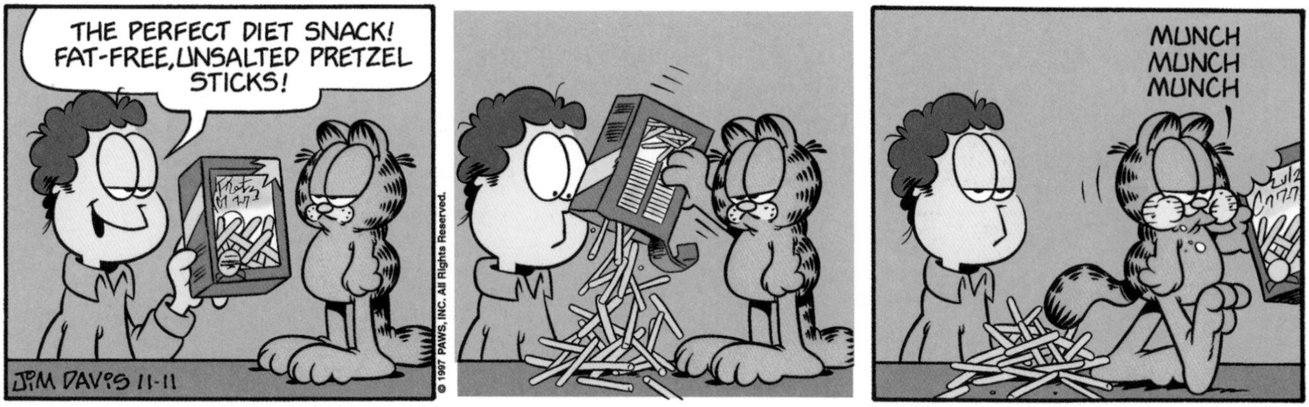
THE PERFECT DIET SNACK! FAT-FREE, UNSALTED PRETZEL STICKS!
JIM DAVIS 11-11
© 1997 PAWS, INC. All Rights Reserved.
MUNCH MUNCH MUNCH

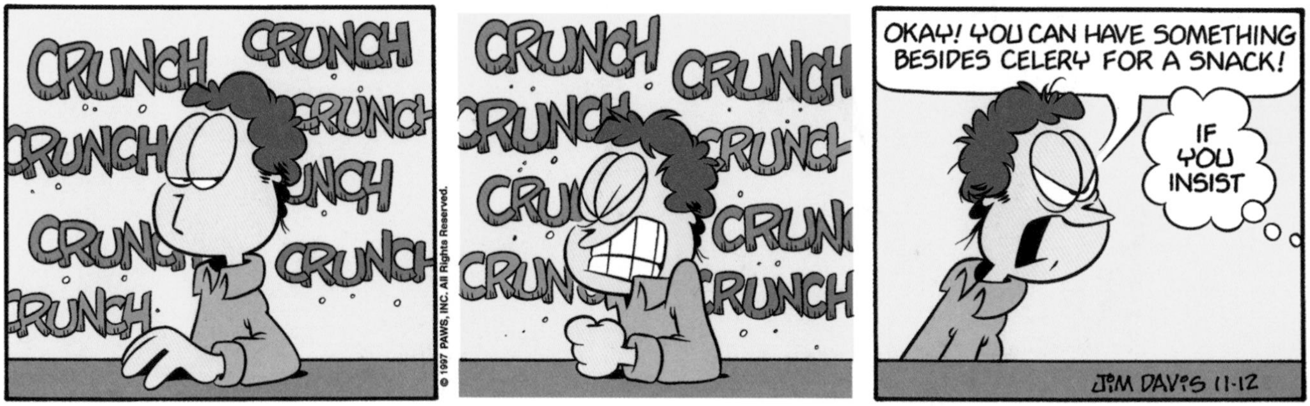
CRUNCH CRUNCH CRUNCH CRUNCH CRUNCH CRUNCH CRUNCH CRUNCH
© 1997 PAWS, INC. All Rights Reserved.
CRUNCH CRUNCH CRUNCH CRUNCH CRUNCH CRUNCH CRUNCH CRUNCH
OKAY! YOU CAN HAVE SOMETHING BESIDES CELERY FOR A SNACK!
IF YOU INSIST
JIM DAVIS 11-12

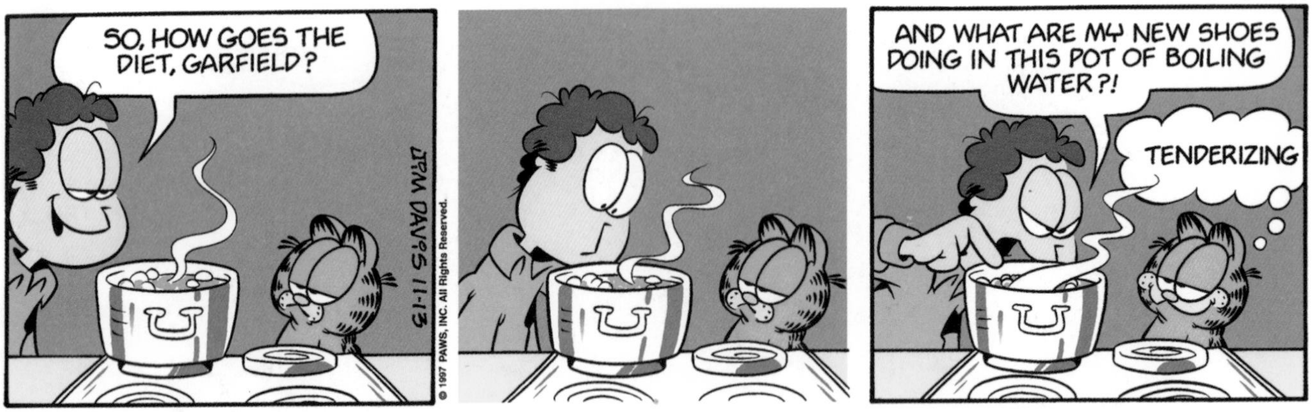
SO, HOW GOES THE DIET, GARFIELD?
JIM DAVIS 11-13
© 1997 PAWS, INC. All Rights Reserved.
AND WHAT ARE MY NEW SHOES DOING IN THIS POT OF BOILING WATER?!
TENDERIZING

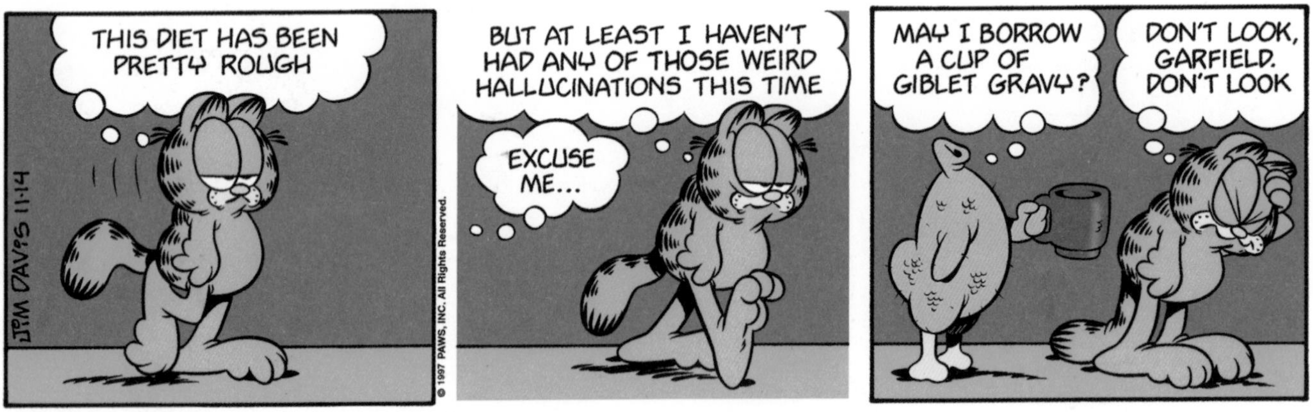
THIS DIET HAS BEEN PRETTY ROUGH
JIM DAVIS 11-14
© 1997 PAWS, INC. All Rights Reserved.
BUT AT LEAST I HAVEN'T HAD ANY OF THOSE WEIRD HALLUCINATIONS THIS TIME
EXCUSE ME...
MAY I BORROW A CUP OF GIBLET GRAVY?
DON'T LOOK, GARFIELD. DON'T LOOK

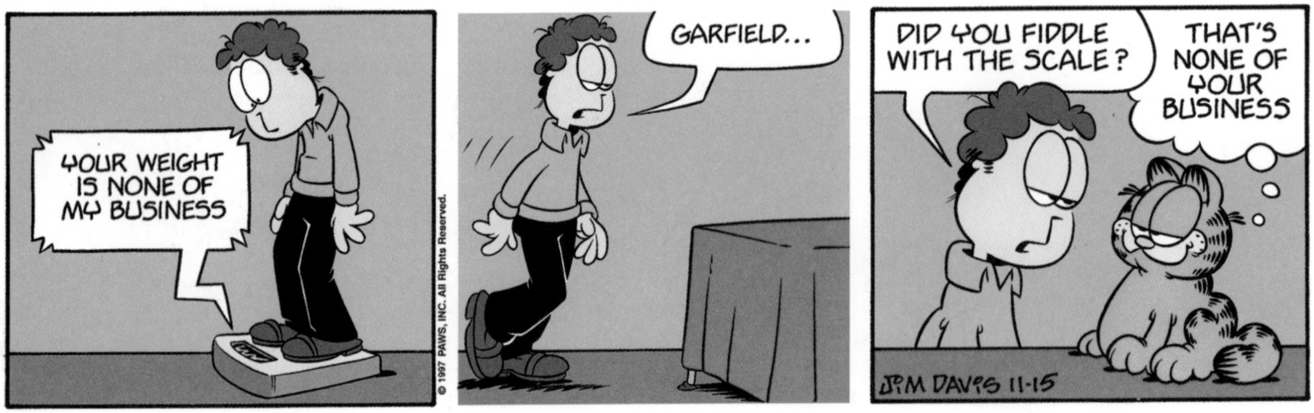
YOUR WEIGHT IS NONE OF MY BUSINESS
© 1997 PAWS, INC. All Rights Reserved.
GARFIELD...
DID YOU FIDDLE WITH THE SCALE?
THAT'S NONE OF YOUR BUSINESS
JIM DAVIS 11-15

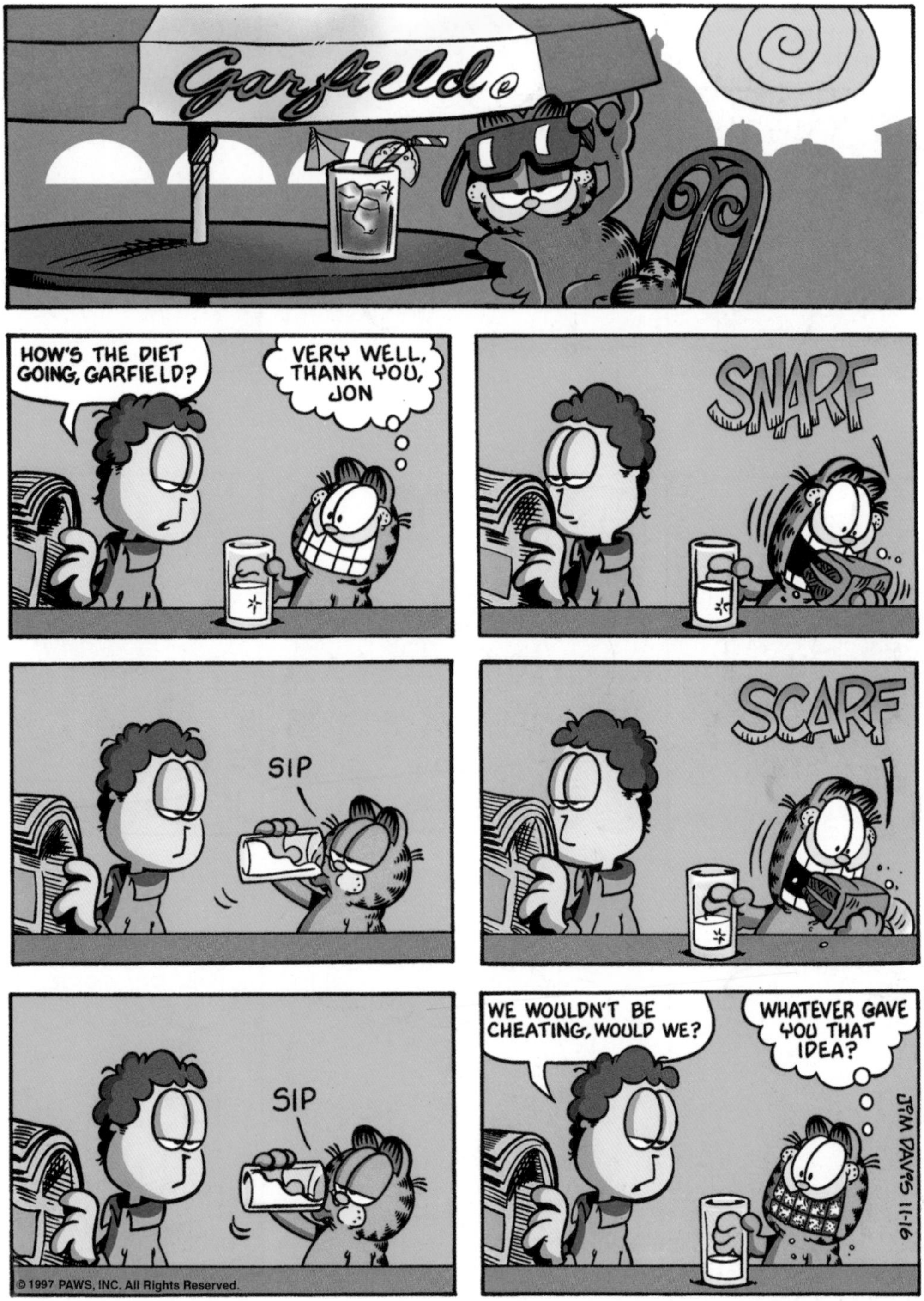
Garfield
HOW'S THE DIET GOING, GARFIELD?
VERY WELL, THANK YOU, JON
SNARF
SIP
SCARF
SIP
WE WOULDN'T BE CHEATING, WOULD WE?
WHATEVER GAVE YOU THAT IDEA?
JIM DAVIS 11-16
© 1997 PAWS, INC. All Rights Reserved.

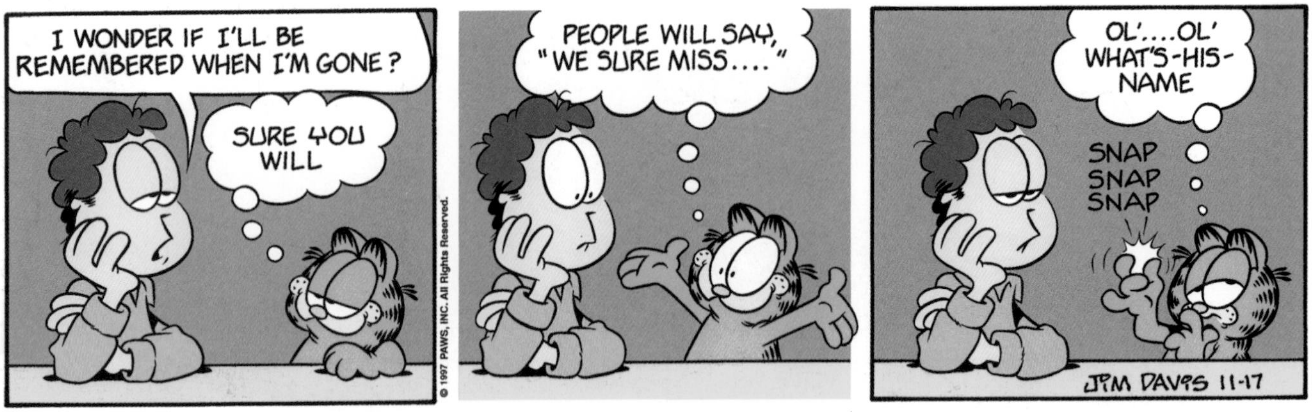
I WONDER IF I'LL BE REMEMBERED WHEN I'M GONE?
SURE YOU WILL
PEOPLE WILL SAY, "WE SURE MISS...."
OL'....OL' WHAT'S-HIS-NAME
SNAP SNAP SNAP
JIM DAVIS 11-17
© 1997 PAWS, INC. All Rights Reserved.

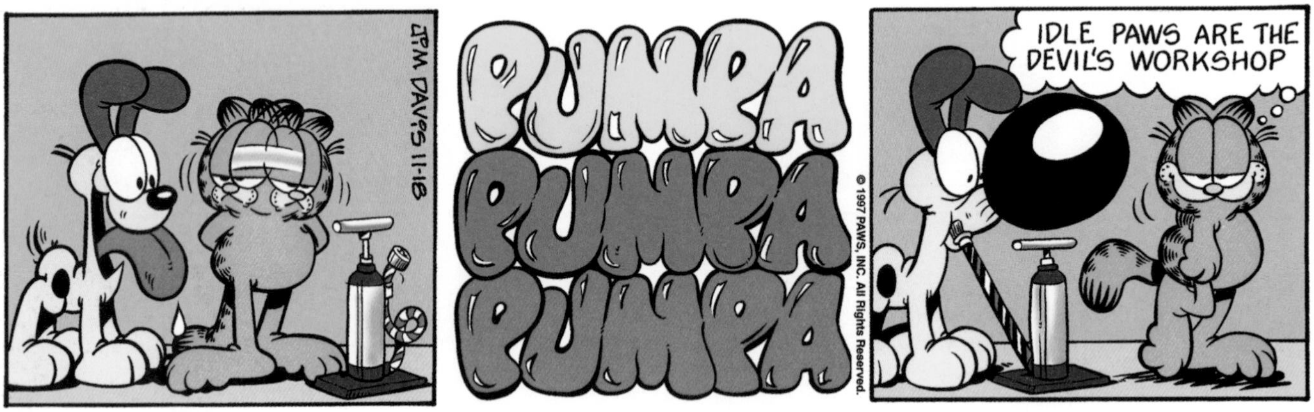
JIM DAVIS 11-18
PUMPA PUMPA PUMPA
© 1997 PAWS, INC. All Rights Reserved.
IDLE PAWS ARE THE DEVIL'S WORKSHOP

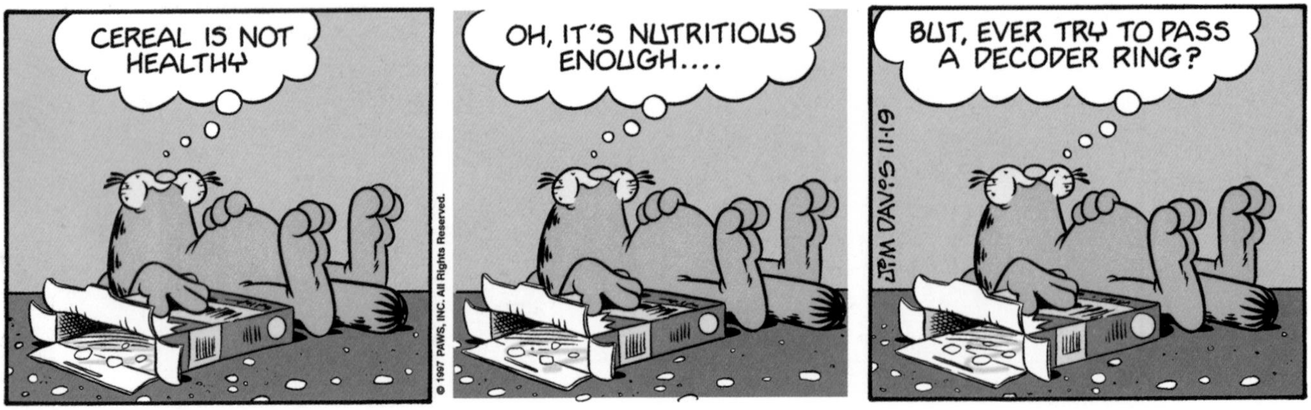
CEREAL IS NOT HEALTHY
© 1997 PAWS, INC. All Rights Reserved.
OH, IT'S NUTRITIOUS ENOUGH....
JIM DAVIS 11-19
BUT, EVER TRY TO PASS A DECODER RING?

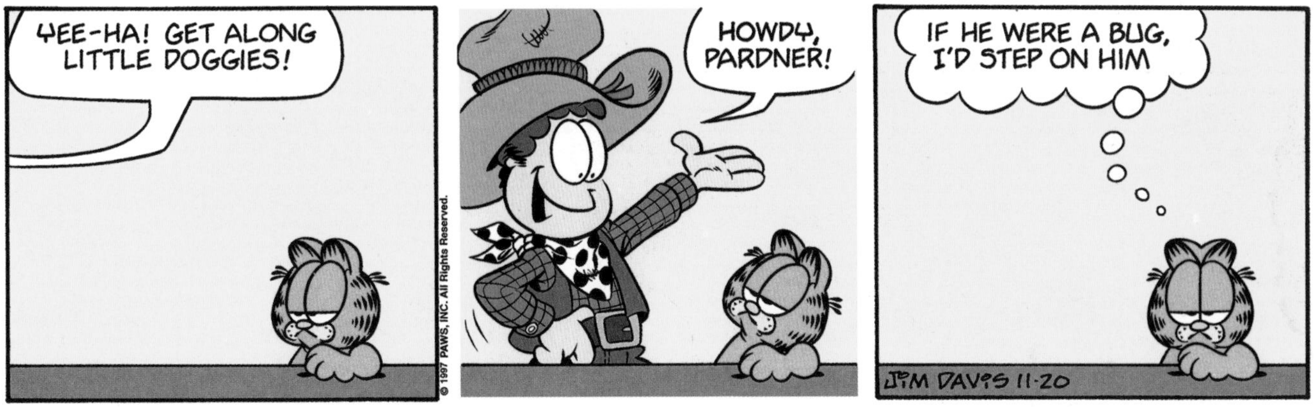
YEE-HA! GET ALONG LITTLE DOGGIES!
HOWDY, PARDNER!
IF HE WERE A BUG, I'D STEP ON HIM
JIM DAVIS 11-20
© 1997 PAWS, INC. All Rights Reserved.

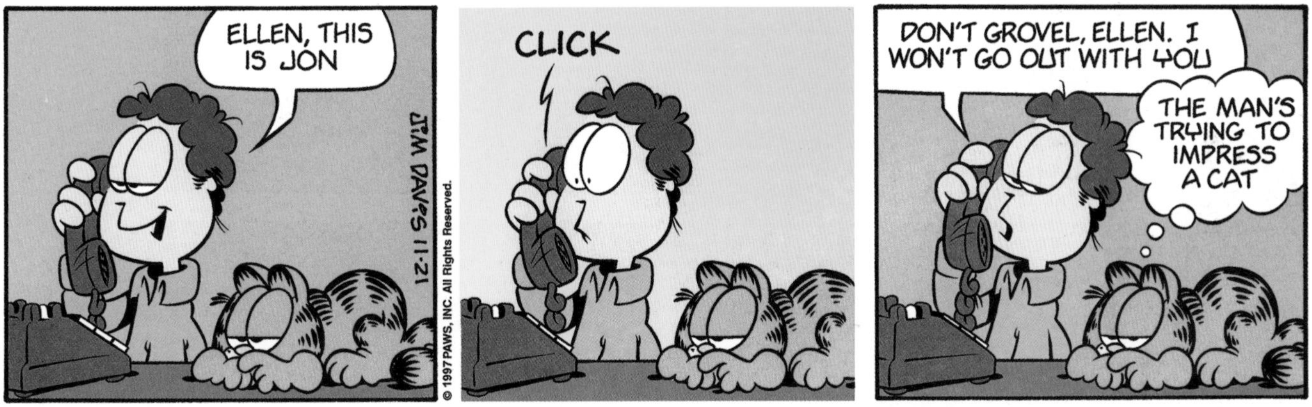
ELLEN, THIS IS JON
CLICK
DON'T GROVEL, ELLEN. I WON'T GO OUT WITH YOU
THE MAN'S TRYING TO IMPRESS A CAT
JIM DAVIS 11-21
© 1997 PAWS, INC. All Rights Reserved.

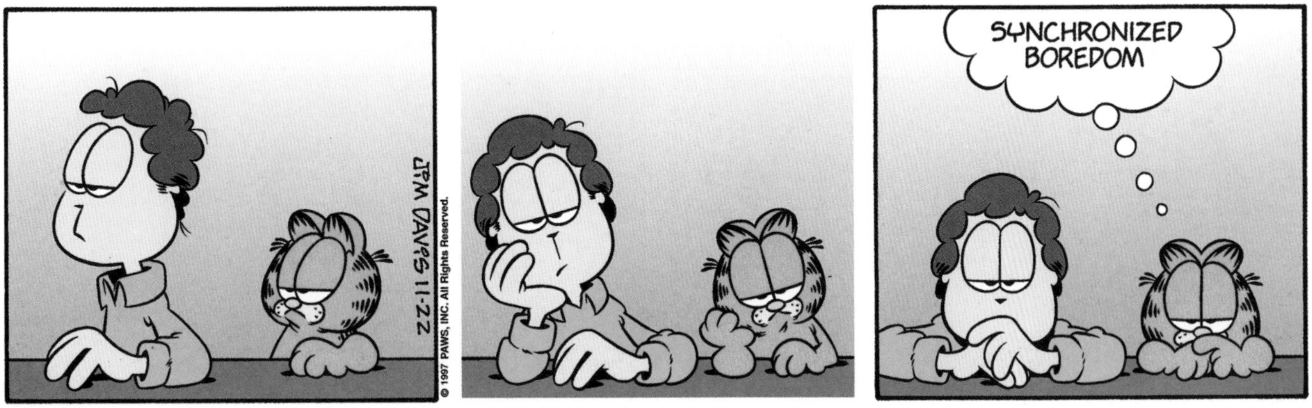
SYNCHRONIZED BOREDOM
JIM DAVIS 11-22
© 1997 PAWS, INC. All Rights Reserved.

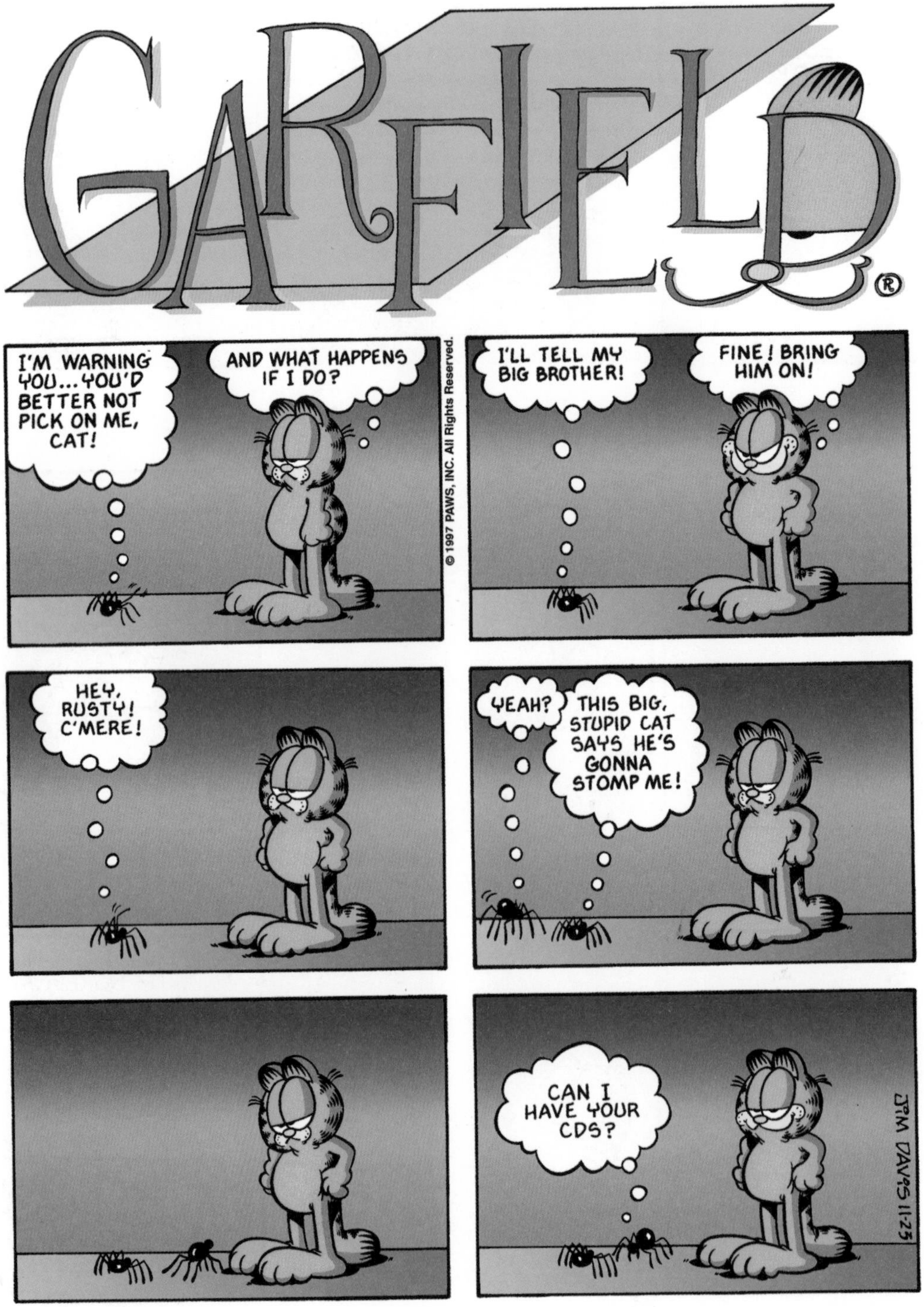
GARFIELD®
I'M WARNING YOU... YOU'D BETTER NOT PICK ON ME, CAT!
AND WHAT HAPPENS IF I DO?
I'LL TELL MY BIG BROTHER!
FINE! BRING HIM ON!
HEY, RUSTY! C'MERE!
YEAH?
THIS BIG, STUPID CAT SAYS HE'S GONNA STOMP ME!
CAN I HAVE YOUR CDS?
JIM DAVIS 11-23

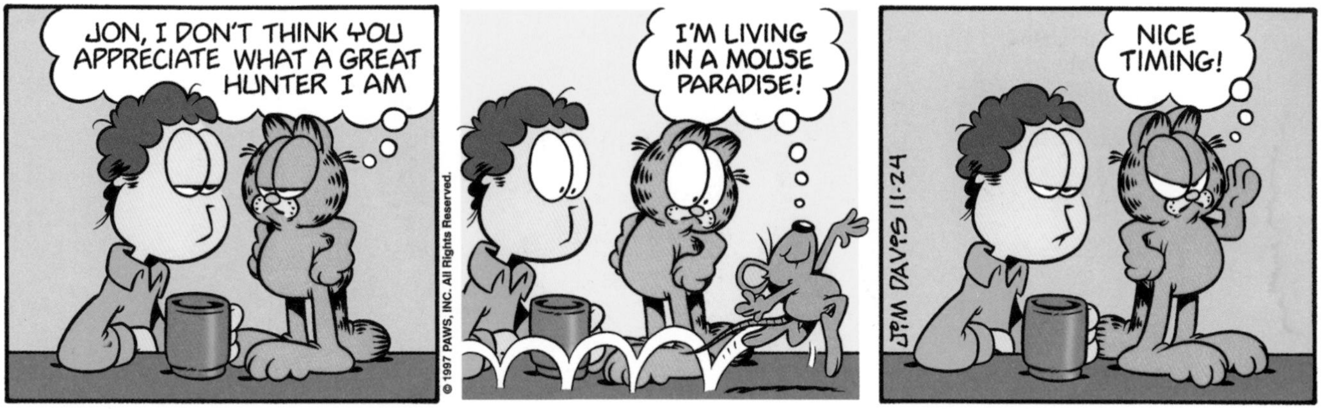
JON, I DON'T THINK YOU APPRECIATE WHAT A GREAT HUNTER I AM
© 1997 PAWS, INC. All Rights Reserved.
I'M LIVING IN A MOUSE PARADISE!
JIM DAVIS 11-24
NICE TIMING!

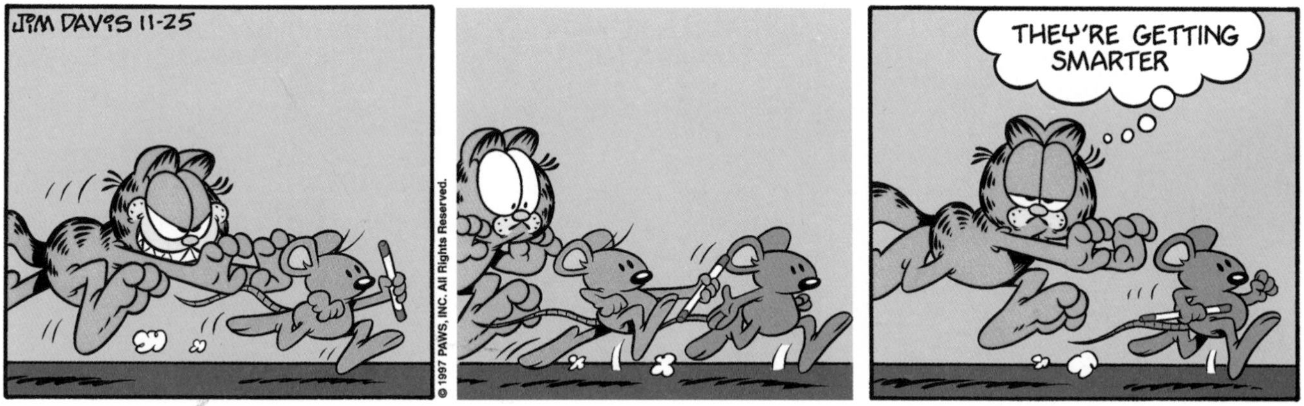
JIM DAVIS 11-25
© 1997 PAWS, INC. All Rights Reserved.
THEY'RE GETTING SMARTER

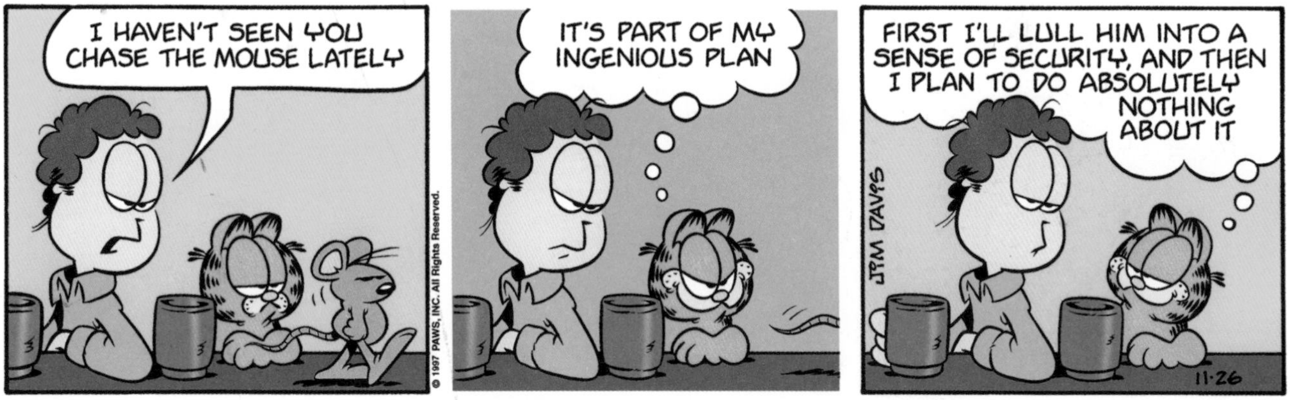
I HAVEN'T SEEN YOU CHASE THE MOUSE LATELY
© 1997 PAWS, INC. All Rights Reserved.
IT'S PART OF MY INGENIOUS PLAN
FIRST I'LL LULL HIM INTO A SENSE OF SECURITY, AND THEN I PLAN TO DO ABSOLUTELY NOTHING ABOUT IT
JIM DAVIS
11-26

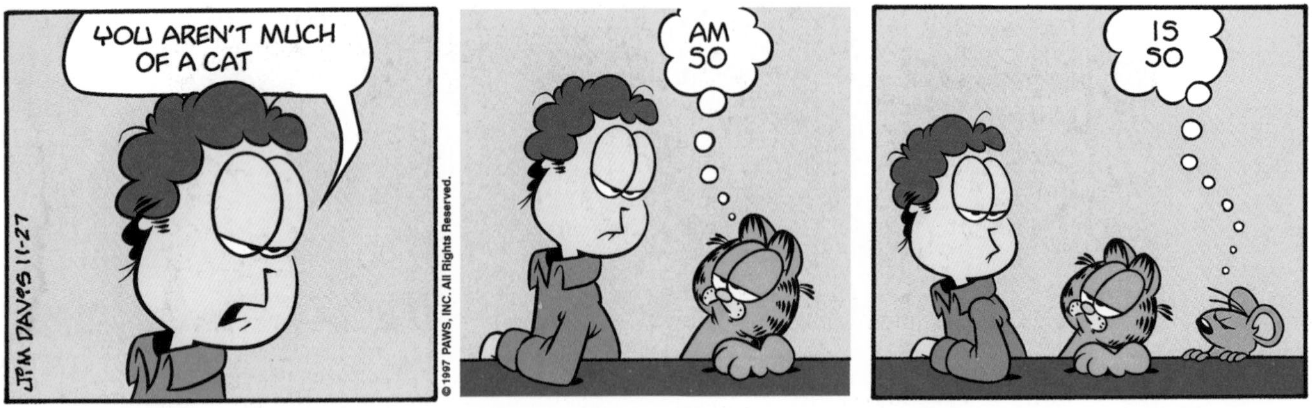
YOU AREN'T MUCH OF A CAT
JIM DAVIS 11-27
© 1997 PAWS, INC. All Rights Reserved.
AM SO
IS SO

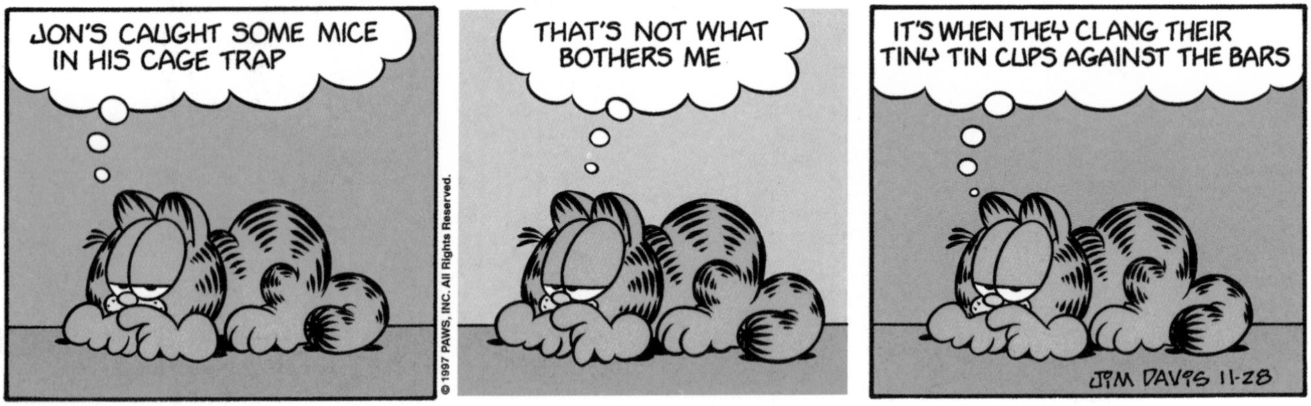
JON'S CAUGHT SOME MICE IN HIS CAGE TRAP
© 1997 PAWS, INC. All Rights Reserved.
THAT'S NOT WHAT BOTHERS ME
IT'S WHEN THEY CLANG THEIR TINY TIN CUPS AGAINST THE BARS
JIM DAVIS 11-28

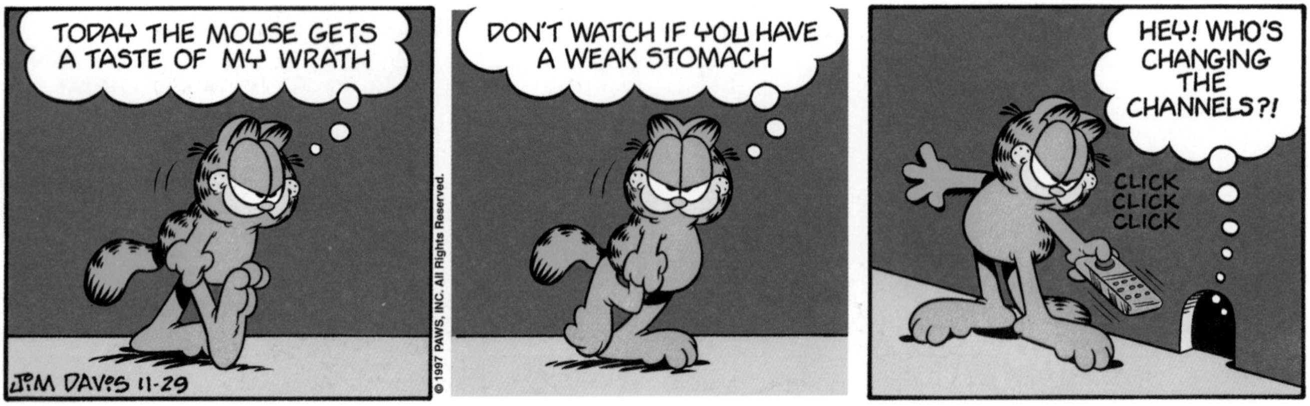
TODAY THE MOUSE GETS A TASTE OF MY WRATH
JIM DAVIS 11-29
© 1997 PAWS, INC. All Rights Reserved.
DON'T WATCH IF YOU HAVE A WEAK STOMACH
HEY! WHO'S CHANGING THE CHANNELS?!
CLICK CLICK CLICK

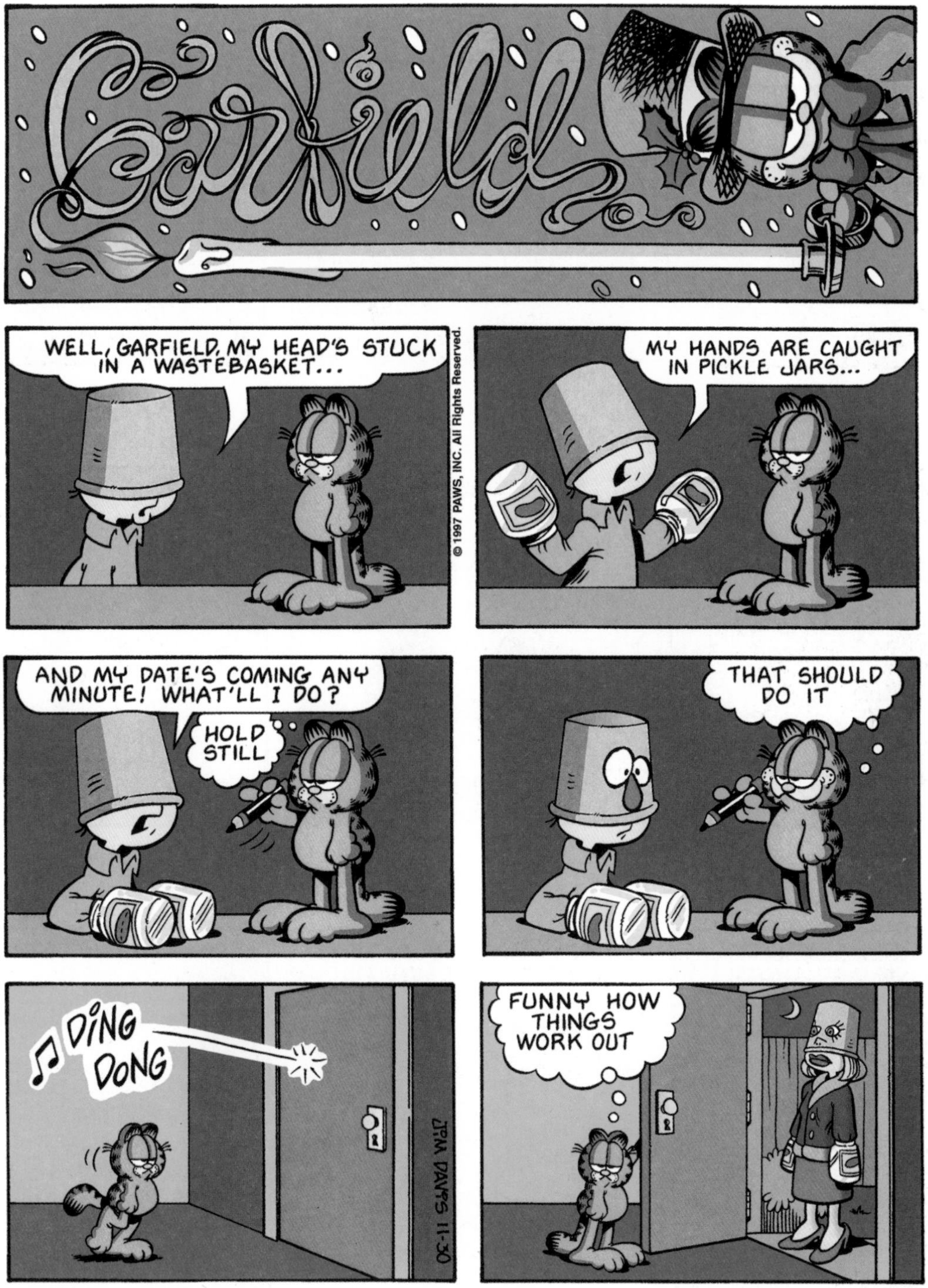
Garfield
WELL, GARFIELD, MY HEAD'S STUCK IN A WASTEBASKET...
MY HANDS ARE CAUGHT IN PICKLE JARS...
AND MY DATE'S COMING ANY MINUTE! WHAT'LL I DO?
HOLD STILL
THAT SHOULD DO IT
DING DONG
FUNNY HOW THINGS WORK OUT
JPM DAVPS 11-30

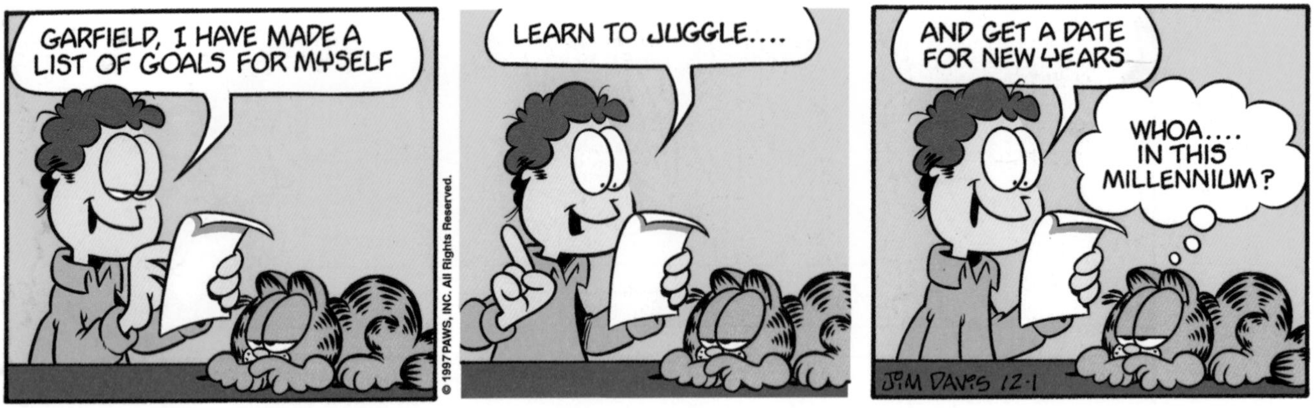
GARFIELD, I HAVE MADE A LIST OF GOALS FOR MYSELF
LEARN TO JUGGLE....
AND GET A DATE FOR NEW YEARS
WHOA.... IN THIS MILLENNIUM?
© 1997 PAWS, INC. All Rights Reserved.
JIM DAVIS 12-1

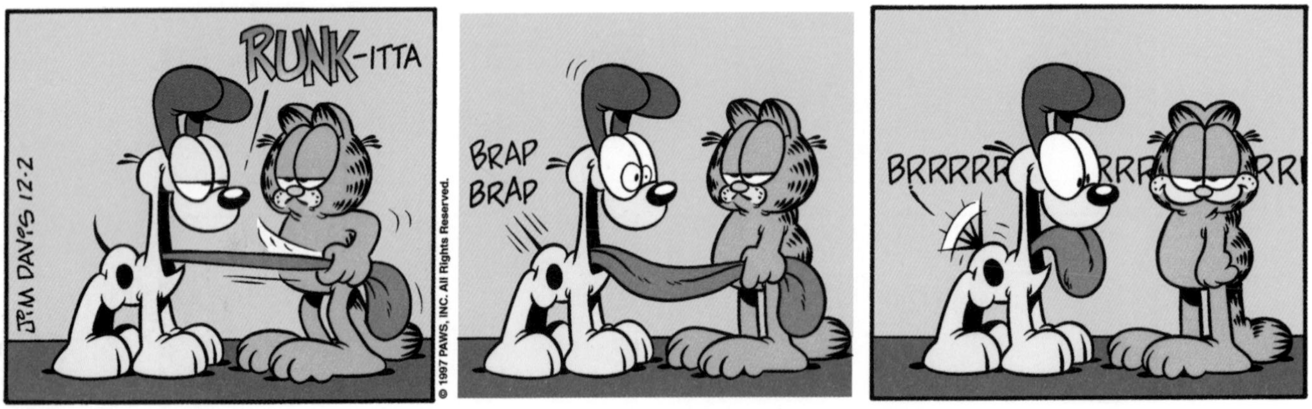
RUNK-ITTA
JIM DAVIS 12-2
BRAP
BRAP
BRRRRR
© 1997 PAWS, INC. All Rights Reserved.

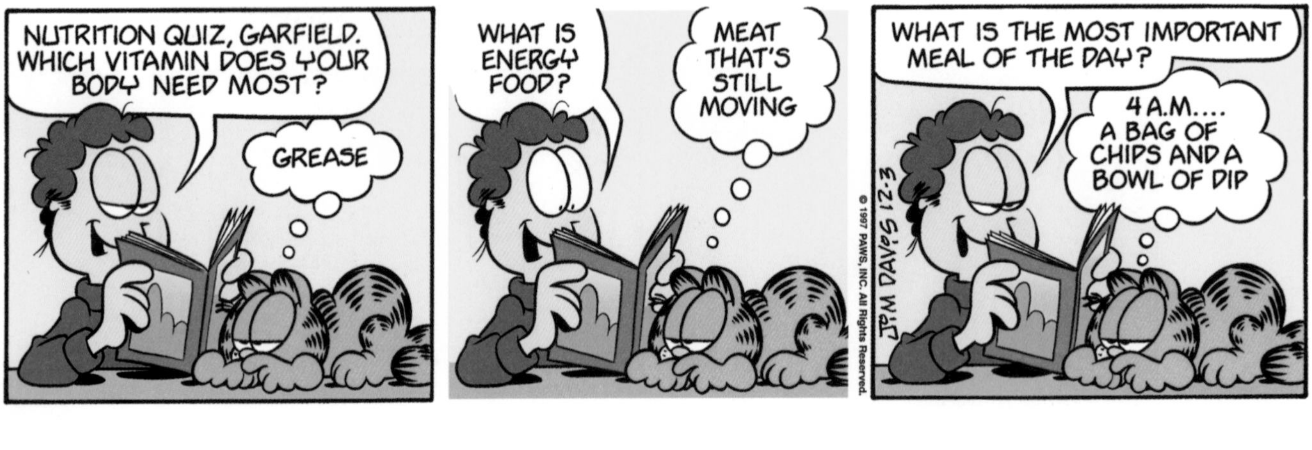
NUTRITION QUIZ, GARFIELD. WHICH VITAMIN DOES YOUR BODY NEED MOST?
GREASE
WHAT IS ENERGY FOOD?
MEAT THAT'S STILL MOVING
WHAT IS THE MOST IMPORTANT MEAL OF THE DAY?
4 A.M.... A BAG OF CHIPS AND A BOWL OF DIP
© 1997 PAWS, INC. All Rights Reserved.
JIM DAVIS 12-3

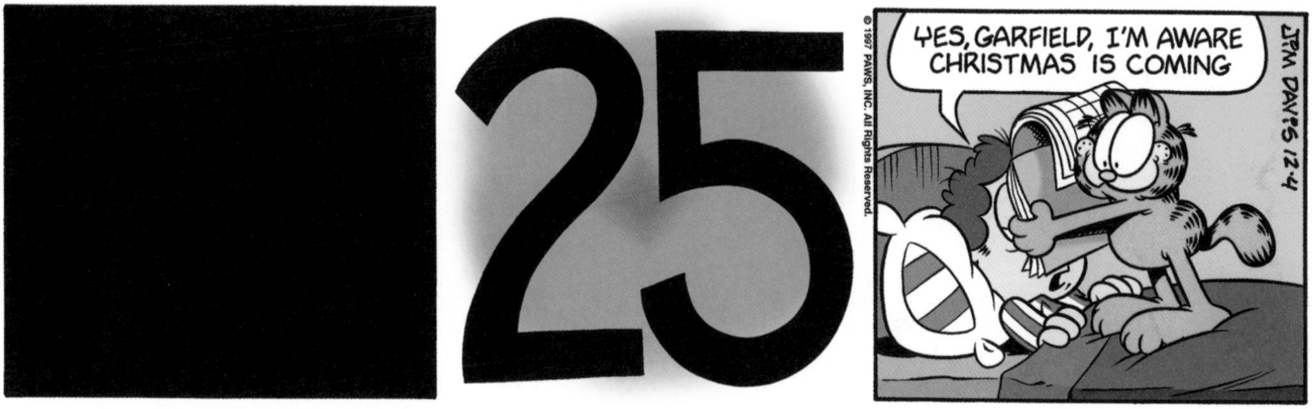
25
© 1997 PAWS, INC. All Rights Reserved.
YES, GARFIELD, I'M AWARE CHRISTMAS IS COMING
JPM DAVPS 12-4

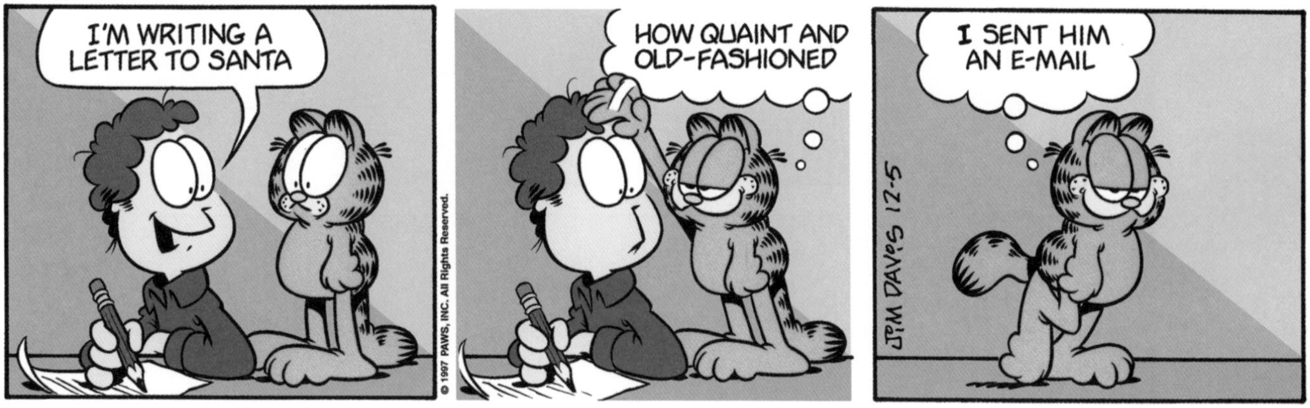
I'M WRITING A LETTER TO SANTA
© 1997 PAWS, INC. All Rights Reserved.
HOW QUAINT AND OLD-FASHIONED
I SENT HIM AN E-MAIL
JPM DAVPS 12-5

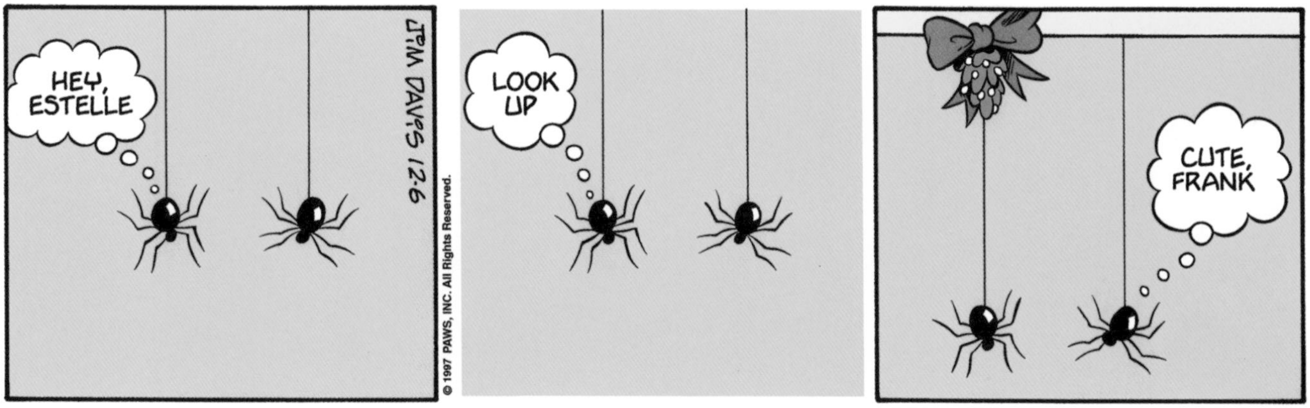
HEY, ESTELLE
JPM DAVPS 12-6
© 1997 PAWS, INC. All Rights Reserved.
LOOK UP
CUTE, FRANK

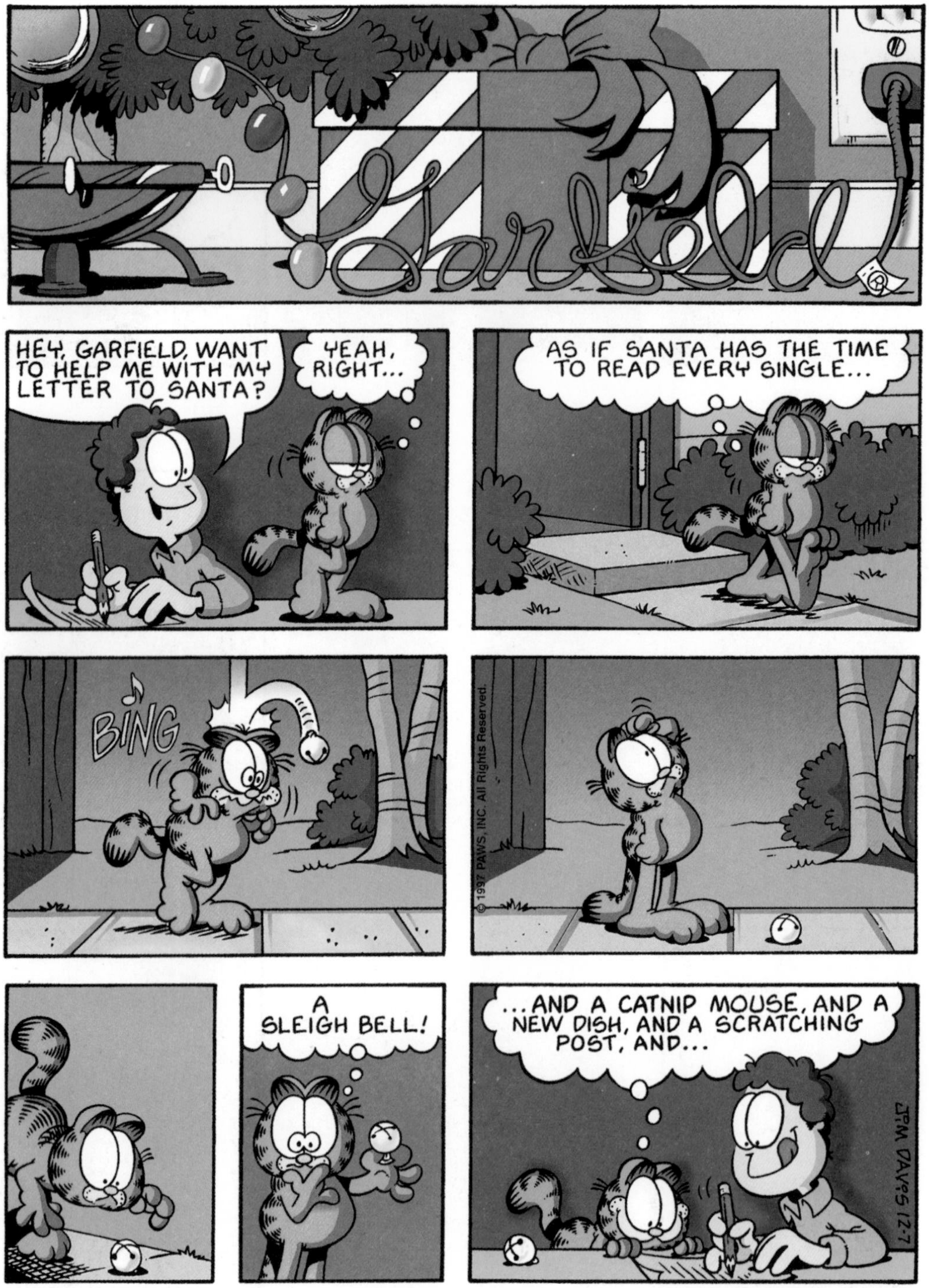
Garfield
HEY, GARFIELD, WANT TO HELP ME WITH MY LETTER TO SANTA?
YEAH, RIGHT...
AS IF SANTA HAS THE TIME TO READ EVERY SINGLE...
BING
© 1997 PAWS, INC. All Rights Reserved.
A SLEIGH BELL!
...AND A CATNIP MOUSE, AND A NEW DISH, AND A SCRATCHING POST, AND...
JIM DAVIS 12-7

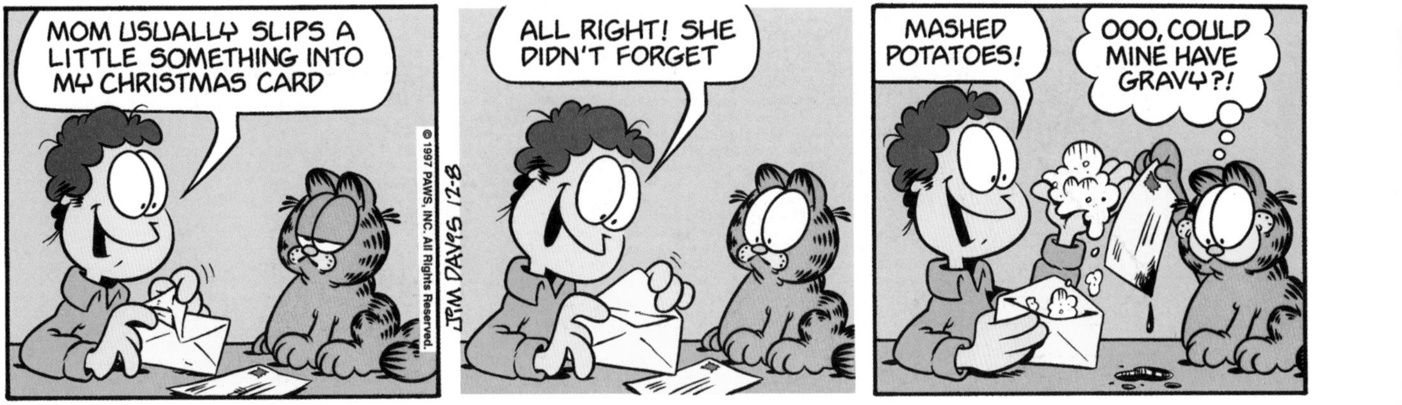
MOM USUALLY SLIPS A LITTLE SOMETHING INTO MY CHRISTMAS CARD
© 1997 PAWS, INC. All Rights Reserved.
JIM DAVIS 12-8
ALL RIGHT! SHE DIDN'T FORGET
MASHED POTATOES!
OOO, COULD MINE HAVE GRAVY?!

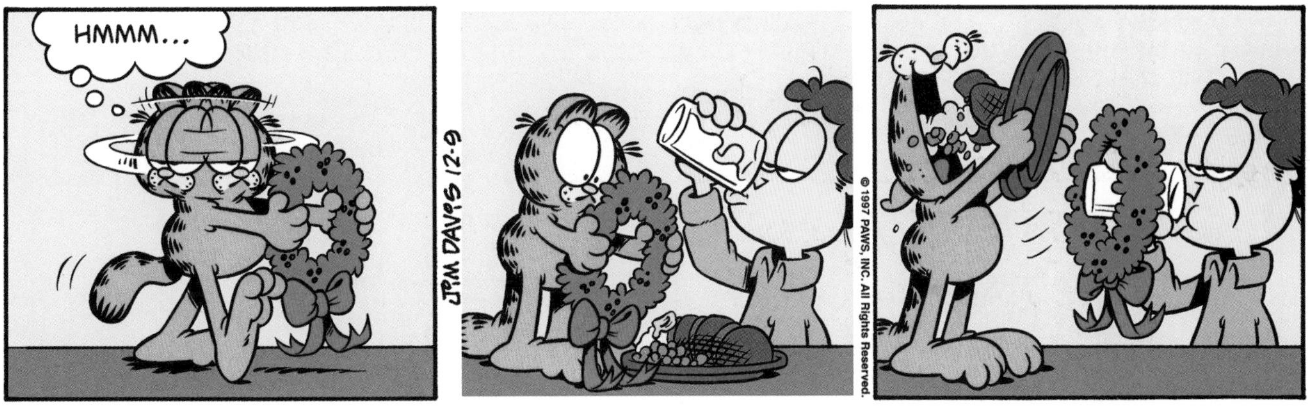
HMMM...
JIM DAVIS 12-9
© 1997 PAWS, INC. All Rights Reserved.

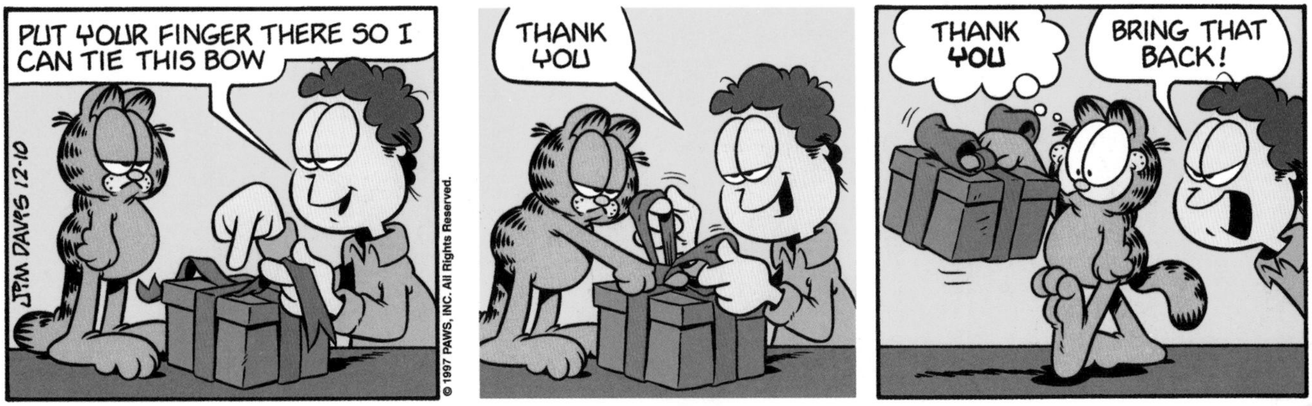
PUT YOUR FINGER THERE SO I CAN TIE THIS BOW
JIM DAVIS 12-10
© 1997 PAWS, INC. All Rights Reserved.
THANK YOU
THANK YOU
BRING THAT BACK!

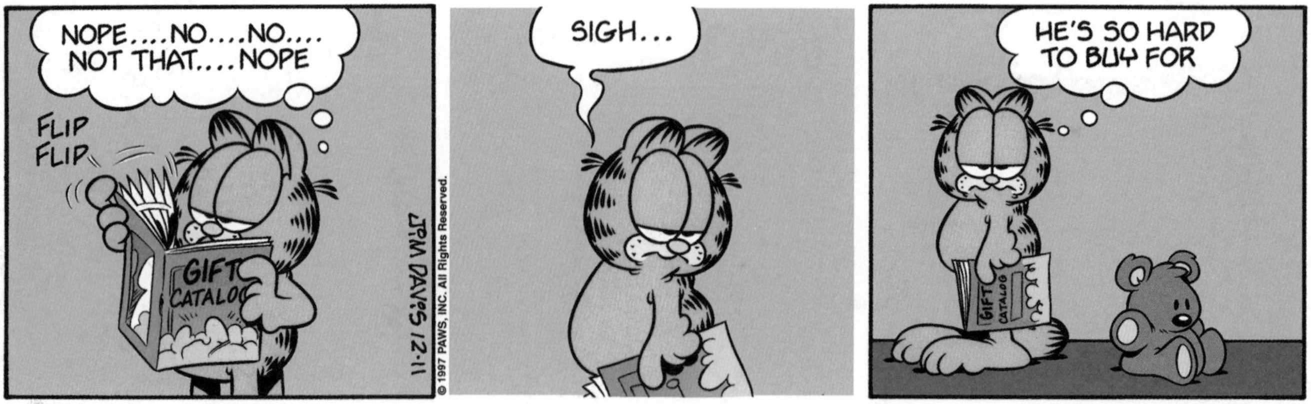
NOPE....NO....NO.... NOT THAT....NOPE
FLIP FLIP
GIFT CATALOG
JIM DAVIS 12-11
© 1997 PAWS, INC. All Rights Reserved.
SIGH...
HE'S SO HARD TO BUY FOR

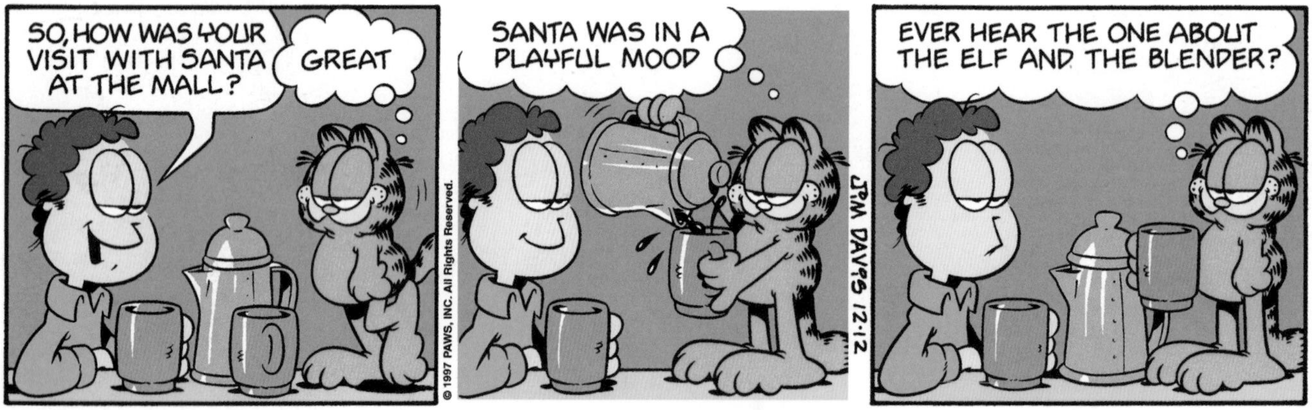
SO, HOW WAS YOUR VISIT WITH SANTA AT THE MALL?
GREAT
© 1997 PAWS, INC. All Rights Reserved.
SANTA WAS IN A PLAYFUL MOOD
JIM DAVIS 12-12
EVER HEAR THE ONE ABOUT THE ELF AND THE BLENDER?

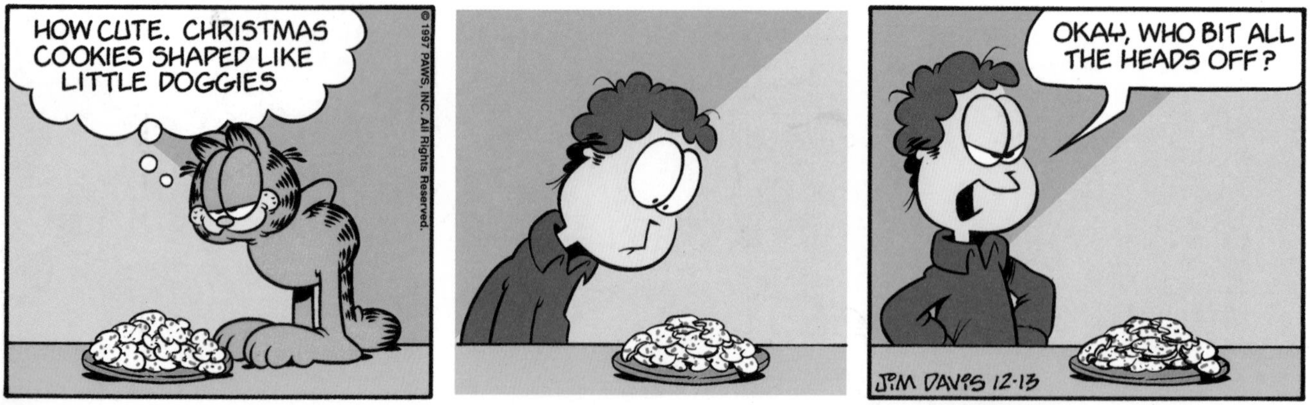
HOW CUTE. CHRISTMAS COOKIES SHAPED LIKE LITTLE DOGGIES
© 1997 PAWS, INC. All Rights Reserved.
OKAY, WHO BIT ALL THE HEADS OFF?
JIM DAVIS 12-13

GARFIELD'S PAST LIVES

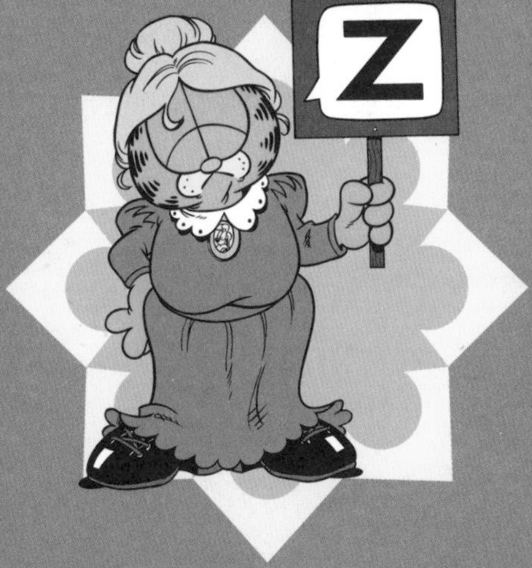
Z

SNOOZIN' B. ANTHONY

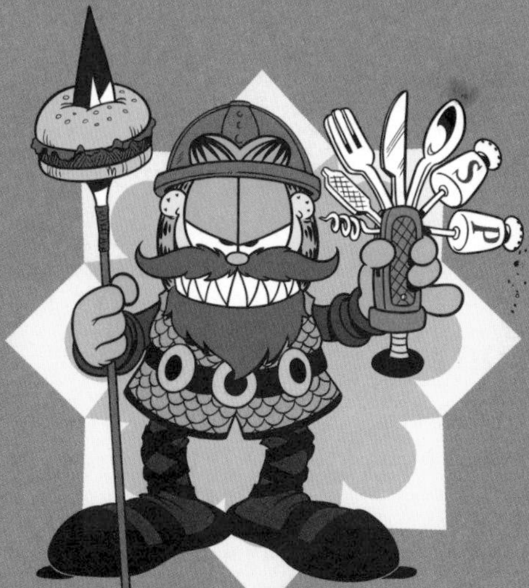

ATTILA THE HUNGRY

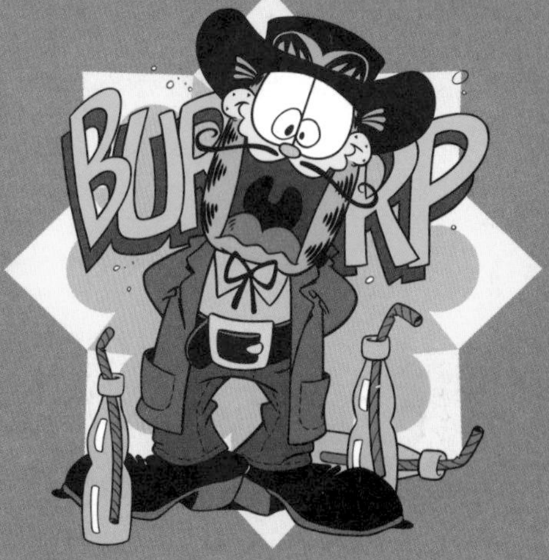

WYATT BURP

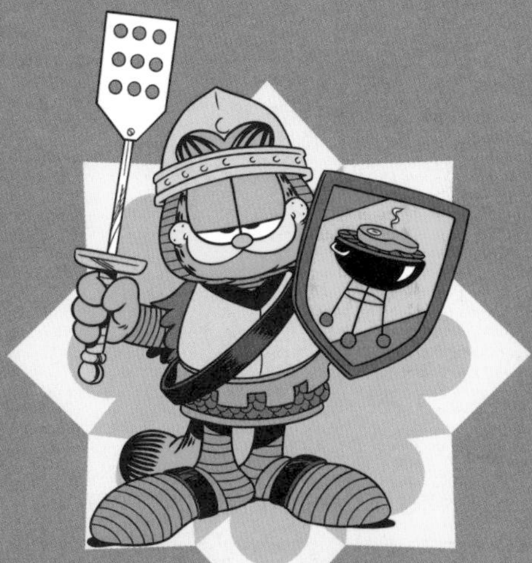

SIR LUNCHALOT

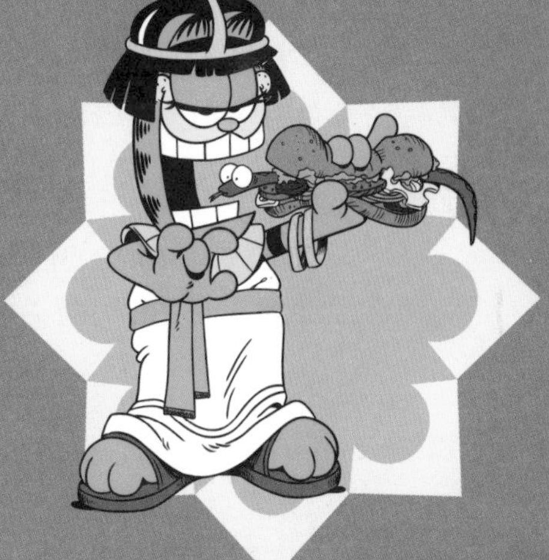

CLEOFATRA

Watch. Read. Shop. Play.

DON'T FORGET THE SNACKS!

garfield.com

* **The Garfield Show**

  Catch Garfield and the rest of the gang on *The Garfield Show*, now airing on Cartoon Network and Boomerang!

* **The Comic Strip**

  Search & read thousands of GARFIELD® comic strips!

* **Garfield on Facebook & Twitter**

  Join millions of Garfield friends on Facebook. Get your daily dose of humor and connect with other fat cat fans!

* **Shop all the Garfield stores!**

  Original art & comic strips, books, apparel, personalized products, & more!

* **Play FREE online Garfield games!**

  Plus, check out all of the FREE Garfield apps available for your smartphone, tablet, and other mobile devices.